Strongneck Books

Internal Affairs

External Affairs

And

Last Grafts

Or

The Internal Affairs Trilogy

To the King

Of the Universe

IA-Foreword to a Trilogy

Greetings. I know that things such as these are rarely actually read; but this one is different; so please take the time to read it. I will work to stay interesting. Also it's worth noting that in this work they actually are a part of the story in and of itself; and you need not worry about them spoiling the plot. (This paragraph does not apply to others added on later after initial publication)

First of all I need to let you know that on a few occasions some of the horrors of history will come up. I am not comparing them, or at least not intending to. I strictly mean to point out the existence of similarities; or the lack thereof.

Also fair warning. This book is a neoclassic; no relation to neoclassicism. Admittedly it's not the easiest read in the world; but it is by far not the hardest. My inspirations are very numerous, some of which are not even books; some others of which will later be discussed. Just to name two are *Varney, The Vampyre* (James Malcolm Rymer) and *Civil Disobedience* (Henry David Thoreau; also known by other titles; the book, not the author); but is much easier to read. Another is *Go Set a Watchman* (Harper Lee).

(insert mule picture here)
Houston

And no, it isn't written in Victorian egghead speak, it isn't about racial issues, and it certainly isn't about vampires! I could split hairs, I'm very good at it; but I won't. Additionally unlike James Malcolm Rymer I know how to get to the point; if anything I'm too good at it.

Additionally this is an especially unpleasant book. Just as *1984* was written as a warning. It is a story that needs to be written; only it's at least as much a warning against what is as it is against what could be. Fair warning; if you're anything like me, this will be a very difficult book, and not for the reason you were given fair warning of in the last paragraph.

And just as some of the quotes in the afterword (will discuss later on) require some thought, seeing as their applicability isn't always apparent at first glance. So also this work must be read carefully. There are issues that I wrote a whole book primarily to discuss that and that issue alone. Meanwhile issues of approximately equal importance are only granted a few sentences. Being as there is just so much; I'm, to quote a journalist "drinking from a fire hose" here.

Admittedly there will be some bad cops in this work; actually a lot. But before you tie me in with the blueaphobes, you should realize that you just picked up either a book called *"Internal Affairs"* or a trilogy bound together called *"The Internal Affairs Trilogy."* What do you expect?! If you have a problem with that, you should just put down this book right now (or delete the E-book) and pick up another procedural.

I also know how many people will point out the good that there are cops to, and call me a hater. Well I'm here to ring alarms, as for the other there a plenty of other people doing that. This work, is an alarm. Also I so many times have heard many times people crying how we need the police to be safe. First of all, while it's one of the issues I have elected to put in the category of "just don't' have ink to address this." A real problem we're having in some places is either not having enough police, or not having enough officers on patrol. To borrow (not for the last time) a real story from the place this book just happens to take place; and not as a slap against Houston PD in particular. The Oak Forest Neighborhood of Houston TX (near the Loop 610) has had to raise money to hire security; it most assuredly is not a gated community. Second; Get Real! No one's gunu get rid of law enforcement; no one is even suggesting truly getting rid of law enforcement. Closest is individual agencies being abolished has been suggested in different directions; by different groups; at different times. As in not even just one political side.

Furthermore this work is not meant to be anything against the Houston Police Department, or any other law enforcement agency; I arbitrarily chose to set this in Space City U.S.A.

Do you remember that show *How I Met Your Mother*? If not I'll briefly recap. In short it was a dad telling his kids in the future how he met their mother. It was a flashback to present day. What does that have to do with this work? Well the story itself, nothing! But how it was told, everything. You see, with slight exceptions, this book was written from the future, published in what is our present. It is a flashback to our near future, their past. Approximately present day.

(insert mule picture here)
Houston

About the book in and of itself: First you have Captain W.X.Y.Z. Olaf's novel *Internal Affairs*; which more has the feel of a TV mystery series in book form; though not exactly. Even the First chapter is different from the rest of the book as much as, and in the same way that most shows' pilot is different from the rest of the series. In it you see more than mere IA work, and he even comes clean to some of his own corruption. Next you have the novella *External* Affairs; which has its own preface, so I need talk about it little. But I will say that it explores the world of law enforcement left without anyone to answer to. The replication to those they are sworn to serve; and themselves. Finally there is the *Last Grafts* novelette. And every part of this work is written in a way like almost no other book. Even the structure, which does not relate to the plot (though this book is the closest I've ever seen), is like no other; or at least no book I've ever read; what it is arranged closest to is *The Jungle books* by Rudyard Kipling (and even then it's not close).

And as for how to classify this book; this book is rather omnigenera; it touches on almost every genera; and many sub-generas. While it is not worth noting the numerous generas; I will note that of these generas; is a new genera. I must explain. There are many sub-generas of horror (Ghosts, Asylum, Vampires, etc...); but they are all of the traditional form or horror. This (while has elements at times of the other) is a tale of terror (and fury). But as opposed to The Phantom of the Opera (Gaston Leroux) and the Asylum series (Madeleine Roux); it is It Can't Happen Here (Sinclair Lewis) and the Jungle (Upton Sinclair).

Also this is NOT a procedural. As such there will be finer points of law, and certainly of police procedure, that are straight-up wrong.

This being written anonymously some people might begin to speculate that this truly was from the future. Well I can tell you here and out, once and for all that the stories in this work are not true; while not completely made up fiction; it is completely fictionalized. There is No Captain W.X.Y.Z. Olaf, no Jane Doe, and certainly no superscandal.

But I will tell you what is real. There is police corruption, cops lie, take evidence without a warrant, do whatever it takes to get a confession, and generally work to find whatever way around people's rights. And none of this is even a crime!

The problem that cops are rarely called out; and when they are it's usually on something bogus. Or in at least one case, blown out of proportion. And coming from me that's really saying something! And as a result there are 2 groups of people, those who believe the police can do no right; and those that believe that the police can do no wrong. And while a few very specific things may be more solved than not. The net effect is worse, and most of the real brutality, most of which boils down to police militarization, goes swept under the rug. Sure there were some people calling them out, but not enough; and I'm hearing less.

And before you call me crazy you should know a few true stories. There once (true story) was a girl whose mother was having kidney problems, and no one could reach her. For all they knew she could have dropped dead at home. She was using her phone in the classroom at school, so she could get cell service; but wasn't disturbing. The wanted to "confiscate[1]" it. She wouldn't give it over, so she was tackled by three large school district police officers in the hallway; someone else recorded it on their phone. But she was lucky compared to the child who was sleeping on a couch; when the condo was raided. It was later found that it was a drug raid; on the wrong᾽ address. They came in in a spray of bullets; she was killed and her father shoved face down in her blood.

There have been many militaristic raids, some they were even told to keep quiet and what lies to tell to their kids' school about homework on "confiscated computers". And usually in such raids they almost universally kill the pets, whether it's a harmless dog or a pit bull. Sound's crazy; but it's true. Doesn't end there.

There are people getting tazed to death and shot over petty disputes about getting out of vehicles, showing their hands, preventing escape, etc… Which is not to say that they should have been doing that; but it's not worth risking killing someone over! And no, stun guns are not non-lethal weapons. That is a straight up lie, possibly from the manufacturers. If you're really old, or have a bad heart, or or or, it's at least potentially lethal. The list continues.

And by this point I'm sure you are pretty skeptical. And if you can forgive me for quoting the X-files, "The Truth is Out There." Facts will confirm everything I tell you. But I will give you one precise example that I'm sure you will have at least heard of. Some time back in Chicago a 12 year old boy was playing with an apparently convincing toy gun in a park. Police were called out, and quickly shot him dead. The grand jury did not indibt; and as insults to injury the city went on to send a bill to his mother for hundreds of dollars for the ambulance ride to take the boy's body to the morgue. You know the case I'm discussing. But let us delve deeper; examining it form the perspective of not just the prosecutor and journalist, but also the philosopher and physicist (bear with me). They could have slammed on the gas; in fact if anything that would have been safer. And as an added kicker let us not forget, it was actually a toy gun. Let us delve deeper still. All people are created equal, ALL. Which means that the author's life is as valuable as the cop's life, as the fry cooks life, exc… But the one true (law would differ) exception is children. No matter your philosophical or spiritual beliefs (or mine), it is undisputed that children, by their young age, haven't gotten as much time spent alive. Cops however are required to be adults. Let us step back and see where we are so far. They (the police) shot and killed him (a child) in order to prolong their own lives; when they have already lived longer than him. And being 12 you know they could have looked at him and told at least that he was a minor. Meanwhile they could have simply fled with most likely less personal danger, and safely had the situation handled from a distance. And don't forget the kicker; unbeknownced to them, they were never in any real danger. Wait, I'm not finished. I know that many people would point out the fact they might have had families of their own, children to come home to. But know this. The egg heads teach us that our view of time as we know it is straight up wrong; and no, I'm not going off topic. Instead everything that has ever happened, right now as I edit this in, and will ever happen is happening simultaneously. That means two things. First, you are reading this very sentence as I am creating it; hi there. Second, that teaches that if he ever had children; he already had them. Admittedly almost defiantly in the future. As such while the cops' kids may have lost a parent; his were wholly blotted from time. Which is worse? You may not agree with me; but you no longer can call me mad, except if you mean angry.

---

[1] In the story of Robin hood; the rich stole form the poor ve sa ve completely lawful taxes; as opposed to a traditional criminal theft; home invasion, highwayman robbery, purse snaching etc…

Sometimes it's a larger scale. A major problem is cops just want to cover the collective blue butt, I mean line. They certainly don't want to turn in one of their own. They just don't want another scandal breaking that makes them all look like monsters. Sometimes however it goes beyond that. In Philly there was a real scandal in the 1970s in which it was found that the police were beating people into confessions in order to keep their conviction rates up. The journalists that broke the story, won the Pulitzer. In 2000 a movie about it came out called *The Thin Blue Lie*. So you can check that out yourself with ease. Also that teaches us how you in fact can have something to hide and not be up to anything; what if the police had caught the story in time!

Most police brutality is rooted in trying to keep the officer safe, not being willing it accept any danger whatsoever, like in the above story from the City of the Broad Shoulders and most all cases of police militarization. But sometimes the problem is not what the police do; but, as I have earlier touched on. What they have not done. Let me begin with a (brief) true crime story from a true crime show. A couple had just hosted a dinner party. It seemed a calm evening, they guests had left. Suddenly shots rang out. The wife was killed, and the husband injured. Despite being injured (and later nearly dying) the police said the shooter might still be in the house; so he had to get out on his own. No-one with a bullet proof vest came in to help him. Who did it? At first they suspected the business partner. He was like a part of that family. He did get over there pretty fast. Turned out the wife was sleeping with him; that affair was why she was on the phone with him at the time; which was how he got over there so fast. Earlier that day he had been shooting on the range, so he was covered in blowback; and he had been shooting the very same kind of gun used in that crime. Was he guilty? No. Turned out the son had gotten a criminal to do it; even left things open for him to get in. The criminal, when caught, claimed that the son made him do it. I do not recall them ever showing proof otherwise. Why? For that we must go back. At ten he was thought to be this perfect little boy. In time he became involved in drugs, and was beating up his mother, or at least physically overpowering her. The sent him off to numerous military schools and boot camps trying desperately to get him straightened out. He simply had to be straightened out. In time he was sent off to a place in American Samoa. The whitewashed term for it ever rang alarm bells. However he eventually grew to like it there. Except he didn't. He was in shock the entire time. I have never heard literally one word of investigation into that camp. Not the only such horror story I've heard. In another a boy at a military school / boot camp just wouldn't do what he was told, and ended up beaten to death. The son was convicted. But I can't help wondering; did they deserve it? No, I am not calling for vigilante justice; but it is a matter of reasonable doubt, I would've done all in my power to see him acquitted. Our legal system is based on the principle that it is better for 100 guilty accused to be exonerated; than for one wrongful conviction. 1% doubt is admittedly very small; but, the for mentioned statistic actually calculates out to under 1% (food for thought).

Meanwhile back at the ranch; police incompetence is quite probably about as big a problem. That book I'll let someone else write. But I will say how unless it's something serious, they won't make any attempt to solve it. And even if it is, they never go to the extreme that you see on TV, to say anything more would be splitting hairs.

But incompetence doesn't end there. While this work is completely fictionalized; a real scandal in the Houston Police Department was when their crime lab was found to be run so amuck that none of the innocent or guilty verdicts could be trusted.

(insert mule picture here)
Houston

And to blur the lines between corruption and incompetence; here's a few fast facts for if you're ever on a jury. Criminal science is far from what is believed to be. Beyond the formentioned scandal, I will just say a few things; seeing as I will leave the book on the many numerous weaknesses of criminal science to another author. But to tell you how much a joke it is. Lie-detectors at best can only detect nervousness. Bite mark analysis is one of the worst; there was a conviction based off marks that were later found could have come off a crawfish. It is not proven that no two people have identical fingerprints in fact if anything the opposite is true. Identical twins often have the same fingerprints; and fingerprints from crime scenes are often smudgy and / or blurred. Not to mention just part of a finger print. And as a cherry on top; they aren't run through computer system. Rather someone just does a visual side by side; and it has been confirmed that their yea or nay can be swayed (try reading that out loud). So bad is it that in the Madrid train bombing fingerprints were linked to an American who was held by the Federal Bureau of Investigation for weeks. Totally innocent; and you know something like that will have the very best there is. Admittedly not all criminal science is this pathetic; but it is very far from what we see on TV. And many of the tests that you see even on procedurals are almost never done in real life

Witness statements can be just as bad, or even worse than criminal science. When you remember something; you are pulling different things from different parts of your brain and re-creating the memory. Have someone dash into a room and steal a purse; and everyone will not be able to truly recognize the thief; they won't remember or will remember him much scarier. Cops (accidently even) can ask suggestive questions and ruin a witness statement; much like handling evidence with your bare hands. Even confessions can be a farce. Such was the incompetent railroad case of Jonbenet Ramsey; (will discuss more later). There was multiple separate confessions.

Getting away from incompetence (wouldn't we all like to); doesn't end with police. Prosecutors get convctions by confessions that were the product of nine hour interrogations; unless it is on the charge of treason in which case to prevent that very thing the confession must be made in open court. Suspects just want it to be over like it's a scientology audit. Use evidence that should have been thrown out of court. Threaten contempt to get the jury verdict they want. The list continues. Admittedly there is a lot more for the defendant once you've been charged with a crime. But you're far from out of the woods.

Even the court-building itself is not neutral in all this. When the jurors are being escorted to the water closet by the bailiff because the accused are so scary (true story) there probably is some unethical jury swaying afoot.

By all rights brutality doesn't end with the police either. Admittedly a prosecutor will not be out electrocuting someone; but it is an established fact that the greater danger doesn't come from the one with their finger on the trigger; rather the one with their finger on the button. The Slenderman stabbers being tried as adults, 11 year olds being locked up over drug offenses, the MacDonald murder case, someone or multiple people being executed *in modern day* when multiple people were in fact guilty of a murder plot that left a smaller number of persons dead (like, say, one), DA Devan Anderson locking rape victims up in jail just so they'd testify soasto obtain a conviction. When they would be violating their 5th amendment rights and testifying against their will; and then the local police not only did squat; but even carried it out! And so the list continues.

And don't think that prosecuting as an adult is only dangerous teenagers. I once heard of a 12 year old girl in Florida being tried as an adult for pinching a boy's butt at school. (And as another kicker; he liked it and wanted her to do it again)

Also in case you're still not with me on this; except of course in the case above. Know this; I have seen highlighters (made to look like pills) that were ages 14 and up, charms that were not for ages 15 and below. The list continues; but most everything here; less is more.

But just as there are good cops; not all prosecutors are bad. The prosecutors were in fact the heroes of the Jonbenet Ramsey case. Yes, that was a great, fine shining example of both common police incompetence, and common corruption. Also like in many murder cases; the police jump to one at least initially plausible conclusion. Then they just can't let it go. Unfortunately; there was no justice for the cops' crimes. There, like everything else in this portion of the foreword, as well as this work as a whole, is just so much that I can do no more than scratch the surface! This is not the first time in this work that there will simply be too much to enumerate. Every time you think you've hit metaphorical rock bottom. You find something else, and something worse; there is even more with everything in this section, but less is more. Being so high profile I won't take the time to go into details here; just know that there is a lot of junk; a lot of lies out there afoot. Also it does illustrate, along with many historical events, that compliance may actually not be a good thing.

It continues on beyond the district attorneys. Another scandal from the Bayou City area was when a bunch of juvenile court judges were found to have taken bribes to convict the accused; (the kiddie jail was privately run and doing those bribes made more profit). Juries?!?! Please?!?! They were not executed for kidnapping; but we know what happens to cops when they end up in jail. I would imagine the same happens to judges; I know jail is hell for those the hurt children.

And often judges could stop something that they should; usually without breaking any rules! However, they rule otherwise.

Jailors are also reached. Beyond not doing what they should and making the jails and prisons safe; there was a scandal in which it was found that the jailors were forcing the inmates to fight each other. They betted and generally were just having a good old time as if it were dogfighting. Those who refused to fight faced, tazing, pepper spray, beating, it was bad!

But furthermore, Alief ISD (in Texas) has an "alternative" school that is truly a jail school. In fact it originally was a sanitarium, nuff said. And all school districts inspect lockers and so on without a warrant. I have heard many stories as well of things such as kids (I believe they complied) having to take their shirts off to be checked for gang tattoos. Also we've all seen the dystopian movie where the people present their papers for being out in public to the police; but how great is the difference between that and presenting a hall pass? But perhaps the worst offense is when they are required to medicate their children for ADHD / ADD and the medication often is a reckless off-label-use that really only makes them drugged and / or it is not an off label use, but for that child presents a real medical danger.. And if you can't take that medication; you simply can't make the school district suck-it-up.

None of this is new. For examples, in the old wild west, the most dangerous man (not my words) may have not been a famous outlaw at all, but rather a sheriff known for his blonde hair down to his shoulders.

(insert mule picture here)
Houston

Another example was when Nickola Tesla died; there was a raid. No warrant. No nothing. All his notes and stuff he had been working on were seized. To this day; lost forever; a mystery of history. It goes back farther. The Boston massacre could very well be counted as law enforcement brutality; thought technically not police brutality because they were solders. Even in our constitution there was an attempt to prevent some of this stuff. It goes back farther still; in fact I'd be shocked if it didn't go as back as far as history itself. In semi-more recent times there have been even more cases. In this work's hometown I have found more cases there still. During WWI there was an attempt at a violent rebellion after an extremely bogus arrest, racially related. Following that those behind it (black solders), some were quickly and quietly hung. Few of the rest ever saw the light of day again. And a less violent side another more remembered case is Miranda v. Arizona;

It continues on; like for example how the border patrol can create checkpoints and stop everyone as if it were the border, so long as it is within 100 miles of some coast. Or city pounds that grab up pets and kill them within days at the most. And won't even call you if you don't have *their* special tag. Ordinances that place the burden of proof for having had a legitimate reason for having certain markers on the accused minor (not the only instance in which the burden of proof is on the accused) Like with everything else in this section and this work as a whole; there is far more to say. But I believe that such matters belong in something more political.

I imagine you may be thinking me to be pretty nuts. After all most all of this is a bit of a non-issue. But someone must pull the alarm, for people to realize the building's on fire. But even before the alarm is pulled; there is smoke. There is crackling. Take prosecuting as an adult. Most people rarely think about it one way or the other. But I have seen instances of the light of realization beginning to come on. People beginning to think twice. This is an issue that came up and was well discussed in the book *Battle of the Ampere* (Richard Paul Evans; part of larger series; series not related to prosecuting as an adult). Also there is a television series about people serving life sentences for things they did when they were 17 years old and younger; I haven't the stomach to be able to watch it. Also the formentioned slenderman case has at least drawn a slight amount of media attention; not anywhere near enough. Should be O.J. Simpson. Also let us not forget that there was a day in time, far enough back, in which no one batted an eye against slavery; no one thought a thing about it; who is to say what will have changed from being something undisputedly acceptable to undisputedly abhorrent come the passage of centuries. It is always far easier to see the horrors of previous generations in the days of old than in the days in progress.

Unfortunately, just as this text is unreadable seen in a mirror; so not all talk about the matters in this work are in our favor. By that I mean that there is a lot of programs out there glorifying police corruption and brutality. Or at least justifying it. That last sentence will seem contradictory to messages I will make later in this work. But instead I believe that authority needs to be hyper-accountable; because what if they're not on the up and up? And unfortunately such programs are not a fringe element. Shows such as *The closer* and *Major Crimes* are all too common. They're many more; but I just can't stomach such programming. Also it isn't just television programs; other forms of media also have similar problems. Also there are those that it's blurry, for example *The Heat* (a buddy cop movie) could possibly be put into this awful category; which is not to say that these programs should be banned, no, freedom of speech runs

(insert mule picture here)
Houston

both directions. As for that movie in particular; it would seem to glorify, except that it takes things to the degree of silly and absurd; so it's hard to say for certain.

You may very well believe, but let me anticipate your reaction, beyond simply a worry for your fellow human beings, let me include here, at the risk of how I may have already come across, a very brief classic:

I Didn't Speak Up by Rev. Martin Niemoeller

In Germany, the Nazis first came for the communists, and I didn't speak up because I wasn't a communist. Then they came for the Jews, and I didn't speak up because I wasn't a Jew. Then they came for the trade unionists, and I didn't speak up because I wasn't a trade unionist. Then they came for the Catholics, and I didn't speak up because I was a Protestant. Then they came for me, and by that time there was no one left to speak for me.

I'm not nuts, we're closer than we think. You may say that these things are rare (how rare is rare). But they are straight up bad. As such rare is too much. And we're closer than we think. No offense to Sinclair Lewis; but it *can* happen here. All it took to turn the major American city of Boston into what was tantamount to a strong-extreme military dictatorship was two bozos with broken pressure cookers, and on top of that all that was a failed attempt to catch the one still alive. Furthermore if the goal of a terrorist is to terrorize, and not to kill, than mission accomplished. Not the only case; similar issues with true stories of police violence, brutality, vandalism, and related happened in the Big Easy after hurricane Katrina. "Never let a crisis go to waste" I suppose.

Also at the end of this trilogy I have compiled, a collection go quotes, adages, proverbs and etc. as an afterword; admittedly some are better than others. Some touch on issues in which there was no place to touch on, some build on earlier points made, and etc… They have been put in no order whatsoever, as such they, unlike the rest of this book, can be read in any order; thought their pertinence, or full meaning, may not be seen at the first glance. However some of the quotes I will include here; seeing as they apply instead to this work in-and-of-itself.

"*How these papers have been placed in sequence will be made manifest in the reading of them. All needless matters have been eliminated, so that a history almost at variance with the possibilities of later-day belief may stand forth as simple fact. There is throughout no statement of past things wherein memory may err, for all the records chosen are exactly contemporary, given from the standpoints and within the range of knowledge of those who made them.*" –Dracula, by Bram Stoker. These words here are for all intensive purposes the preamble to the most famous vampire novel of all. And they apply to this work just as much as they did to that one.

(insert mule picture here)
Houston

"*The pen is mightier than the sword*" – proverb. Just as The Jungle (Upton Sinclair) brought about big changes; so I hope this work does also.

"*Style is but the faintly contemptible vessel in which the bitter liquid is recommended to the world*" – The Bridge of San Luis Rey

"*The business of literature is not to answer questions, but to state them fairly*" – Chekhov

Hi, I'm Captain W.X.Y.Z. Olaf. Currently I'm HPD captain of internal affairs; But most of this book will be flash backs to near present day in no particular order. However this chapter will take place in the future. Also most of it will be in 3rd person, but sometimes I will have to break in to make it make sense.

"Good morning Captain Olaf." said lutenant Stein.

"Good morning Lutenant Stein, Lutenat Wong-" Said Captain Olaf.

"We need to skip the formalities, just get to the Chief's office." said Lutenant Stein.

"What? What's going on?" said Captain Olaf.

"Beats us, It's on a need to know basis, and we didn't make the cut. But whatever it is big and important." said Lutenant Wong.

Later at the Chief's office:

"Hi captain, hurry in and shut the door behind you," said the Chief.

"What's up? What's going on?" said Captain Olaf.

Click

"Does the name Jane Doe ring a bell?" said the Chief, "Cus she's dead

"Isn't that what we used to call a female whose name was unknown? Course now they're all just Sam Does," said Captain Olaf.

"Correct, however it's also a Disobeyer name," said the Chief.

Ok, this is a cut in. Nowadays there aren't many traditional Christians left in America. They are a downtrodden class, and I am one of the very last civil servant Christians left. The Disobeyers are the largest group of Christians left. Founded back in 2014 in Paris France by Madelyn Cousteau. She was murdered in America at the age of 10. She is believed to have been working as a detective, but there is no proof. She was the daughter of Madelyn Murray O'Hare type atheists. That's also why she was sent to America. Nowadays they are the Global Siblinghood of the Sivil Disobeyers. (No I didn't spell that wrong.) Originally they were just the civil Disobeyers, coming from the Civil Rights leader Rev. Dr.

(insert mule picture here)
Houston

Martin Luther King Jr. Though in the interest of full disclosure they, among many other things, do have great admiration for Thoreau (wrote Civil Disobedience) they are mostly just exactly what we should be. However they have a few nutty views regarding running away from home; and there are a few crazies here and there. That is used to fight them, but they won't back down. They usually get murdered before they become adults, and those that do live into adulthood have stared many religious groups. And usually they do not have Christian parents, but most kids eventually become disobeyers, often before being Teens, or even tweens. Yea, life's hard for them. Also I would tell you how they will also have a disobeyer name which they take when they become disobeyers, much like when someone becomes a priest, monk, or nun. It's usually very weird, like Jose Wong or Mohammad Stein. Also they seem to have their own independent intelligence service that helps kids run away from home among other things, good things. Usually abused kids, but sometimes just those in big trouble or something else equally excusable. But they also use that service to expose real life villains of all kinds. Now, back to the story:

"O-k, Not sure why I'm here, 5.6 Disobeyers are murdered here In Houston proper per day, plus those that we don't know it was murder, if we ever know, probably like 14.1-14.8. Even if a cop did it, what makes this so-" said Captain Olaf.

Are you done rambling?" said the Chief.

"Yes Boss," said Captain Olaf.

"Don't call me by my first name," said the Chief.

"Why? Everyone calls everyone by their first name? Even my kids call me by my first name," said Captain Olaf.

"Coroner Alztimer, can you please explain to Captain Call Letter the gravity of our situation?" said Chief Boss.

"Yes, Boss," said the coroner, "We have till midnight tomorrow night to solve what is about to be the most high profile murder at least since the assignation of Pres., Kennedy was it?."

"Oh, well sooner or later we'd have a real live, one of those beat the clock, cases. But why can't we just have a stay of execution?" said Captain Olaf.

"Because it happened last night," said the Chief.

"Say what now?" said Captain Olaf.

"Yea, I was the one doing the autopsy," said the coroner.

"Why was there an autopsy?" said Captain Olaf.

"As of at least 3 months ago, all human deaths must have an extremely extensive autopsy, no matter how obvious the cause of death is or was. As I was saying, I always start by confirming the identity, but the prints didn't match," said the coroner.

Here I must cut in again, ever since way back in 2016 all persons must have their fingerprints and DNA in "the system" from birth on. Now I return you to your previously scheduled murder mystery which is already in progress. Just kidding.

"O-k, then what?" said Captain Olaf.

"I'm glad you asked, I ran her prints and DNA. DNA said it was her, but the prints were no match," said the coroner.

"Then how do you know there wasn't a body switch, or was there. Did you go old fashioned and have family or close friends or co-workers ID the victim?" said Captain Olaf.

"DNA, and Dentals. But it didn't still didn't add up. But at least the Autopsy results didn't add to confusion," said the coroner.

"How so?" Captain Olaf said.

"Well, strictly forensically speaking, the cause of death was execution by carbon monoxide poisoning. But that ID thing was so weird that I couldn't declare a cause of death. So I made a chat straight to cyber-crimes. Results just came in. That print thing was done by a Hacker in Moscow named Paydahack. Don't know who "Paydahack" is other than an expert hacker for hire. Course the New USSR is always so very helpful and friendly in such matter to begin with," said the coroner.

"Yes, Yes, I've had the pleasure a few times myself," said Captain Olaf, "So do we think this was a murdered disobeyer or an E-homicide or possibly both? Either one is so very bizarre." He said sarcastically.

"It's clearly a murder by execution for hire." said the Chief, "and it still gets worse."

Now I will start writing in the first person, this is getting old, cutting in and out like this.

"How so?" I said.

"We thought Jane Doe, or Jane Timmyson to use the real name, was the Tuesday night killer," said the Chief.

"That serial killer I paid little attention to," I said.

"Well unlike most, The Tuesday night Killer kills randomly in random ways. The only two things that connected the murders were that, as the name implies, they all happened on Tuesday night, and a very distinctive mark was left on all 93 bodies. One the police never released till the trial. The Tuesday night killer was, or probably is, good. However there were prints on the last crime scene. It gets even better," said the captain.

(insert mule picture here)
Houston

"She was young," I said.

"Precisely, the murder happened the night before her 13th birthday, the day after that birthday she was arrested," said the Chief, "Apparently the other 92 murders were enough for her to be tried as an adult, but in-adminisble in court. She alibied out on some. The Disobeyers have been wanting to take down prosecuting as an adult for quite some time calling it 'an evil double standard'," the captain shook his head and them said "And I guess they were right for once."

"How long did it take for her to be killed? And what does this have to do with Internal Affairs? And what about DNA evidence?" I said.

"She was killed the night before the first anniversary of the murder," said the coroner.

"Part of the new electric chair express lane?" I said; obviously not the legal term for the law.

"No, just didn't file for an appeal, wanted to get it over with and even had the date moved up," said the coroner.

"How did the parents allow that?" I said.

"Out of their hands," said the chief.

"When this gets out it will be a mess, so let's keep this quiet as long as possible, which is till we have to release the death certificate, with is abbreviated autopsy results and the cause of death," said the coroner.

"But still, what does this have to do with Internal Affairs, and where did DNA evidence come in?" I said.

"Nothing, but this is such a disaster we need out cleanest cop on top of this, and no DNA evidence was submitted by the prosecution, which was the defense's main defense. But still Jane was convicted," said the Chief.

"Who was this judge?" I asked.

"Justice Crayer," said the Chief.

I blanched.

"What? the name ring a bell?" said the Chief.

I shook my hands up and quickly replied "NO No, no, nothing, nothing. Well. I believe. that in such. a. murder case is this. standard procedure is. to start by. in addition to. the. Normal.-" I studdered.

"Spit it out man!" said the chief.

"procedures of any murder. Interview the judges and prosecutors," I said, "Say, who approved Jane to be tried as an adult? Let me guess. CRAYER!" I said.

"Uhhh, yea, how'd you know?" said the Chief.

"Lucky guess," I lied.

Later in Crayer's layer, I mean Chamber

"So detective, what can I do you for?" said the villain, I mean Crayer.

"Captain, and does the Name Jane Tommyson A.K.A. Jane Doe ring a bell?" I asked.

"Yes, I believe we had her gassed last night, I do believe," He replied.

"Well, that execution has now proven to be a murder. Standard procedure says we must question the bail judge, the case judge, and any other justices involved. You are all of the above.

"Well, I believe the greater Newer York City area has had only one other Murder by execution; back in 20-16 was it. I'm surprised that you have a standard procedure. Also I thought you were Internal Affairs," He said.

I should let you know that Houston is often called Newer York or New New York. You can guess why. The DFW area metroplex is new California and I can't remember what city is New San Francisco.

"True, and that one homicide really cleaned up forensic science. Who knows what this will clean up," I said.

"Then out the window I saw Juvenile News Network's world famous news corner (really big screens, next to each other, taking up 2 sides of a building) overlooking Herman Park. It went from a snowy Alaskan scene to the headline "Innocent Child Executed in America." Busted.

I rushed back to 1 P.P.

At the Chief's office:

"The disobeyers are making a huge deal out of this. As we feared. Tonight they will have a "Peaceful riot" outside the criminal courthouse. Not sure what that means, but it doesn't sound good. Also the victim's best friend and twin brother John Tommyson A.K.A. John Doe is here to be interviewed as a next of kin," said the Chief, "Whenever there is a bit of corruption against them it is a huge deal."

(If only what he had said was true)

Later at the interview room.

"Ah! Glad to see there's a brother on the case," said John.

"Yu, yea, yea," I said looking at my, well they say that it has nothing to do with demeaning us, we (we being Christians and disobeyers) just must wear demining markings safety pinned onto our close everywhere so that others can isolate themselves from "Ideological disease." Obvious lie.

(insert mule picture here)
Houston

Poor kid, his scrubs were all a mess (everyone wears scrubs nowadays, it's just the style). Looked like he'd been crying all night, which he probably had. Seeing his black band (yes, people have gone back to that custom) next to the marking pinned on his shirt so represented the fate of all us Christians.

"Look, I imagine you're mad and just want to spit in my eye, but I'm not trying to squeeze some trumped up or hate speech confession out of you; or some stupid lead. I have a real mess on my hands, I just want to find the real killer," I said.

"That's what the other detectives said," said John.

"I'm Internal Affairs, I lock up 'the other detectives'," I said.

"Just-start asking questions," Said John clearly trying to not cry.

"Did your twin sibling have any enemies?" I asked.

"None in particular, but being a disobeyer Jane faced the prosecution of today. And I know what you're going to say, It's not Rome, or Iran. But this is different. Rather than government paid hangmen we need to look out for it's social hate. Hate speech sentences, underage religious practices, Christian free zones and stores, micropersicution, Chsirtiphobia and Disaphobia, serial killers, police graft, and other attackers. I would know. We all would," said John.

"I pointed at the mark pinned to my uniform and said "sib, I am no stranger to this."

He just broke down.

The next morning:

"Things have gone from bad to worse," said the Chief.

"I know, I was there," I said.

"I also want to put you to work finding who shot that officer. You know, he died at disobedience hospital," said the chief.

"Solved," I said.

"Really? Who did it, Let me guess, no no don't tell me it was one of those-" said the chief.

"Me," I said.

The captain reacted as would be expected.

Let me make this part make sense to you. For starters the peaceful riot was keeping anyone from entering the main courthouse, never mind there was no one but janitors and security guards on duty. Maybe someone that forgot their HoLo (mobile device) at the office. And as for that crazy hospital, you'll see.

(insert mule picture here)
Houston

After a lot of studdering the chief said "This is the worst thing since the disobeyers stole Intel and exposed so much anti-disobeyer corruption a third of the department was sent to jail, three months ago."

"Yes, I remember, been a long time since I raided central station. I had you in tie bands, in this very office," I said.

"Yes, do not think for a nanosecond that I have forgotten," said the chief.

"No jury would convict me," I said.

"Well, do you remember when the terrorists looked to this city, they imploded Galleria 2 and blew up the water to the med center, which they then burned down, and we also lost 4 refineries and the Oak Forest neighborhood. And to make things worse, the disobeyers were the ones that fundraised to rebuild the med center. So now it is one big private religious hospital," The chief steamed and said "Should have been free, and secular, like in Canada, or Cuba. But now people are inclined to come here and skip all that. Now where was I?"

"11k dead," I said.

"No, no, no, the point of that," said the chief.

"Your guess is as good as mine, actually since you were talking, better," I said.

"Oh, right, do you remember the disaster after the great NYC cell phone heist," said the chief.

"I'd hardly call that a disaster," I said.

"I would, they made off with quadrillions of dollars in stuff, cops just happen to aggressively storm the wrong place, next thing you know there is 19 dead officers, 22 dead minors that we couldn't prove guilty, and way too disobeyer friendly schools," said the chief.

At this point I'll let you know that what happened was stolen or "confiscated" stuff went Robin Hood. Stolen back to give to the rightful owners

"You mean equal rights," I said, "Because that still hasn't happened."

"Watch your toung captain, I'm still looking for a reason to terminate you," said the Chief.

"Just skip the, well, well, well what is the point of this?!" I said.

"There's somebody from GSSD to talk to you. It looks bad, real bad," said the Chief.

"For me or for you?" I said.

"JUST GET OUT OF HERE WILL YA?!?!?!" shouted the Chief.

later at the designated meeting place.

(insert mule picture here)
Houston

"Oh where is the person? This is the place and time," I thought out loud.

Then she arrived, maybe fifteen, and no point in dwelling on it, but really looked like she had been through the gutter of life.

"Hi, I'm Ming Rain," she replied.

"Anyone else?" I asked.

"No, I don't need a translator," she said.

"Well, I know from the news reports that when something like this happens, you make request, or demands, depending on the news source. To improve the bad conditions you live in, so where do we start?" I asked.

"Well, you're wrong, we make demands to make the world a better place. For example I have just exposed the largest scam in German history, and in Geneva, as you may remember, we had twice the casualties of the police, and half the hostages we saved weren't even disobeyers. Disobeyer intelligence exists to make the world a better place. We're not perfect, but when you look at the facts, you see that were not nearly as bad as you thought. Also I'm surprised they'd have a disobeyer on 'the force'" she said.

"I'm not a disobeyer, But I am Christian. There is a difference, albeit small, that has been forgotten," I said "And why do you want me to be the one that does the negotiations?"

"Ah! just is there is a forgotten difference, in that there are Mormon or messianic disobeyers, but admittedly not many. As for why you, that doesn't concern me," she said.

"I'm surprised that they'd send only one person," I said.

"Well, I'm a detective, basically it's our equivalent of an MP. Whenever I'm called in it's big and it's bad. However usually it's a leaker, defector, or spy. But, let's get to business," she said.

"Yes, I think you should go far," I said.

"Well, we may be forcing the hand of the senate on this surrender treaty, but we still should not push our luck," she said.

"Last night, you had a peaceful protest. 43 of your random members, mostly not even those in disobeyer intelligence, the youngest being 2 going on three, were shot to death because they came prepared and shield themselves from flash grenades and bean bags. Push as hard as you please," I said.

She said "Well, police militarization ended at NYC phone, and well, there is those incessant 'hate speech'-

"Yea, that would be pushing it too far," I said.

(insert mule picture here)
Houston

"You're right, but we do want changes in Prosecuting as an adult," she said, "For everyone."

"Only changes?" I replied.

"Yea, minimum age 16. No exceptions. Even if caught as an adult. Also adult maturity level must be proven beyond a reasonable doubt," she said.

"Done." I said.

"And no trumped up charges, against anyone," she said.

"Wouldn't work. Already we have such laws. Events like this clean things up, but that's all that cleans things up. More laws will just be ignored," I said.

"Oh, well, that makes sense," she said, "Also, no taking forensic evidence without a warrant or permission."

"You know what is already on file for everyone. What's the point?" I said.

"Advancements are coming soon, didn't hear it from me. Also there is more than DNA and fingerprints.

"Sold, err, done," I said.

"Well, what else is there?" she said.

"You should ask for police to be banned from lying. And try to get these to be retroactive so we can prosecute some of these animals," I said.

"No, no, tis always better to bury the hatchet. And I'm not so sure about police lies. That being said we have had many of our own get killed because of police lies and secrecy," she said.

"Well, there is just one person that I-" I said.

"You've got some personal grudge-" she said.

"No," I said, and while I didn't mention my personal 'dealing' if you will I did say, "A very long time ago I came to a crime scene. A judge had been knocked out with a mallet and his six year old daughter had been cut in half above the hips with some form of samurai sword. At first the forensic evidence said it was the older brother. He had been at karate but had slipped out for some unknown reason. But he said that his dad had told him to do that. After being transferred from juve to adult prison, bearing in mind that he was 11, he was found in his cell, strangled. An investigation and autopsy proved it wasn't murder or an accident. However the same night the twin brother of the victim was found behind a police station, stabbed in the neck to death. At the time of the incident he and his mom were at the pediatrician's. When I told him about the murder he said he felt a lot of guilt for having not been a better brother, and him, being from a Christian upbringing, said he just wanted to go join his sister on the other side-"

(insert mule picture here)
Houston

"Sounds like an early disobeyer," she said.

"Not really, the coroner said it was self-inflicted, called it an accident. I like to tell myself it was," I said.

"Well, while I don't know about that young, but such things, let alone to this degree, are very rare among disobeyers, and are always made the face of disobeyer intelligence. Even though we do so much more," she said.

"Well, it was all so crazy that I had to look into things, turns out that judge was about to be arrested for taking bribes to approve children to be tried as adults, sometimes under completely absurd circumstances-" I said.

"It's always absurd. Furthermore, I guess being told his big brother did it pushed him over the edge, no sicko pun intended," she said.

"None taken, as I was saying it was a long and hard investigation, going much farther than normal, still have no proof, but the judge somehow thought that that would get him off, and, somehow he was right. I've seen a lot but that, for some reason, is still what comes to mind when I hear the word 'evil'" I said.

"Let me guess, that was Crayer," she said.

"Correct, bingo, affirmative," I said.

"Done, we'll take him. Let's say that we're just using him as an example, may have to go after the prosecutors as well. But we can go easy on them. What about nowadays?" she said.

"Well, he still has no more children, adult or otherwise, and his wife never knew, but divorced him. As for the subject of lying cops-" I said.

"Wait, what about the big brother?" she said.

"Oh, yes I almost forgot, his 'dad' I later uncovered pulled strings to have him tried as an adult-" I said.

"Did he have priors?" she asked.

"Yea, besides a room that looks like a ninja layer he had been a serial biter." I said, "Earlier had served nearly 4 months."

"Are you sure Crayer didn't do that to save him from juve, or the son was the one pulling-" she said.

"Why would he-" I said.

"Never mind, never mind, we stopped that warden, what was that about lying cops?" she said.

"O-k I'll assume I shouldn't be worried," I said.

"You need not worry anymore. Please go on," she said.

(insert mule picture here)
Houston

"Well I'll have to tell you a story from when I was working in suicide," I said.

"Say what?" she said.

"Yes, I started out as a beat cop, then assessing accidents, then suicides, then a homicide detective, then internal affairs, then captain of internal affairs," I was sure glad that it didn't come up that I was a Crayer victim.

"Oh, please go on." she said.

"Ok, where should I start?" I said.

"How about the very start of it all," she said.

And so I began:

"Ok, what've we got?" I asked.

"I see the coroner beat you this time," said a regular officer.

"The coroner is here, take me to him," I said.

"Her," he said.

"Hu?" I said.

"Her, the coroner is-" he started.

"What-ever just take me to the coroner," I said.

"Funny you should say 'whatever, '" said the officer.

"Oh no, not one of those," I said.

"Fraid so," said the coroner.

"Oh, Coroner Parkinson," I said.

"Ironic to have someone die in the Texas Medical Center," said Coroner Parkinson sarcastically.

"Ok what've we got?" said I.

"Looks like another jumper, what is it about this garage? 11th death this year, and only February," said Coroner Parkinson.

"Yea, last one was this lady in her car-" I said.

"Pills?" said the officer.

(insert mule picture here)
Houston

"No, stroke, mid-90s, not the point, had officer Wells check to see the roof because it looked a little funny," said Coroner Parkinson.

"How so?" I said.

"Well, usually they aim for concrete, but sometimes they will hit something different, like a brick wall, or if it was an accident, no telling," said the Coroner.

"Hit something weird, and do signs of an accident, maybe something fishy?" I said.

"Can't declare anything till I get her to the morgue, but this I have never seen before," said Coroner Parkinson.

"Headfirst into a parking ticket dispenser?" I said, "Could have missed, has this trapped those in the garage?"

"Just from getting in, could have been a coincidence. But to be safe I had him look on the roof. Also it's weird that she wore no socks and took her shoes and watch off," said the coroner.

"Watch?" I said.

"Yup, found it in her shoe," said the officer.

"Well, probably just letting us know that it wasn't murder. Anything to ID the Jane Doe?" I said.

"Only thing on the body, besides clothes of course, was this driver's license, just old enough to drive by months. Presumably to help ID. But once again, will have to get her back to the morgue to be certain of anything, except that she's dead." said Coroner Parkinson.

"Well, any car of hers here?" I asked.

"Looked, cameras say she walked in off the street. But as a bit of weirdness, did find socks half way up in the stairwell," said the officer.

"Well, if they're hers, that will help the family to confirm their worst nightmares. You did say you bagged em? Right?" I asked.

"Right here," he said, handing me the socks.

When I got to her family's apartment, which was only one block away and 6 floors up, I found cops were already there, I was just the man to confirm their worst nightmares.

"Hello?" I said.

Another one?! Why are you here and not out looking-

"Then what?" she said.

"Sorry, that part is still, after so many years so hard to regurgitate, could I just do a quick overview?" I asked.

"Sure, sure," she said.

"Well, she had a 13 year old brother, he instantly snapped, said his parents may as well have just stabbed her. Been easier on her if she had had her brains blown out; than driven off a cliff. Would've liked to have known him, to have been joking at a time like that. I tried to calm him down, but he grabbed a gun, shot my gun out of my hand, and said he was going to kill his parents. (pause) " and just turned the gun on himself."

"Sounds like one of those stories that we obsess over, you know as a face of disobeyer intelligence," she said.

"Yea, then I saw that the four year old sister saw and heard everything." I said.

"What then? And why did the sister-" she said.

"Just about everything teenage, grounded, forced to break up with her boyfriend, phone taken away, just generally the works," I said, "That is my single most traumatic memory. Years later I got to talking with another officer who had had a semi-similar experience. He asked when to the flashbacks stop? I simply said 'they don't."

"Horrible, but what does that have to do with lying cops?" she asked.

"I, and I still wonder if I was lying, thought that it was really that he just couldn't stand living with his parents. I said if he just came with me there would be no prosecution and he would never have to come back. before that I was just another liar. But that straightened me out. He even said how you couldn't trust anything a cop says. Sadly he was right about that," I said.

"Well, no more police lying-" she said.

"Also I think you should ask, no demand legislation that will get our organizations to actually work together," I said.

"I don't think that would work," she said.

"I think that it would still get past," I said.

"I mean the law wouldn't work," she said.

"I don't know, and it has gotten so bad that a little kid is shot to death, and they just assume it was suicide or an accident and the gun somehow walked," I said.

"Oh, ok then, If this works the battle of Britain is over," she said.

"Battle of Britain? What does WW|| have to do with anything? Oh right," I said.

(insert mule picture here)
Houston

"Gotten so bad we are saying, besides safety tips, just 'keep calm and carry on'" she said.

"Done," I said.

epilog

Just by putting together their evidence and our databases we stopped 90% of it in just one day.

Jane Doe's murder was never solved. I had to acknowledge the idea of some degree of an inside job to make all this happen, or any one of dozens of other theories. But I think it was just the Tuesday night killer wanted out, or to be a new killer. And Jane Doe was just a perfect scrape goat (yes, that's how people say that nowadays).

The prosecutors pled down to 10 years suspended. The judge's murder trial was a mega trial that was all people talked about for some time. Here are the only worthwhile highlights

The central part:

"Mr. Crayer, did you approve Jane Timmyson to be tried as an adult?" said the prosecutor.

"Yes," said the villain, I mean Judge Crayer.

"Did you sentence her to death?" said the prosecutor.

"Yes," said Crayer.

"Mr. Crayer are you familiar with Nuremburg?" she (the prosecutor) asked.

"Objection to relevance," said Crayer lawyer.

The judge paused and decided the whole case in one word "denied."

"Yes," said Crayer.

"What was their defense?" she asked.

"We were just obeying orders," said Crayer.

"Were they convicted?" she asked.

"Yes," said Crayer.

"Mr. Crayer, who ordered you to approve Jane Timmyson as an adult?" she asked.

"No one," he replied.

"Mr. Crayer, who ordered you to sentence Jane Timmyson to death?" she asked.

"No one," he replied.

(insert mule picture here)
Houston

"Your honor, people and persons of the Jury, I rest my case" she said.

The victim's family statement, delivered by John Doe:

"Well, never really thought I'd be here. Never thought she'd be convicted, never thought that the police would become honest and actually do their job. I'm not perfect, As I'm sure you know I at one point started to satanically murder Judge Crayer, but had a change of heart when a saw his toddler daughter. Still spent 8 months in jail. Funny, she gets tried as an adult and killed, I just got a few months, and then released just in time for her execution. As a Christian and a Disobeyer I'm trying to forgive him, and the killer, but it's still a work in progress, and probably always will be. I know that we'll eventually be murdered, all disobeyers know that, but you still somehow think that it won't really happen to you. You know, you'd think I'd just be crying all the time, but really, I just keeping thinking about all that Jane will never get to do: will never get to be an aunt, never get to be mum, never remarry, never get to go vertical cliff wall camping in Scandinavia, the list goes on. Yes, remarry, like most disobeyers Jane did marry. And it was the typical case.   Never not to live together, but they were great together. He was a part of our family, and Jane his. At least she lived a good life, well, shouldn't use the past tense. But unlike most disobeyers her parents and all her immediate family and most of her in-laws were disobeyers and / or Christians. It is hard, but I am comforted to know that she's back together with Wolf, her late other half, obviously a disobeyer name; who became a crime statistic years ago: that was hard enough. This has been hard on my other siblings, Sam, Charlie, Avery, and Taylor. My sib Dis is just a baby so 'I'll never really know it. Trying to be a good big brother and help us all through this. If possible this has been even harder on our parents than me. They've had their faith challenged. I briefly snapped and defected to deliberate devil worship. But right before I satanically killed the defendant I came back. I just like to focus on the fact that my twin is better off than ever. And someday I will join her outside the boundaries of space and time," said John.

The last words from Jane Doe as she was strapped down at 11:59 pm:

"Well, I know you all have been through so much. But hang in there. Mourn if you must. But I'm just glad to have lived such a good ling life. My sibling in law had the same date of birth as me, but died over 10 years ago. You may feel sorry for me; but don't. Actually I am to be envied. I'm getting off easy, and have had 12 good years, and one ok year. Sure there's regrets, there always is, should've tried harder to remarry, should have been a better family member, should have been a better disobeyer, should have been a better lot of things. But, while I didn't want to be convicted, I actually got the ending I wanted. I only fought the death penalty because to not do so, would have been suicide, which is murder, which is wrong. But, there are worse ways to croak I suppose. I am glad to have lived long enough to see so many disobeyer victories of different sizes and forms. I had a good run, and I will be able to do whatever job is waiting for me on the other side with peace now that I am sure that my brother is back on this side, and free. I have nothing to complain about. But, if i may have a dying wish, it would be that this somehow has a good outcome, preferably on a large scale," she turned her head and said "Ok, I'm ready."

(insert mule picture here)
Houston

Also congress (against their will obviously) gave into all their demands that were done in what was really just a surrender treaty. What we did, did far more good than harm.

In case you were wondering the proceeding was not the only dealings I had with Judge Crayer. And F.Y.I., he has no connection the 30's judge whose murder took 90(ish) years to solve, hasn't been yet solved at the time of this being published. I still remember my first day as captain like it was yesterday, because it was. Ok, just kidding I'm writing from the future; and sending it to your present day.

RIIP

"FREEZE" screamed a woman. The officers reached for their guns, but paused when they saw the bomb vest. "NO sudden movements, slowly reach for the ceiling, and move to then center of the room. As they did so she then said "Here's how it will be, this is a hostage situation. If you shoot me my hand will go off the detonator, and blow us all to hell. If I shoot you and you shoot me, then well. Now then, Phones, Tasers, weapons, all in this recycle can," she said as she took one off the officer's weapons. "Now, you there, in the plain close, slowly put that phone on loud speaker and call 911."

He did so as everyone else handed all their stuff and weapons over.

"Harris County 911, what is your emergency?" said the 911 operator.

"I'm at 1 Police Plaza, central station," said the woman.

"Do you, need an ambulance?" He replied.

"No, there's a hostage situation," said the woman.

Thinking this to be a joke he replied "Should I send officers?"

"No need I have, let's see," then counting out loud she said "17, 18, 19, 20' 20 officers, what? What's that? No? Just, just 19 officers and one, somebody," she said.

"Then how is there a hostage situation?" said the operator.

"Bomb vest," she said.

"And you are the 20th person?" said the operator.

"No, I'm the person taking the hostages. You! You there! With the badge around your neck, who's the head of Internal Affairs?!" she said.

"I believe lutenant call letters, just made It." she replied.

"Real Name, please," she said.

"Captain Olaf," she said.

"I will only speak to Captain Olaf, head if internal affairs." she told the operator, "And by the fact that I have 19 cop hostages in the largest police station, probably in the state, and I do believe I see security cameras, I do believe, you should take this threat very seriously." And she hung up.

Then I arrived.

"You were right, that place does make the best dogs outsidea New York-" I said.

"I assume you're phone was off. Thank goodness you're here, we've evacuated the building, but there's 19 or 20 people we can't get out," said another Captain.

"What was that?" I said.

"A hostage situation," said the man.

"What does that have to do with me? I never worked in hostage negotiation? I have to get to work." I said.

"You can't," he replied.

"Oh, really," I said.

"The hostage situation is at 1PP," He said.

"What? How it that even possible?" I said.

"Bomb vest," said the man.

"OH NO! But, what does this have to do with me? Is it a cop taking hostages?" I said.

"Don't think so, but, everything about this case has been so insane nothing would surprise me. Now hurry!" He said taking me by the hand.

"I know you aren't trained in this, and I can only take time to tell you to keep her-" He said.

"Her?" I said.

"Yea, as I was saying keep her on the phone and remember that if she's talking, she's probably not hurting hostages. Also keep her calm, same reason. Don't even know how this could have a happy ending. Well, good luck," He said, handing me a phone.

"So, Uh, Hi, You wanted to speak to me?" I said.

"You the head of internal affairs?" she said.

(insert mule picture here)
Houston

"As of today, yes," I replied.

"Why should I believe you?" She said.

"Turn on a video cha- you know, if you don't believe I'm who I say I am then you'll never believe anyone about who they say they are," I said.

"You could show your badge over a video feed," she said.

"Or someone else could just as easily show my badge over a video feed," I said.

"Good point," she said.

"So, whatdaya want?" I said.

"My demands are that you kill justice Crayer!" she said.

After the uncanny shook I said "Kill, as in dead-kill?"

"What other kind of kill is there?" she said.

"Good point. Any particular reason that you what him dead? Or did you just wake up one day and decide to have someone killed and the dart landed-" I said.

"DON'T BE A SMAR-" she said mad.

"Why?" I said being about as annoying as possible.

"Do. Not. Toy. With. Me." she hissed into the phone.

"Good point, but seriously, there must be a reason that you took 20 folks hostage with a bomb-" I said.

"Indeed there is, Judge Crayer approved my son to be tried as an adult when he was 13," she said, "And I could just kill him myself, but if I can make *you* cops kill him, Any furthermore you cops did nothing but help him. And we all know it's a common military school technique to punish the group so that they'll make sure the one won't-"

"And that makes it ok?!?! Shoot- No wrong choice of words-" I said.

"Get to the right choice of words," she said.

"I mean that there should be a union to prevent stuff like that-"I said.

"Just be glad I'm not scalping and lynching cops" she said.

"Get real, Like you could," I said, "And what did he supposedly do?"

"No, No, no, years ago, and does it matter?" she said.

"I. Guess, Not. But, why this now? Took this long to plan?" I said.

"Nope, got killed in jail yesterday," she said sounding mad.

"My sympathies-" I said.

"Look, uncase you haven't figured it out yet, this is NOT going to be a normal hostage situation. You think you're going to keep me on the line to keep your people safe, till you can kill me; unless I comply to a t and then it will only be life in maximum security jail? Not gunu happen. If my plan works out as planned I won't survive. But know 2 things number uno: We will only talk, and only like this, when I have a reason. Number dose: for every hour you keep me waiting, I'm going to kill one of your boys in blue. And obviously any attempt to not comply with *me* will result in the death of all hostages, and any that attempt to invade. Any questions?" she said.

I got an idea and replied "Yes, one, does it matter how we kill Crayer?"

"No, as long as I can see that It's him and he's dead. I'm a lot of things, but not a liar. I have no motive to kill these hostages, except to make you do what I want. But there's just one little problem," she said.

"What's that?" I said.

"You can never expect people to fully believe a threat unless you first break a few fingers," she said.

BANG!

"Any other questions?" she said.

"Yes-" I said.

"Yes I killed him. I'm having another hostage send pictures to the news to make sure believe me," she said.

"That wasn't the question, the question was does the countdown start now?" I said.

"About 10 seconds ago," she said, setting a timer on a phone, "Anything else?"

"No." I said. Then she hung up on me.

"OK! LISTEN UP PEOPLE! She's Avenging The Death Of Her Son. If ya'll can figure out who her son is, that could help." I shouted.

"On it," said hostage rescue officers.

(insert mule picture here)
Houston

"And I want paramedics and firemen in case she does blow!" I shouted.

"Way ahead of you," said the lead official from the fire department.

"Captain," I said.

"Yes, Call letters?" He said.

"Let's get to Crayer's," I said.

Later in his chambers

"Dude? You ok there?" said the judge's assistant.

"Yea, yea," I said.

"And you are?" he said.

"Captain Olaf, head of HPD Internal Affairs. A.K.A. Captain call letter-" I said.

"You look like you're still in your rookie year," he said.

"That I am," I said, "I will have been on the force 1 year next month."

"How does an officer end up rising through the ranks so fast?" he said unbelieving.

"Being framed for murder at 10 because they can't solve it leaves them without much of a choice in the matter-" I said cutting myself off, "Oh Judge Crayer, Crayer!"

"Yea?" he said headed into his chambers.

"Need to talk to you, now," I said.

"Great, call my secretary to secdule it," he said.

"I'm sorry, was there an 'if it so please your highness' in what I just said," I said.

"Watch your tongue lutenant!" he said.

"It's captain, and this is the hallway, you can't put me into contempt here," I said.

"O-K, I'll bite. Whatdaya want?" he said extra crabby.

"Does the name Greg Ross ring a bell?" I said.

"No, and before you continue, I ask you why should I care about whatever this waste of my time is?" he said.

"Tried as an adult, about 20ish years ago. killed in jail yesterday-" I said till I was cut off.

(insert mule picture here)
Houston

"Yea, lots of that has happened in my court room-" he said.

"I was talking, and I know. Well, his mother is avenging his death by holding 19 cops hostage, with a bomb vest. Every hour we let you live she kills another cop," I said, "Already one dead."

"Sounds like I need police protection," he said.

"Keep dreamin," I said.

"Captain please-" said the hostage rescue captain.

"Captain, could you go, say, make sure the car is sitll black and white, or something," I said.

"O-K, don't want to mess with Internal Affairs," he said.

"Let's take this to your chambers," I said.

"Good, but can we make this quick," he said.

"It'll take however long it will take," I said.

"I have an appointment!" he said.

"Then if it runs over I will personally tell them to get lost," I said.

"So, ya gunu kill me?" he said.

"No, If I was going to kill you I would have done it a long time ago," I said.

"Threatening a judge is crime CAPTAIN," he said being so snotty.

"Hey, you want a threat, I can give you a threat!" I said.

"You watch your tongue officer!" he said.

"I'll say whatever I want you you'll find a way to live with it," I said.

"CONTEMPT!" he said reaching to ring for a bailiff.

So then I slapped his hand away, shook his gavel above his head, and said "I run Internal Affairs! There is no one to arrest me!-"

"You've got priors," He said.

"Not guilty verdicts that backfired on everyone!" I said, still holding the gavel, but calmly.

"From my courtroom!" he said.

(insert mule picture here)
Houston

"EXACTLY!" I said. I really wanted to put it through his skull. Remembering the horrors, all the PTSD counseling, um, well, not important.

"You want someone to hear us," he said.

"I want you to-" I said.

"Yea, not the first cop that wanted me to not do something," he said.

I had been watching over this guy and then it all became so clear, so much, (dramatic pause) evil "You are, and you killed, and you, and me, and you probably know who-" I was unable to complete a thought before another gasp came to mind.

"HOW ABOUT I JUST KILL YOU AND MAKE THE WORLD A SAFER PLACE!" I screamed, just as the appointment stepped inside and see me raising the gavel over Crayer.

"Is this a bad time?" she said.

"Yes, get lost," I said.

"O-k," she said.

Then I put the gavel down as they left.

"So? you going to kill me?" he said again.

"Judge, if I was going to kill you, I would have done it a long time ago. That being said it still is on the table." I said.

"Refresh my memory, which one were you?" he said.

"Oh you've done it so many times, on my birthday, my big sister of close age and little brother -" I said.

"Oh, yea, the birthday boy, didn't you come close to-" he said.

"Nearly ended up where I am before 12, that's how bad it looked," I said.

"Sounds like you blackmailed your way to where you are now," he said.

"Number 1, I didn't really blackmail, number two, I've done all my jobs well number three, pots should not call kettle's black, number four, you can't come forward without confessing to-" and then the other captain came back.

"Hey, I heard shouting and nearly got trampled by a swarm of bailiffs, fortunately I was able to chill them, everything ok?" he said.

"No, we have no 18 of our own in front of a firing squad," I said.

(insert mule picture here)
Houston

Bing Bing

"17," he said.

I had to stop myself from cussing.

"You may remember in William Shakespeare's' classic 'The Tragedy of Romeo and Juliet-'" I said.

"What does the world's most canned love story have to do with anything?" he said.

"Actually the world's most canned love story is friends-not just friends, anyway I'm glad you asked, Juliet Capulet, or I guess at that point It should be Juliet Montague-" I said.

"Get On With it!" said the captain.

"Right right, well, she, before the final bad ending, I never liked-" I said.

"Get on with it Officer," said Crayer.

I took a moment and couldn't think of a better response so I just said "That's Captain to you."

In a little shock the captain said "seriously?"

"As you may remember Juliet faked her own death, making her seem dead. That might just solve our not so little problem," I said.

"I thought you didn't believe in lying, and I don't think he'd cooperate," said the captain.

"There is an exception to every rule, and, Do we have to give him a say in the matter?" I said.

"Yea!" he said.

So then I said, "I may not be able to make you fake your death, but I can make you come down to 1PP." So then I grabbed him by the ear, twisted and made him follow.

"OW ow ow ow," he said.

Then in front of nearly a dozen bailiffs I said "Pipe down or you'll be the first judge to be shoved in the trunk of a squad car.

I then rushed back to 1PP and was told to keep Crayer away. If the bomb was powerful enough then it might be detonated in the hope that the blast would take out Crayer.

"So, you killed him?" she said.

"If I did, that would only encourage people like you-" I said.

(insert mule picture here)
Houston

"We so sure that's a bad thing?" she said.

I paused and then said "I never claim to know what someone's going through, but I will say that your son was a Crayer victim, so was I. But what about these cops? I can't let you go, and that's the only way that Crayer could get killed. But what about the hostages? What did they do? What is their crime? Crayer's a monster, but even he didn't even try to kill Greg, unlike a certain somebody else. Just, be logical, reasonable, and rational. I can understand wanting to be some vengeful judge killer, but is-" I said.

"You're right," she said.

BANG!

I wasn't sure what happened, and everyone else waiting for a bomb to go off.

Then a man came on the phone and said "She did herself in, was cornstarch, fake bomb, all clear."

"Who is this?" I said.

"Officer Eduardo Garcia," He replied.

Then I had the pleasure of shouting "FAKE BOMB!! ALL CLEAR!!

By now you're probably sick of prosecuting as an adult; ditto. Also any good murder mystery series needs to have some solved mysteries. And you're probably wondering where the Internal Affairs really comes in. Well, this one should take care of all three.

"But, since I am not a liar, like you I will admit that I am looking for a legitimate reason to fire or to arrest you. And yes, I do hate you-" I said.

BANGBANG BANGBANG a meer meer a meer meer meer meer mcmeer-

"Hold that thought detective, hello, Captain Olaf, head of Internal Affairs' cell phone Captain Olaf speaking," I said.

"Captain, we have a situation," said the assistant Police commissioner.

"What's going on?" I said

"We have a dead officer," He said.

"Oh-D-dear, but, what does that have to do with me?" I said.

"We have a diner full of witnesses, mostly old people, and they're all saying the same thing; it was a cop," he said.

"I thought we already knew that," I said.

(insert mule picture here)
Houston

"No, no, no-" He said.

"Wait, Cops killing cops?" I said.

"Singular on both counts, but yes, please just hurry down," he said.

"Ok, where?" I said.

"The Denny's where T.C. Jester intersects the loop; in the Oak Forest Neighborhood," he said.

"East or west?" I said.

"There's only one Denny's, please! hurry! This is a nightmare," he said.

Later at the crime scene:

"Ok, I've worked in homicide; what've we got?" I said.

"I think we can rule out natural causes," said the ME.

"Coroner NPH?!" I said; yes this city has a lot of medical examiners that seem to have been named after forms of dementia by some silly author. Not me.

"It's just me, but I highly doubt they will be able to plea an accident," he said.

"What happened?" I said.

"Well, the one thing witnesses can agree on is that Officer Park here was pulled over by a fellow officer on our force. And in one of the old white and blue sedans at that," said an officer.

"Any description?" I said.

"Nothing reliable, except that he looked legit," he said.

"It's a he, that narrows it down a tiny bit," I said.

"Not really, can't even positively confirm that, most witnesses think it was a man, but almost none can confirm it, one confirmed it was a woman," he said.

"#yea," I said sarcastically.

"Gets better, no one got a plate number, and the killer either is very lucky or knew this little eatery a little too well. Every camera on this tiny lot is fake," he said.

"What about neighbors?" I said.

"Gas station has none, storage has none pointed the right way, and the only one near here that could have caught it wasn't recording and no one was watching the feed at the right time," he said, "Believe me, we have scoured the area."

(insert mule picture here)
Houston

"I assume you've canvased the area and are taking statements," I said.

"Done and Done, the Restaurant and gas station both have been very hospitable, for nearly 2 hours each was a makeshift police station. Denny's was absolutely packed and everyone raced to a window when they heard shots fired," he said.

"Well, I guess that's good, I assume both are now closed?" I said.

"Correct, err, tecnically" he said.

"Now, Mr. NPH what is your expert statement?" I said.

"9 high caliber shots to the face, all a bull's-eye and from less than 2 inches from his face. Something big, I'd guess about a 50 caliber, but can't confirm anything without an autopsy when it's this shredded. This does go along with how it seems to have played out," he said.

"How's that?" I said.

"Pulled over into this parking lot by a fellow officer, or more likely a fake officer, and instead of license and registration, this," said the officer.

"Sounds like a pretty determined and / or mad killer," I said.

"Extremely," said the officer.

"Also lets check GPS database just in case it was somehow as it appears to be. Also have cyber-crimes scour the internet for anti-cop hate-threats. It's a needle in a needle stack, but might get lucky," I said, "Also call the family, see it there was anything personal that might have lead to this. Oh! And I'll look through records; see about incidents that could have led to this, arrests that just got out, use of force, and so on and so forth."

"Guys, I hate to break up the memorial service; but we just got a call from 99 in the Galleria district," said another officer.

"Area, not district like Westchase," I said.

"Whatever, we just lost another one of our own," she said.

"What!? When?! Same M.O.?!" I said.

"No, *more* violent, better hurry before your crime scene gets covered in bird poop, and while the buzzards are still circling" she said.

"There are no buzzards at the Galleria!" I said, "But you're right, I should hurry."

Later at the crime scene:

"Yikes, that is, is, in all my years in homicide, I, I can't even be sure that's a person!" I said.

(insert mule picture here)
Houston

"Tons of witnesses, many saw it from tall surrounding building, driving past, the largest mall in Texas is catty corner across the intersection, they can't seem to agree, but we're up to our eyeballs in witnesses!" said the officer.

"What about cameras?" I said.

"So far nothing good, but was caught on several cameras, just not deliberately pointed at this corner," said the officer.

"Shesh, cop chopped up in the street, literally. What is this city coming to? What about coroner report?" I said.

"What happened is obvious," said Medical Examiner Lou Gerick.

"Louis, captain obvious, what can you tell me?" I said.

"Well, I don't think it was a stroke, however been wrong before. I never confirm anything till an autopsy; but it looks like he was chopped to bits. I don't believe this was accidental; nor do I believe it to have been suicide-" said the coroner

"Just get to the point," I said.

"Captain call letter, this appears to be a very violent attack, smattering of the brains, removal of hands, feet and limbs, the list goes on. For once I don't think you even need me here, so, can I go back to watching the Dynamos now?" he said.

"Go annoy somebody else," I said.

"Any evidence left behind?" I said.

"Oodles, ax was left next to the body tazer was left in the car-" he said.

"Wait? Tazer? Car?" I said.

"Yea, he deliberately hit the squad car to make the officer stop, tazed him by surprise, and well, you know the rest." he said.

"And he put the tazer in the squad car? Was there any suspects in the back at the time?" I said.

"No, and no, he put the tazer in his own car," said the officer.

"And he left of foot?" I said.

"Nope didn't leave," said the officer.

"It did happen in the middle of the road, a jam is already forming, was he hit-" I said.

"Nope, initial responding officers, err, officer arrested him, he was just sitting on the curb waiting for them. According to the arrest report he complied 'to a t' go figure. At least makes our jobs easier, that's a silver lining I guess."

"Well, let's see what he knows about the other murder," I said.

"Other murder?" he said.

"You weren't told?" I said.

"No, another ax murder?" he said.

"No, used a gun, impersonated a cop, was near the Oak Forest neighborhood," I said.

"Yikes, whatever is going on is bigger and scarier than we could have ever imagined. Better solve this one quick," he said.

"Or we're just missing the main piece of the puzzle. Better go to 99, see if I can get the killer to cough up something before things go triple," I said.

"Juve," he said.

"What?" I said.

"Killer was a teen, 16, maybe 17," he said.

"O-k, I, Um, well, I," I shuddered, "Well, I'll still see what I can get him to cough up about the murder."

"You do that," He said.

"Say did he leave DNA on anything? Or prints?" I said.

"Everything, seems to have not even made any attempt to get away with it," he said.

"Think he just wanted to go to jail?" I said. "Nothing today makes any sense!"

"Anything's possible, but I doubt it." he said.

"Anything making it make sense from witness statements yet?" I said.

"Not really, the witnesses are remembering him as super scary, also the only thing that the reliable ear witnesses seem to agree on is that this was revenge for his sister. Those lip reading from 9 stories up and 1,2,3 blocks away we might as well not even listen to," he said.

"Well, the other scene is seeming to be the preface crime, so call me if the evidence begins to change. This should be pretty open and shut," I said.

"Will do," he said.

(insert mule picture here)
Houston

A little later at central booking:

"Where is he?" I said.

"Where is who?" said the booking officer.

"The cop killer, just arrived-" I said.

"Dead," said the officer.

"DEAD?!?!" I said, "dead?!"

"Yes, dead," she said.

"How'd he die?!" I said.

"Not sure, we were just taking the usual precautions with such a suspect, but he had somehow died on the way here. At first we thought it was a trap to somehow hurt or kill more officers, but we were wrong." she said.

"Are you sure he's really dead?" I said.

"We did AED, whole 9 yards, he croaked," she said, "Hope we don't get sued by someone saying that our precautions caused a care delay that killed him," she said.

"I hope ya'll weren't wrong in the first place," I said.

"How so? About guilt, I thought you were certain-" she said.

"No, about him being dead," I said.

"What? you know something?" she said.

"This whole storyline has been so insane and self-contradictory I wouldn't be terribly shocked by anything!" I said.

"Still you do sound a little crazy," I said.

"Where's the arresting officer?" I said.

She took me to him

"Now normally IA could and would fire you for not speaking, but I have higher ethics. Officer Johnny Benson, Would you like an attorney?" I said.

"I-Guess-so, now that you mention it," he said.

Later:

(insert mule picture here)
Houston

"My Client has nothing to hide, I am instructing him to answer all questions and hold nothing back," said the attorney.

"So, officer, Take us through what happened," I said.

"I had been in an elevator responding to a domestic disturbance in a hotel room inside a hotel inside the Galleria shopping mall. Then I heard the murder being called in by bystanders over the radio. I radioed in that I was coming and then called for backup. I raced to the scene. He was just sitting in the driver's seat of his car with the door open and facing outward. I put his hands up and said 'It was me. It was all me. It was just me.' He complied with me. As I was doing initial reports he said 'You know I'm guilty, don't you?' I didn't respond, and he seemed casual the whole time. It was scary. He after a moment he said 'He deserved it.' Before reports I looked to see anyone else hanging around. There was none. And people at the bus stop confirmed his story. I got special permission to skip my station and-

"The 99th I assume," I said.

"Yes the 99th precinct, and take him straight downtown. It was granted. He just sat back the whole way quietly. I thought he had gone to sleep." He said.

"Anything else?" I said.

"No, what? You don't think?" he said.

"I don't know anything, nothing about this makes sense.

"Captain, just got the fallen officer's records. As is often the-" said my assistant.

"Let's talk back in Internal Affairs office, 9 floors up," I said.

"Ok," he said.

In my office:

"As is often the case in fallen officer murders, they both were with a very good record. Officer Park had been on the force 19 years. Was only 3 weeks from retirement-" said my assistant.

"I remember him!" said Lieutenant Khaff.

"You did?" I said.

"Yea, he had a above average record, but a week ago he fatally tazed a 14, almost 15, year old to death for lipping off. Good record so only got sudpentionary probation-" she said.

"He killed someone and didn't even get suspended?" I said clearly ticked.

"Y-e-s, anyone else would have just looked the other way," she said.

"Now about recent arrests and releases?" I said.

(insert mule picture here)
Houston

"Plenty, and there is family to also have motive-" said my assistant captain.

BANGBANG BANGBANG a meer me-

"Capta-" I said.

"Yes, this is detective Mine from HPD homicide. I think we cracked it," he said, "Just go down 2 floors."

"On my way," I said.

click

"The Law and Order theme song as a ringtone?" said Lutenant Khaff.

"Yea, and Togotta and Fude and g minor is perfectly normal," I said leaving.

"Well, It's befitting Internal Affairs," she said.

"No befitting would be the one with the packed choir singing alleluia," I said.

"You mean-" she said.

"I have to go," I said.

Later at homoside:

"As you may know officer Park-" said detective Mine.

"I do so hope you have dragged me down for something more than just the tazed teen. Because I already know," I said.

"Oh, so much more!" I believe we've cracked this case!" he said.

"That teen, his mother came home to find this:

Dear Olivia,

  Prepare yourself

  As you may know our beloved son Gabriel, was killed. We thought that the police would actually do something. We were wrong. Internal Affairs is just as much a blue line towing band of crime scene cleanup thugs as the rest of the police. I will not stand for this. That monster must be made an example of! I have hired a hit man to take him out. Don't bother calling the police. By the time you get this the assassin will have done his job. When he comes looking for the rest of the money at the appointed place, he will see that I jumped. For the sake of not being buried as a John doe, I will tell you that the meeting place was Med Center garage 5-

I will interrupt the story to tell you that that garage is the same one form the flashback in Epi 1. See what I mean about bees to a beehive? Anyway back to the story:

I would tell you how to find the hitman, but I don't want to put you in danger. I hope you can forgive me; everyone else, except for the almighty, I just don't care.

I remember when we lost Rafael, right after he was born. I can't go through that again. And when Olive is born; don't tell her about this. Let her think she had a good father, and let her think she was an only child.

-your unworthy lesser half,

Urieal MacMonth

"You see what she knows about the other killing and the John Doe now being Autopsied. I have to go yell at a police lutenant," I said.

"Actually, management has confirmed that no officer on the force was close enough to have carried it out," said a detective.

"Does no one tell me anything?!" I said.

"Just came in minutes ago," said the detective.

"Well, still doesn't rule the cops out, GPS can be tampered with, and there's always someone whose Lojack is busted," I said.

"Fat chance," said several officers.

BANGBANG B-

"Yo, what's happening?" I said.

"Please proceed to the Harris County Mortuary, your autopsy results are ready. Please proceed to the Harr-" said the call.

"Robocalls from the morgue, at least they save them for us cops, I think!" I said.

Later at the morgue:

"Good morning, Captain, right?" said Coroner Alztimer.

"Yes, captain," I said.

"Well, I thought you were promoted to Internal Affairs?" I said.

(insert mule picture here)
Houston

"I was, err am, It looked like a cop was at least in on it. And has still not been disproven, Also I am technically heading this, so, what've ya got?" I said.

"Well, with Officer Park, Coroner NPH was right. Ready to send the slugs to ballistics. With Officer Grace, well, not a lot to find left that's not abundantly obvious. But did find stun gun marks, so that can be totally confirmed," said Coroner Alztimer.

"What about the killer John Doe?" I said.

"Right here," said Coroner Alztimer.

I took a glance and said "Suicide?!?!" I said.

"Oh yea, took a lota heart pills. Surprised that wasn't found dead at the scene," said Coroner Alztimer.

"Still a John Doe?" I said.

"Yea, nothing popped in nearby school systems, or 'the system'" said Coroner Alztimer.

"Speak- oh, you havn't run that," I said.

BANGBANG BANGBANG a meer meer a meer meer meer meer mc-

"Yes?" I said.

"We've made a breakthrough!" said a homoside detective.

"I'm on my way," I said.

Later there at 1PP:

"I assume you have a lead as big as that note," I said.

"Correct, ID'ed the car from the Galleria-" he said.

"Speaking of that note, did the widow tell us anything about John Doe?" I said.

"She told us everything she knows, but she knows nothing about nothing," he said.

"Are we sure that she's telling the truth?" I said.

"Everything she says adds up, isn't showing of the tell tale signs of lying, but under the circumstances you can never be totally certain," he said.

"I-so-pose that she could still be in on it," I said.

"Doubt it," said another detective walking in like in the TV mystery series'.

"How so?" I said.

(insert mule picture here)
Houston

"Checked out that "THIS IS FOR MY SISTER!" thing, 4 days ago Officer Grace tazed a 4 year old girl to death," he said.

"Let me guess, she has a brother," I said.

"Yup!" he said.

"Maybe it was a blackmailed kill, did the tazed teen, I thing Gabriel was his name, have any siblings?" I said.

"Nope, but it wasn't her brother," he said.

"Another sibling? And how can you be so sure?" I said.

"Far as I can see, didn't have any, but, daughter of a single mom, father unknown, who knows?" he said.

"Ok, but like I said, how can you be so sure it wasn't her brother?" I said.

"Was 5, same situation, so probably half siblings. Also I know you said 'blackmailed kill' but he was at her funeral during the time of the murder.

"Well, I guess that rules him out, Anything from, and what was her name?, the mother?" I said.

"Having the normal reaction, as not helpful as possible, dead end," he said.

"And I assume we can't talk to the brother," I said.

"Correct," he said, "Tried to serve a warrant at the funeral home to compare DNA, but was already cremated."

"That's slightly fishy, but not very, could we get DNA from ashes?" I said.

"Not once they've been scattered," said the officer.

"That's more fishy!" I said.

"Yes, but, once again, can't prove anything," he said.

"Could we get DNA from the brother?" I said.

"Would need a warrant, and that's such grasping at straws, it wouldn't work," he said.

"Are we sure he said 'sister'?" I said.

"What are you getting at?" he said.

"Well, he was 17, and she was four, well, Now I'm grasping at straws. Say, didn't you say something about John Doe's car?" I said, "And for Pete sake! What was her name!"

"Charlie, Charlie Sam Smith, brother was Sam Charlie Smith, no points for names," he said.

"About that car?" I said.

"Right, Right, right," he said, "We ran the plates, and that's when things, got interesting."

"What kind of interesting?" I said.

"That car was owned by someone in the same general neighborhood as the murder of Officer Park," I said.

"And just as I was beginning to believe they might be unrelated!" I said.

"Yea, gets better, Had a son. Took a little digging but looks like John Doe and the son have the same basic description. If it was the son he had no license;

"Sounds like he-" I said.

"Boy was reported missing, car stolen. Was overshadowed, but now we're bringing them in to ID him," he said.

"Any siblings?" I said.

"No, " He said.

"Any connection between Gabriel and Charlie? That we can find?" I said.

"Only connection that we can find between the families is that Charlie seemed to have lived across the street from where John Doe's father worked. But, with no one co-operating, can't be sure of anything," he said.

"Gabriel have any sister?" I said.

"No, but a brother," he said.

"Do tell," I said.

"6 months old. Dead end. But was named Michael, so, at least we got all 4," he said.

"Anyone else we have found that could help?" I said

"With everyone not co-operating, are we talking to those surrounding the main characters in this, Already dug up John Doe's Scoutmaster. He thinks that he didn't do it. And not without grounds too, you know he was going to have been an eagle scout," he said.

"Why am I always the last to know anything?!?!" I said.

briiiiing! briiiiing!

"Hello, HPD homoside," he said.

(pause)

"Oh, It's for you," he said.

"Hello?" I said.

"Coroner Alztimer here," said Coroner Alztimer.

"Yes, this is Captain Olaf; head of Internal Affairs; and this homicide investigation," I said, "Not that they are doing a good job of keeping me in the loop."

"Well, that's all about to change," said Coroner Alztimer, "Remember that John Doe that you say killed an on duty officer,"

"How could I forget?" I said.

"The alleged parents just became not alleged, It's him," said Coroner Alztimer.

"And does that mean we might get close to finding the missing piece of this puzzle?" I asked.

"Nope, they're accusing the department of simply murdering their son, a total dead end," said Coroner Alztimer.

Clicktickbuzzclick

"Sorry, got another call coming in," I said.

"Hello," I said.

"Yes, I believe I need to speak to the head investi-" he said.

"Speaking, and you are?" I said.

"Sargent Ceaustu, head of ballistics division of the HPD crime lab," he said.

"Yes, yes, everyone that's anything knows who you are! Why are you calling?" I said.

"The bullets from Officer Park's face and head are a match to several contract kills-" he said.

Clicktickbuzzclick

"Got to take that," I said.

"Hey, Hi, Olaf, and you are?" I said.

"I solved it," she said.

"I doubt that, do tell, please," I said.

"The now childless widow gave us a free pass, she seemed truly surprised when she learned of her husband's use of the dark web, so I don't think she was in on it," she said.

"Let me guess, hired a hit man that is suspected of other kills," I said.

"How'd you know?" she said.

"Just got off the phone with ballistics, anything you can tell me about the mercenary," I said.

"Just that he, or possibly she, operates out of the dark web, and this was just another notch in the pistol, no pun intended," she said.

"Well if anyone learns anything, have them let us know," I said.

"Will do Captain," She said hanging up.

"Ok folks! Good News!

4 days later

"So, Captain, have you turned up any new leads?" said Detective Mine.

"Not really, it looks like 2 unrelated murder suicides, and one lone high quality, high price hit man. But there's enough loose ends that I can't be sure of anything!" I said, "Guess this one becomes a crime statistic."

"Never say nerve cap'n. You never know, the big break might just fall into our laps yet!" he said.

"MAIL CALL," said the rude mail girl as she dropped in my lap.

"Let's see, junk, junk, WRONG ADDRESS, I'll take that to the mail room later, HEY!" I said, "You were right! Literally!"

"Looks like a hand written letter. From someone you've been wanting to get in contact with?" he said.

"You could say, It's from the killer," I said, "Let's get this to the crime lab so that they can confirm nothing's phony."

At a press conference that evening:

"As I am sure you already knew, a few days back 2 seasoned Houston Police Officers were violently murdered. At first we believed that they were connected. And while we still are not absolutely certain there was no connection. We have found no real evidence of any connection, but no proof otherwise. Also initially it was believed that at least 1 HPD officer was involved. As such I was brought in to lead the investigation from behind. And while our deepest sympathies go to the many people killed during the course of these events, I still stand before you with every cop's worst nightmare, because both officers deserved it. Not enough to get the killer's off completely but mitigating circumstances were still great. At 6:32 Pm several calls came in from a restaurant on the loop 610, near the Oak Forest neighborhood.

He was murdered by a serial killer for hire. We cannot ID the contract murderer; but I can tell you that Officer Park fatally tazed an unarmed, young, minor, cardiaclly disabled, teenager. The father took the law into his own hands when my own department failed to do our job. I admit that while I was unaware, my apparently mismanaged department was not. And that puts blame directly on Internal Affairs, and indirectly myself. At 8:59 PM one Officer Grace, was on his regular beat in the Galleria Area, near the namesake shopping mall. His squad car was deliberately hit by another vigilante. He had fatally tazed one Charlie Sam Smith of four years of age. She was scared off and he was too lazy to chase, so he tazed. Internal Affairs did nothing. In both cases technically no procedure was broken. As such I have to see to it that criminal charges are pressed by HPD against itself, for their role in the death of these of these Officers. Officer Grace was tazed by surprise by his victim's big half-brother, Initially we were unaware that he was a half-brother and she was the product of a secret affair. And then violently chopped to pieces in the street. Not before the vigilante poisoned himself to death; dying almost imeadatly after his crime. Officer Park's vigilante also took his own life following the crime. It didn't add up at first, but in the case of Officer Grace, the vigilante sent a letter to your truly to show the error of our ways. A letter close to a sympathy card to his step mom of sorts. A suicide note revealing that this pushed him over the edge to do himself in to his 5 year old step brother. And 3 to the press. All were confirmed and obtained using warrants and without actual police violence. Following these tragic events, I arrested an officer who did not break procedures in fatally tazing an 88 year old man walking through the park without any close on. He, along with the police commission, is charged with voluntary manslaughter. Any questions?

Hey, I was worried you weren't coming. Where have you been?!?! Anyway, not important. I am sure that the last one was a welcome relief from prosecuting as an adult. It was for me. Also it was a welcome break from Crayer. Anyway, in keeping with the spirit of things on a grander scale, I have decided to do this story next. Also it's about high time we visit NYC. In my humble opinion, you can't have a good mystery series without at least one mystery in The Big Apple. So, here we go! And F.Y.I. I was there on a brief exchange program; this is also a true story.

"Detective Olaf? I believe," said NYPD detective Jones.

"That's the one, I go back home when a spot opens in Internal Affairs," I said.

"Internal Affairs?!?! You're one of them?!?!" he said.

"Going to be," I said.

Whoosh!

"Oy Vey," he said reading the message.

"What? Too by the book? And what was that sound?" I said.

"No, not that, and it's supposed to be a subway going past non-stop," he said.

"Ah! Thought it rang a little bit of a bell," I said.

"Yea right, cowboy," he said.

"No 1, It's true, No 2, don't use that as an insult and No 3, I am from the forth largest city in the nation, admittedly not the inner-" I said.

"Blah, blah, blah, weave a murder to get to!" he said.

"Weave, like knitting?" I joked.

"Not helping, let's go!" he said.

Later at the scene:

"Whata we got? Glaucoma?" he said.

"Bad one," she said.

"In my city the coroner's are named after forms of dementia, not eye diseases," I said.

"Ignore him; what's your report?" he said.

"Found by one of our own patrolling here in the park," she said, "Strangulation, about 5, maybe 6 years of age, female, no defensive wounds, was dressed for the weather," I said.

"A Jane Doe?" I said.

"Probably, a medical ID bracelet says she lives on Park Avenue, a likely story," she said.

"Any idea of time of death?" I said.

"About 1-3 this morning, wasn't found till 6," she said.

"Hey! That's a very expensive coat! Maybe it wasn't a con," I said, "however could be hot."

"Or fake," he said.

"Either way, how does a six year old end up going from wherever it is she came from, to half buried in the snow?" I said.

"Not sure, but that probably fake bracelet is our first lead, in answering that question, and this mystery," he said.

"Speaking of snow, anything like prints to recover from the crime scene," I said.

"After that snowstorm, nothing would be left," he said.

"Sorry, Texan, gulf coast," I said, "Well, adopted from Scandinavia, but was an infant at the time."

"Yea, I know," he said being so rude.

(insert mule picture here)
Houston

"I'll autopsy her, see if that can tell us anything about what happened in her last hours," she said.

"We'll go to that address, make sure it's fake and all," he said.

"I'll assist in case this becomes a notification to the family," I said.

Later there:

"NYPD," he said knocking.

"Yes officers?" said a man I fast realized to be the butler.

"Is anyone home?" he said.

"Yes, should I summon him?" said the butler.

"Yes, please, my good man," said Detec. Jones.

"Master Harold! Some policemen to see you," he said over the intercom.

"Coming Geves," he said, "Sup dudes? Oh, everything ok?"

"You ok there?" I said.

"Yea, yea, just another headache, nothing contagious. Like I said is everything ok?" he said.

"Don't worry, was just wondering if anyone would recognize an object," he said.

"Oh, where are my manners, please, come in, come in, he said cautiously, "Geves, I think I can handle this, you can go now."

"Yes sir," he said as we came in.

"So officers, what can I do you for?" he said.

"Do you recognize this object?" I said.

"Yea, that's my little sister's. I doubt the police would bring in detectives just to return it. I repeat, is everything ok?" I said.

We (Jones and I) just looked at each other and I said "Who was the last person to see your sister?"

"She's at school," I said.

"And who took her to school?" said Jones.

"Our Nanny, Mrs. Miniver, seriously, what's going on?!" he said beginning to panic.

"And where is she now?" I said.

(insert mule picture here)
Houston

Chimes sounded and he said "Other side of the door," and pointed.

I opened it and said "Are you Mrs. Miniver?"

"Yes, Why?" she said with a basket of laundry.

"Did you take his little sister to school yesterday?" I said.

"No, he did, why? Harold is everything ok?" she said beginning to worry as she stepped inside.

"Doubt it, and no you did," said Harold.

"No, you did, as you often do," she said as she closed the door.

"No, it's your job and I wasn't feeling, ouch, good so I skipped it," he said.

"Well I didn't take her to school!" she said.

"Did either of you get her up this morning?" I said.

"No, I didn't get her up, or ready," said Harold.

"Nor did I," said Mrs. Miniver.

"Probably was just one of the parents," I said forgetting time of death.

"Nope, they never do, nowadays she often gets herself up with nothing more than a clock radio, and prepares herself for school," said Harold, "I was feeling bad so I didn't bother."

"Do you have any other siblings or staff?" I said, "And when does she get up?"

"You've met Geves, and Mrs. Miniver, this is the maid's day off, and the chuffer took Mother and Father to work early. Both have a big meeting. Need all the time they can have to prepare. Now Tell Me what's going on!" said Harold.

"Siblings?" I repeated.

"Brother, lives in a real slum far from here. Stopped by just last night. Has she vanished? Is she Dead?" said Harold, really panicking.

"One last question, where to your parents work?" I said.

"Dad, union negotiation for American Telephone and Telegraph Company. Mom's a Wolf on Wall Street," said Mrs. Miniver.

"Where exactly do they work?" I said.

"They don't want us coming to their work for obvious reasons. You'll have to ask the chuffer," said Harold.

(insert mule picture here)
Houston

"I'll take the phone man, you take the wolf," I said as we left.

On the phone with the coroner:

What've ya got? I said pulling into a garage.

"Name: Katy Mills-" said Glaucoma.

"Back home we've got a mall by that name, sorry, go on," I said.

"Cause of death: Homicide; strangulation Legal guardians at time of death: Mr. Harold C. and Mrs. Katy M. Crayer Mills-"

"Maden name?, Crayer? that is?" I said.

"Well, that's what the documents say," said Glaucoma.

"Any connection to Justice Crayer in Houston TX?" I said.

"Let me check," said Glaucoma.

A long hold time later:

"Yes, cousins, why?" she said.

"Um, possibly not important, go on, up, nope, wait never mind. I'm already at destination," I said.

Later in the lobby:

"Welcom-" said a receptionist.

"W. X. Y. Z. Olaf- HPD / NYPD," I need to speak to Harold C. Mills I said flashing by badge.

"Um, Uhhh, guard, can you take him to his office," she said.

Later at the office

"Hello, can I help you?" said his secretary.

"Yes, I need to speak to Mr. Mills," I said.

"Do you have an appointment?" she said.

"I'll be seeing him without an appointment," I said.

"You won't be getting in without an appointment," she said.

"Yes I will," I said.

"No, you won't, and if you don't go away I will have to call security," she said.

(insert mule picture here)
Houston

"That won't work," I said.

"Then we will call the police," she said.

"Best of luck," I said, finally showing my badge.

"Oh, that can't be good," she said.

"Just let me talk to him," I said.

"I'm afraid he's in a meeting," she said.

"We have to interrupt it," I said.

"It's his biggest meeting of the year, and it's much more important than it is most years," she said, "Yearly labor negotiations, if it ends badly again today there will be strikes. The CEO has even come," she said.

"Big negotiations, curious," I said under my breath with the first clue, "I'm sorry, this is more important."

"4 years ago a fake cop came in and got the last person to hold my position to try to do what you want. It was a con, and that's how I got this job," she said, "If by some change that is true, I need to know what 'earth shattering' thing could ever be so important."

"I probably shouldn't tell you even this much but, you don't want to be the one to have to tell him," I said.

"A likely story," she said.

I showed her a crime scene photo. "Just let me in that boardroom, and I guarantee you will not be fired," I said.

Fearing not cooperating in something like this she said "right this way."

At the boardroom:

"And that's why-" said the CEO.

"Detective Olaf HPD / NYPD," I said.

"Elizabeth, what on earth were you thinking letting him in here?!?!" he said.

"I'm here to speak to Mr. Mills?" I said.

Everyone looked to the man at the far end of the table.

"WHAT are you doing? Interrupting this tremendous meeting!" he said, "Do you have an idea-"

"I don't care, and neither will you," I said.

"What is that ungodly interruption about?!?!" he said.

"Just step outside," I said, trying to be as nice as I could, while not telling him here and now.

"I will not! Call security!" he said trying to not look to be at blame.

"That won't work," I said, "You need to step outside."

"What is this?! Some crazy arrest?!?!" he said.

"Please," I said.

"I don't care if you are a cop! You will be gotten rid of!" he said.

I was very desperate, so showed the ID bracelet in the evidence bag.

"Wait, what now?" he said, totally taken off his game, and recognizing it.

"Please, step outside," I said.

"O-k-k," he said, "I-'ll be back in a few."

As he left I said, "No, he won't be back anytime soon."

"Ok, detective, you've made me ruin a perfectly good pair of pants, and have gambled a perfectly good carrier. I assume you have a good reason," he said.

"If you are concerned about losing your position, I assure you that under the circumstances your employer will not have fair legal grounds for termination," I said.

"Blah, blah, blah, cut to the chase," he said.

"I, err, we regre-" I started.

"I said cut to the chase, hiding his fear," he said.

"A body was found deep in Central Park early this morning. It was Katy," I said.

"W-W-what? That, that, that cannot be right, this must be, be, be, well, how do you know it's her?!" he said, " Get me out of here, I don't want to be seen at a time like this."

Later after they IDed her:

"I know this is-" I said.

"I watch true crime shows, did she have any enemies, no," but as he broke down he said: "BUT I DO!"

"You think that this is some by-product of the union negotiations?" I said.

"No, they are not that low down, It's Harvey," I said.

(insert mule picture here)
Houston

"Harvey? Whose Harvey?" I said.

"Her big brother," he said.

"The one that doesn't live at home?" I said.

"Yea, he didn't do it," he said.

"What makes you so sure?" I said.

"Look, even if I was him, It's still my fault," he said.

"How so?" I said.

"We did nothing, and when we finally did act, I'm sure we did it wrong," he said.

"I don't understand, what are you saying?" I said baffled.

He sighed and said "His side of the story is probably closer to the truth."

Later,

"How'd it go?" I said.

"Mom's in shook and too upset to really talk. All I could hear was blaming us for not having enough men on the street to prevent this in the first place. You have any better luck?" said Jones.

"Little, Dad's beating himself up, and has regrets. But there is an older brother, didn't say how but said he bot0,h thought it was him, and knew it wasn't," I said.

"That makes no sense," said Jones.

"Yea, he's gotten even loopier, something about the maid, but I think he means nanny," I said.

"What about the Nanny?" he said.

"I think something along the lines of thinking he didn't bother to raise her," I said.

"Nanny Guilt, heard of that before," he said.

"Well, I think I'll talk to the older brother, you see what you can learn about this union thing, there's been union violence before, but I've never heard of it being this low down." I said.

"And I'll send some other lower detectives to canvas the building and get camera footage, see anyone saw anything," he said.

"Good, good," I said.

Later at the apartment:

(insert mule picture here)
Houston

knock knock

"Who's there," said a woman.

"Police," I said.

"A likely story, now why don't you tell me why you're really here," she said.

I put my badge up against the hole in the door.

"Sorry, in this neighborhood you can't be too careful, most plainclosemen are phonies," she said.

"Understood, may I come in?" I said.

"Sure," she said unlocking and opening the door, "Feel free to sit wherever, just bewhere it may be moldy."

"What was that sound?" I said.

"Probably just a rodent," she said, "This is about Harvey's baby sister, isn't it."

"How'd you know?" I said.

"Sr. Harold told Jr. Harold, who told me," she said clearly upset.

"And you are?" I said.

"Ms. Amy Mills, used to be Amy Toon, but you know," she said.

"Oh," I said, "And Harvey is,"

"Toilet, whatdayawant?" she said.

"To talk to Harvey, do you remember last night?" I said.

"Well, about 10 PM I went on shift-" she said.

"Where?" I said.

"We're cab drivers," she said.

"We? as in Harvey and you?" I said.

"Yes," she said.

"And where was Harvey?" I said.

"Don't remember, I was on shift, remember," she said, "I do remember that he knew his parents wouldn't be home, so he paid a late visit to his siblings. It's hard for them to get together."

"Why?" I said.

"Let's just say Harvey had really rough teen years, not that CPS or you cops would ever do anything about it," she said.

"What happened?" I said.

BANGBANG BANGBANG a meer meer a-

"Olaf," I said.

"Yea, getting ready to interview the younger brother, want you down to do it," said Jones.

"Ok," I said, "I was, well, I'll tell you when I get there."

Later there:

"So, Harold, what do you remember about the last, 18 hours?" said Jones.

"Well, was as per usual, she came home from kindergarten, went to out to dinner as a family, called Ed-" said Harold.

"Who's Ed?" I said.

"Edy," he said, "Not Ed, Macy's secret boyfriend."

"Who's Macy?" I said.

"My little sister," he said thinking I was insane.

"You have another little sister?" I said.

"No, Katy usually went by Macy," he said.

"Oh!, silly me," I said, "Any idea how to reach him?"

"Oh, just a couple blocks up the street from our apartment," he said," I have his cell phone number."

"His cell phone number? How old is he?" I said.

"Younger than my sister, but not my much as he always says," he said.

"Oh," I said, having had that theory go out the window.

"Tell us about your older brother," said Jones.

"Oh good grief! Not this!," he said.

"Whatdaya mean?" I said.

(insert mule picture here)
Houston

He sighed and said "What happened was at least as much my fault as it was anyone else's. And as such I'm sure Macy's murder is my fault also."

"How so?" I said.

"Hell if I know, but at this point my best guess would be that I was just too busy having a headache to protect her," he said.

"What about your brother?" I said.

"I never stood up for him, you know after he turned 18, he tried to kill himself," he said.

"Why?" I said.

"Said he couldn't live without justice, and if he killed his parents, he'd go to jail; so thanks a lot!" he said.

"What happened to your brother?" I said.

"My parents never excepted him for who he is; they just kept trying harder and harder to bang him into the product of their imagination that they actually loved. They just kept trying harder and harder to change who he was. Eventually he was sent to hell in Alaska. AND DO NOT MAKE A HELL FREEZING OVER JOKE!" he said.

"Wouldn't dream of it," I said, "So, was that like a military school?"

"It started with military school!; guess when you're a parent you must make things such that they are not open for discussion. Lest you loose the argument, lest the child wins" he said "It was a 'recreation school' they admitted that it was to completely change who you are. And I just blindly sat down and shut up like a soviet pheasant," he said trying not to completely break down.

"Pheasant?" I said.

"pheasant, pheasant Smesant, who cares!" he said, "After what I let my brother go through I don't even deserve to live." he banged his fist on the table and said "Should've been me."

"How do you even know that you could've stopped them? And did your brother blame you?" I said.

"No 1, blah, blah, blah, and no 2, Exactly the opposite," he said.

"Why exactly was he sent off?" I said.

"Does it really matter?!" he said.

"Did your sister know?" I said.

"Yea, we figured she'd know sooner or later, so us brothers told her, she blamed the parents. One thing in life that really bothered her." he said.

(insert mule picture here)
Houston

"We're you three close?" I said.

"Yea," he said, paused and then said "Nothing unites like a common enemy."

"What do you remember about last night?" I said.

"He and Amy came over. I'm so glad he has her to take his mind off his troubles; someone to lean on. Where was I? Oh! yes, last night. Normal visit, video games, and etc..." he said.

"What was your parent's relationship with Macy like?" I said.

"She was the favorite," he said, "Meanwhile I was just too busy with stuff that doesn't matter like grades to so much as brother to keep her from being murdered!" he said.

"I though you said you had a get together last night?" I said.

"I mean the big picture!" he said.

"I thought you said you were close?" he said.

"Well, I still didn't do things like take her to the park often enough, etc, etc, etc, Kindly quit twisting my words!" he said.

"One last thing, what about helping us contact Edy," said Jones.

Later with the other brother:

"You're back, Last time he missed you entirely, thought that the trade mark blend of invasive creatures and fungi would have driven you off for good," she said jokingly.

"Nope, just called into the office," I said.

"By me," said Jones.

"O-k," she said, "Have you found the killer?"

"I think we may have, but that doesn't mean the investigation is over. Say? Where's Harvey?" I said.

(knocking)

"That's probably him," she said.

"Hello Mr. Mills," I said as I opened the door.

"Oh, have you cracked the case?" he said.

"I think that we have, how did your visit last night end?" I said.

"Parents were going to come home any minute, so I had to leave quick," he said.

(insert mule picture here)
Houston

"Parents don't want you around?" I said.

"Exactly the opposite, I just can't handle being around them after-" he said.

"We know about Alaska, and I couldn't help but notice this 'loft'-" I said.

"Har, lawyer up, Officers, he has PTSD, after all he's been through, he can't handle this," she said getting mad and panicking.

"Him to?" I said.

"What?" said Jones.

"Nothing, nothing," I said.

"Amy chillax, I have an alibi. I'll talk. I'm not in as bad a shape as I was 2 years ago." he said. "You think this is some sort if indirect, riches to rags, revenge killing don't you?" he said.

"Um, no," said Jones.

"Don't tell bad lies, it's very toddleresque," I said, "What happened two years ago?"

"We got married," said Amy, "I remember as if it were yesterday, We met in a support group, first we were just frinemies, then more than frinemies, but simultaneously frinemies, a fine example of 'it's complicated', but enough about that."

"Ok, so we do think it was that, so what now that you know that," said Jones.

"After that I was having a hard evening, so I tried drowning my sorrows at Stienbec-" he said.

"So you were drunk at the time!" said Jones.

"No! If I got drunk every time I had a bad flareup, I'd have ended up on the streets a long time ago. It was just corn beef!" he said, "How do you think I gained so much weight?!"

"About what time did you leave the delicatessen?" I asked.

"Midnight, when they closed," he said.

"That's very interesting, because the time of death was between 1-3 in the morning," I said.

"Well then," he said," I guess it's a good thing I'm a glutton with a bad memory," he said.

"How so?" I said, waiting for this bit of craziness to fall apart.

"Well, after I couldn't stuff my face with corn beef I went for-" he said.

"Cheesecake?" I said.

(insert mule picture here)
Houston

"Close! CheeseSTEAK! But, I could remember the name of this great cheesesteak place, but not the location, took best part of 3 hours to find it. And burned it off in advance I told myself cuz I was too broke for anything but feet!" he said.

"A likely story," I said.

"Hey, their cheesesteak is worth a walk. If you don't believe me, ask my carrier," he said.

"We will," I said.

that evening:

"His alibi checked out. Never even went back to the apartment building or was in Central Park," I said.

"You sure he didn't, just, have a fellow cabbie carry it around?" said Jones.

"So I thought, satellite is accurate down to 1 yard. Everywhere the phone said he was, streetcams backed him up, same with private cameras. He's clean."

"Maybe was the wife, Or maybe murder for hire, or blackmailed," said Jones.

"So I thought, and the wife's alibi checked out, and they're broke. Also, who's he gunu blackmail?" I said.

"Well, that's what I figured," said Jones.

"Then why'd you send me to do all that?" I said, "I did so much apparently unneeded digging that I learned that Harvey had no In-laws. Wife grew up in 'the system' probably how she ended up in that group," I said.

"Couldn't hurt. Wana hear?" he said.

"Sure, sure," I said.

"Well, that canvas, was productive. Round midnight got a special visitor. Believed to be a mob assassin, but sometimes works for others," he said.

"To tell," I said.

"Yea, gets better! Quietly, while wearing a mask, lock picked his way in. 9 minutes later the vic is being discreetly carried out, at knifepoint," he said.

"How'd we learn of that?" I said.

"Building full of cameras," he said.

"Any idea who let him in?" I said.

(insert mule picture here)
Houston

"Was rung up," he said, "Don't have a recording of the intercom conversation, but we do know who rung him up.

"Who" I said.

"'big' Eddie von Husen, VP of the port workers union," he said.

"Really?" I said, "What does he have to do with this?"

"Ever heard the saying 'birds of a feather, stick together'?" he said.

"Yea, but I thought that different unions were like different mob dons?" I said, "In more ways than one."

"Correct!" he said.

"So, let's go pick Eddie up," I said.

"Are you crazy?" he said.

"How so?" I said.

"This was probably just a favor, and didn't even know what he was doing," he said.

"Then let's go straight to the phone co union-" he said.

"You try that and then they'll go to the police, or possibly a different public union, and next thing you know, they're real reasons for striking are hidden, and our investigation has become a threat to public safety," he said.

"Guys, someone to interview," said another officer.

"Who?" I said.

"Edy," she said.

"You chowder heads picked up EDDIE?!?!" said Jones.

"Not Eddie, Edy, remember,-" she said.

"Oh! yea, he might just know a thing or two," I said.

"He's in interview room 2," she said.

"Thanks," we said.

"So, Edy, does the name 'Katy Mills' A.K.A. Macy, ring a bell?" said Jones.

"Y-yes," he said.

"Did she have any enemies?" I said.

"No, why do you ask?" Edy said.

"Are you sure? Was she acting different?" said Jones.

"Yes, I'm sure, but you guys are seriously freaking me out! I'm not saying anything else till you tell me what this about," he said.

"We know about your secret girlfriend, I understand, I'll keep my mouth shut, but-" I said.

He started to worry and said "Fiancé."

"What?" I said.

"Yea, we've been together for little over 2 years. I was 3, she was 4. Been great, no one but her brother, teen brother, not adult brother, knew," he said, "Were going to tell our families today, but she didn't come into school. Then I got this mysterious call to the principal's office. When I saw cops I thought I knew what this was about. Now I just don't know."

"What did you think it was about?" I said.

"I-I-I am not sure, but, only Macy knows. Your past always catches up with you," he said.

"What are you talking about?" I said.

"3 years, guess it's time to come clean," he said.

"About what?" I said.

He sighed and said "Almost 3 years ago to the day. I am not just a big brother, but then I only had a big sister. After then I was an only child."

"What are you talking about?" I said.

"It was an accident, I thought it would shock her, but I didn't think it would kill her," he said.

"I still don't-" I said.

"It was a dumb dare. I talked her into it, I-I- No-no one would have ever guessed-" he said.

"Oh," I said.

"All these years, glad to have that off my chest. Not sure what will happen. I may die, I may be locked up for good-" he said.

"You were two, the law would back that up," I said.

"Oh," he said, "Sure I don't deserve that. So why am I here? And what does Macy have to do with anything?"

"That is strictly coincidental," I said, "What you said that is."

Cold as ice Jones said "Back to the matter at hand. We're you ever 'just friends'?" I said.

"No, contrary to the cover story, but like I said you guys are seriously freaking me out! I'm not saying anything else till you tell me what this about," said Edy.

"Edy, early this morning there was a body found in central park. It was Macy. We're trying to solve her murder." I said.

He knew nothing; but he was a real mess. After we got his parents informed of everything and him home we said it was late enough to go home.

The next morning:

"So? any new ideas?" I said.

"Nope, nothing that can be done; guess this goes officially unsolved," said Jones.

"Never say never, what if we tell everything?" I said.

"What? I'm sure whatever you're talking about would kill our case," said Jones.

"No, everyone everything, we tell the city everything we know, on the 9:00 news. Then we encourage the phone workers to strike against the union until they work with the police," I said.

"Strike against the union? What does that mean?!?!" he said.

"Withhold union dues, refuse to strike, and so on," he said.

"And if they try to get the cops to strike?" he said.

"We start off by saying that part too, every. little. detail," I said.

We did, the union nearly died, and the killers were brought to justice

Hey, you're probably both, wondering the details of my past, and also wanting something not so humongous. Here is what I consider to be my very first case. One that I have much pride in: here goes:

"A toast! To the defendant of the hour!-" said my father.

"Not a defendant anymore!" I said.

"Cheers! / whatever!" said mom.

In ran a teen, about / maybe 16. Turned out he was going on 16.

"Is captain Olaf here?" he said.

"H-here," I said.

He looked like he had been in a bad fight.

"Cap-tain?" he said.

"Going to be," I said.

"You, are captain Olaf? He said quite surprised.

"Take a seat," I said.

"S-sure," he said.

"Who told you about me?" I said.

"Over heard officers talking, then looked you up," he said.

"How did you find us here?" said my father.

"Tried to knock, but doorman wouldn't let me in your building. So had to follow you," I said.

"Well, that's not creepy at all, why didn't you confront us in the parking lot?" he thought.

"I was nervous, then I had trouble getting in this high class place," he said.

"Gee, I wonder why," said my dad.

"That's enough, If I am going to be captain, than this is what I need to get used to," I said.

"How does someone your age get to me IA captain?" he said.

"You first," I said.

"It's need to know," he said.

"Ditto, let's meet up somewhere else at some other time," I said.

Later there:

"Yo, capt-" he said, startling me.

I screamed bloody murder and then started to cry.

"Whoa, sorry bout that," he said.

"It-its ok," I said catching my breath.

"So, captain, how exactly did you get to be captain?" he said.

"Your story first," I said.

"I'm on parol, in fact I just got back out on parol, after I came forward last time I was just accused to lying. If I come forward then it will have to be undeniable," he said.

"Greg, Come forward with what?" I said.

"My guardian, my grandfather is beating the-" he said.

"That's why you looked that way!" I said.

"Yea, it wouldn't be happening if I could defend myself, but if I defend myself they'll send me off to jail," he said.

"Isn't there evidence tha-" I said.

"They said he was the one defending himself," he said, "And not without grounds."

"What are you talking about?" I said.

"I'm almost 16, and I've probably spend a total of 3 years in juve," he said.

"13 months, no convictions, just no bail. Was framed for killing by big sister and little brother. They just couldn't crack it. It was a miracle that I was able to get evidence that they had framed me, even then is was slim evidence, and slim exoneration. Only had one E-mail between them showing a frame. My big sister was very close in age to me; and my little brother wanted to be a coroner," I said.

"Yikes, and that makes you captain?" he said.

"Actually what happened to me in jail, may have been malicious; or maybe just clueless; I don't like to talk about it," I said.

"Oh, that, well," he said.

"It's ok, so, how can I help you?" I said.

"I'm not sure," he said.

Then, the blue blood began to flow to my brain, quickly I hatched a plan.

The next day:

"So, you're actually telling me that you knocked an 83 year old man out in self-defense?!?!" said the officer.

"He was belti-" said Greg.

"Turn around, you're under arrest," he said.

"OBJECTION! I HAVE PROOF!!!!!" I said bursting out of the closet. Yes, I was tazed.

Later:

"So, not even really on the job, and you arrested 9 officers for their connections to an arrest of a known juvenile delinquent, on charges of endangerment of a minor, then you jump out of a closet and arrest 2 cops for 'tazing a fellow officer'. You should know that none of those charges will stick," said a deputy commissioner.

"Just doing my job," I said.

"11 years old, not ever on the job yet, and already-" he said.

"You know that man wasn't the real victim, the charges are open and shut," I said.

"Yea, permanent injuries, and jail," he said.

"You know, you don't want a fox running the hen house, but a wolf wouldn't kill you," I said, and being 11 then howled.

"I really could never have given you the job before you turned 18; but now I will make sure you work your way up the ranks. But you'll be at your destination while still in your rookie year," he said, "Much worse what happened and I would have to be giving you your badge right about now."

"Badge or no badge, this is only the beginning," I said.

"I know, and I shudder," he said.

It has been brought to my attention 2 key details of the proceeding 2 stories have been inadvertently omitted. In the last episode, as you probably expected the old man played the innocent old victim routine.

Oh, at the start I forgot to mention; regarding the story before last, Edy also said "Please, just tell me it wasn't a cruel murder." Only thing he was able to say after he got the news. As I was saying:

Anyway, this is one of the last cases I worked before becoming head of Internal Affairs:

"I hate cops," said this kid.

"HEY! I'm putting my life on the line to keep you safe!" said the officer sitting next to him.

"Yea, right, you're just another thug!" he said.

"YOU LITT-" he said.

"GETTLEMEN!" I said.

He saw my Internal Affairs badge and said "Ho boy! Here we go!"

(insert mule picture here)
Houston

"And who are you?" I said.

"I am Internal Affa-" I said.

"Hey, Captain Asleep at the wheel, where were you while my sister was being murdered; Eating a donut, or killing some else?!?!" he said.

I looked at the officer, then back at him and simply said "Criminal justice is a struggle; and in any struggle there will be some good guys and some bad guys on both sides. Furthermore, justice isn't a smooth and wonderful thing it's accredited as being. Rather, like evolution, it's hard, it, quite literally, is just getting back at someone; not too dissimilarly from a vigilante. I would know."

I saw that he was getting really upset; I told the officer "take 5."

"I'm serious," he said.

"So am I," I said.

"You ever, say, have a younger sibling, that you like to think of your-self as the 3rd parent of, get murdered?" he said doubting I really was a cop.

"Yes," I said.

"Well, while I liked to think of myself as this big deal big brother, It was really a joke, she was almost 7, I am almost 8," he said.

"Recent?" I said.

"4 day ago," he said.

"I'm sorry to-" I said.

"Save the canned sympathy," he said.

"Hope it wasn't a cruel murder-

"Is it ever not?" he said.

"I have connections, I can get someone to actually-" I said.

"PHA!" he almost laughed, "She was murdered by the Fuzz!"

"What?" I said.

"Oh, yea, Supposedly someone was selling some substance you cops don't want people to have, I personally couldn't care less, I was at school, but she was sick. They came in so violently that she was killed, so was spot. Mother and Father were also sick, but survived." he said, "So, what's your sob story?"

(insert mule picture here)
Houston

"It was my 10th birthday, I packed it in early so that I would be fast asleep before midnight; I really didn't like the end of holidays. My 5 year old brother and 11 year old sister were playing with my newest version of Grand Theft Auto; each declaring they would be the superior cop killer. Mom and Dad stepped outside. They had promised me a tree house; but like was the case with everything in my family; they were procrastinators. Grandfather Garcia, in is demented state, didn't understand modern air conditioning so he left a window open. I ran in when I heard my parents scream. Oh God! That awful sound! I thought there could be nothing worse, Then I found them,-" I said.

"A likely story," he said, "Just have to top everyone."

"It's not like that!" I said.

"Go away, just leave me alone," he said.

"Later at the office:" I said.

"I got one boss," I said.

"I am not 'boss' my name is not 'boss' I am Captain Villinovec," he said.

"Either way, there was a manslaughter," I said.

"Not another one!" he said.

"Yea, drug raid gone bad," I said.

"Something like that would have been brought straight to me," said Captain Villinovec.

"Wasn't one of ours is the deal," I said.

"Then what does it have to do with us?" he said.

"Simple, homicide will not do anything," I said.

"Could put some pressure on them," he said, "But if it wasn't us how will we have jurisdiction?"

"It was right in our jurisdiction, I'm already bringing up officers and a dispatcher that wouldn't respond; not that that would have done anything," I said.

"You mean they also goofed up jurisdiction?" he said, "They're in big trouble."

"No, they also had jurisdiction," I said.

"Oh, did we have anyone one on it?" he said.

"Yea, I'll call him in now," he said.

"You do that, and I'll be there with you in the interview room," he said.

Later:

"Captain Clemens was a part of this?" said my boss.

"Yes," I said.

"The head of narcotics was a part of this! You are just trying to bag bigger and bigger game," he said.

"Yes, the police chief said that when I arrested him, if memory serves," I said.

"Yes, then you arrested me!" said my boss.

"Well you did try to stop me from making that arrest," I said.

"Professionally as your boss!" he said.

"Regardless, I take your position in 2 weeks," I said.

"I still think you're blackmailing your way to the top," he said.

"No, no, more pulling strings to the top, I checked with a lawyer," I said.

"Oh, here's captain, um,-" he said.

"Clemens," I said.

"Guys, you said you needed me to come in urgently, is everything ok?" he said.

"Yes, we just need your help," I said.

"Oh, good, they say that you're on a witch hunt, and Captains are your favorite," he said.

I chuckled and said "No, no, A witch hunt implies dishonesty and illegality, and it's not captains, it's detectives."

"Well, that's not reassuring at all," said Captain Clemens.

"Now, you've been informed of your rights, right? " I said.

"Right, " he said.

"Just need to know what federal agent you handed a case over to," I said.

"WAIT! WHAT?!?! What are you trying to do?!?! Bust a federal operation?!?!" said boss.

I turned to him and gave a casual "yes."

"I-I-" studdered Captain Clemens.

(No, no connection to you know who)

"Agent Alexia," he said.

"Give him an excuse to come into your office," I said.

Later when he arrived:

"Good morning Agent Alexia," said Captain Clemens.

My boss, fearing me more than the feds, was too busy cowering under his desk, wedged in, to come. So it was at that moment I jumped out of a closet and arrested Agent Alexia.

"Agent Alexia you are under arrest for your role in the death of a minor child, you have the right to remain silent, anything you say can and will be used against you in a court of law. You have the right to an attorney, if you cannot afford an attorney one will be provided by you by the court. Do you understand these rights as read to you?" I said.

After the usual reaction he said "What? that raid a few days back; so the GPS was wrong, big deal, not our fault. If you must go after someone go after them," he said.

"GPS smPS, I totally blame you," I said.

"Do you have any idea the trouble you coul-" he said.

"You're being held in the largest police station in this part of the country and the force fears me more than ya'll," I said.

Later during the interview:

"My client's work forbids him to answer any of your questions," said an attorney.

"And my work forbids me to take no for an answer: here's the straight skivvy: If you give me over everyone related to this case, and then lead them into my trap. Then I'll put in a good word for you at the DA's office. And yes, the DA does fear me just like everyone else. But if you don't; then I'll put in a bad word for you at the DA's office. An't right-" I said.

"What Dane says 'an't' anyway?!!?" said Agent Alexia, "And furthermore 'an't' an't a word."

"I am not a Dane, I was adopted from Sweden as a toddler, and furthermore I am glad to see I can get you to talk," I said.

"You're adopted?" he said.

"Everyone in my family is adopted, except for one weird cousin, And my youngest brother. Really he is just the crazy uncle before any of his siblings had kids," I said.

"Really," he said trying to change the subject.

"Stop talking," said the lawyer.

(insert mule picture here)
Houston

"Right, as I was saying it AN'T right, but you might even get a shot at the death penalty," I said.

That really scared him. He then agreed to do all that in exchange for a plee deal that will get him only brief probation:

"Hello and welcome to the Drug Enforcement Agency Conference. I know that many of you had to cancel important work to come, but I am very happy to see that all the persons I had ordered to come, did come. Before we begin, I would just like to say," and then I flashed my badge, cops came out of the wood work, and I said "Gotcha! Yea, you're all under arrest."

Regarding the murder you heard about in the last episode, so there I was at Pinkerton. I had just made top level homicide detective:

"Excuse me, is this your umbrella?" I said.

"No, getting an update?" he said.

"Actually no, not getting an update, this is not how we normally receive updates. Actually, I'm about to make internal affairs," I said.

"No kidding?" he said, "Well, I'm here on a personal matter too."

"Well, for me it's just about high time," I said.

"You too?" he said.

"Well, it's really a big part of my life story, and will sound a little crazy," I said.

"You too?-" he said.

"Sounds like it may be very similar reasons why we're here. What say we exchange stories," I said.

"Sound's good, you first."

"It was my 10th birthday, I packed it in early so that I would be fast asleep before midnight; I really didn't like the end of holidays. My 5 year old brother and 11 year old sister were playing with my newest version of Grand Theft Auto; each declaring they would be the superior cop killer. Mom and Dad stepped outside. They had promised me a tree house; but like was the case with everything in my family; they were procrastinators; a real-life manifestation of now or never. Grandfather in is demented state didn't understand modern air conditioning so he left a window open. My parents found them-" I said.

"You're also here because of murder," he said.

"Well, there was no matching MO out there, and whoever did it knew what they were doing. My brother's best friend and probable girlfriend said I had killed before, and that was proof enough! Then came that judge-" I said, "By the time I was out I was a totally different person in a very different family.

(insert mule picture here)
Houston

Everything that happened not only bankrupted my parents, which caused my guilt. But they were able to show that the cops framed me. It wasn't enough to even reprimand the cops, but was enough for a reasonable doubt, and to put me at the top of Internal Affairs," I said.

"Let me guess, Crayer-" he said.

"HOW DID YOU KNOW?!?!" I said felling a rush of different emotions.

"He's the king of prosecuting as an adult," he said, "Most judges I can keep from doing that, but him, he'll even do it when it's absurd.-" he said.

"You a lawyer?" I said.

"Yea, actually a super lawyer that could get anyone off," he said.

"No kidding?" I said.

"Yea, juvenile defense. That being said most of my cases I do for free, either because they're being tried as an adult, or really young. Or both. Basically the closer it is to my nephews case, the more likely," he said.

"They couldn't crack it, so I was framed. I was another notch in Crayer pistol," I said.

"You here to finally get some answers as to why they were killed?" he said.

"Yea-" I said, "Say-Hey, you're Michael W. Sackett, that-"

"That's the one," I said.

"With you around we often don't even try to try as an adult, sometimes even indibt at all," I said.

"Really! I had no idea, I'll wear that as a badge of pride for the rest of my life," he said.

"I don't know how to respond to that," I said, "So? What's your story?"

"I have never been divorced, but I am a widower thrice, over," he said.

"Really?" I said.

"There has been even more craziness in my life, for example I am an only child with siblings," he said.

"Just tell me everything, this is sounding like a quick trip to Crazytown," I said.

"Well, about a year before I was born my brother ran away from home, but when I found out about him I was 17, I then went to live with him and everything changed. I never knew about him for the same reason that when my sister-in law was killed, we thought that dad did it. But she was just a dead ringer in the wrong place at the wrong time." he said, "He has since remarried"

"Oh," I said.

(insert mule picture here)
Houston

"As for his family when his son was 14 his twin sister was murdered. He didn't do it but he did come super close to pleading guilty *for* the death penalty. They were close. And when they found the real killer, they couldn't get him convicted. He is now married with 3 adopted kids. " he chuckled and said" The oldest one can now talk and calls me 'Uncle Grandpa' His younger son is in school and is going to follow in his big brother's footsteps. But instead of a regular cop like my nephew and my wife, he will be a crime scene photographer. He also has a little sister and another on the way." he said.

"Yow!" I said.

"Yea," he said.

"Well, why exactly are you here?" I said.

"Well, to make that make sense, I'll have to go back, way back. Oh! And did I mention that my 8 year old sister died right before I was born?" he said.

"Don't. think. so." I said.

"Well, when I was six I had a good friend named Charlie," he said, "I still miss her. We were more than just friends, but still friend up until the time we were 8. Would have been about a year sooner, but, you know. By 10 we were engaged. At 11 we were both in a bad accident. I saw my sister, and she met her twin brother. Doubting either of us would survive they married us. but we both did. She was one of those that had no family, so my parents then took her in as a foster kid. To this day I will sometimes say something about 'yes, but I was only briefly married to my sister and only one of my sons was a serial killer.'

"Say what?" I said.

"Yea, when we were 13 she accidently killed herself. That was hard. When I was 18 losing my sister in law, I had gone to live with my brother, so I also liver with her threw me back harder than before. When I was 19 the first woman I went out with after Charlie, we ended up married. She was killed in a car wreck. Still miss Avery too. Was a lot of relationships to find Taylor, she was murdered in revenge for an admittedly guilty teen I exonerated. Also tried to kill me. But before her and after Avery I graduated collage, became a lawyer, and adopted Franklyn-" he said.

"Frank-lyn?" I said.

"Yea, because of the right ages people sometimes thought he was how and why me and Charlie had to get married. BOGUS! Taylor lost her only sibling, her brother, as a child. But was with Avery, I met Sam first date after losing Taylor. She's great, a remarried widow, her first husband was a firefighter fallen in the line of duty, and came from a family of cops. her kids, the oldest being 8, are now my kids," he said.

"What about Franklyn?" I said.

"Was a contract killer, at 11 I had to exonerate him. He got engaged at 13, and his would have been father in law killed him for obvious reasons. Only got a few years. Nevertheless Jenny is still a part of our family," he said, "And I always note that Franklyn died a good person, at least as good as anyone ever is."

"Wouldhavebeen daughter in law?" I said.

"Yea," he said, "She just got re-engaged."

"But, that doesn't' answer why you're here," I said.

"Well that's because-" he said.

BANGBANG BANGBANG a meer meer-

"The Law and Order Theme Song? That's your ringtone too?" he said.

"Yea, YO!" I said.

"Really? I thought I was alone in that," he said.

"Hate to break up the reminiscing, but duty calls," I said.

"If the killer was under 16, call me," he said.

later in Memorial Park:

"What've we got?" I said.

"Single shot to the forehead, lots heard, none so far saw anything," said coroner Alztimer.

"Not the best neighborhood, you think a mugging gone wrong?" I said.

"No defensive wounds, and nothing looks to be stolen-" said the coroner as taking me to the body.

"He's old," I said, "And looks like my great uncle."

"Yea, reading the classic Frankenstein in Memorial park. That's what I call an ironic death," said detective Ludwig.

"I'll say, nothing missing?" I said.

"Phone, wallet, keys, ID bracelet, book, wig, nothing's gone." said detective Ludwig.

"Don't be so sure," I said, "look at the crease on the tie, have the photographer get that. Might have been mugged by someone that knew him and also knew the worth of the tie-" I said.

"Either way, just got our first lead. Looks like the last person to see him alive may have been an Uber driver," said detective Ludwig.

"Have him brought in," I said, "By the way? What's the name?"

(insert mule picture here)
Houston

"According to ID, Fred Wong, US citizen. But looks like a permanent ID, thus an old picture. Might be switched," he said.

Later with the Uber driver.

"So, Mr. Phan, does the name 'Fred Wong' ring a bell?" I asked.

"Oh, call me Ned, and yea, don't get too many Geezers using Uber," he said.

"Anything unusual about the ride?" I said.

"Well, like I said, not too many Geezers using Uber," he said, "Other tha-"

"What?" I said.

"Well, he," said Ned.

"What? What?!" I said.

"Chillax! Going to the park, a little, but not very, unusual destination," said Ned.

"That's it?" I said.

"Well, I do this for 12-13 hours a day on average. Baby sister with health problems, and orphaned," he said clearly worried about her, "But, it was slightly weird."

"Please, do tell," he said.

"Well, he said he wasn't up to a lot of walking, but still liked the park. So he bought a book. I think it was Frankenstein; but not sure," he said, "but what was strange was he seemed excited."

"What's so weird about that?" I said.

"Being excited about reading in the park, now that must be a man with no life at all!" he said.

"Anything else? Anything about meeting anyone or buying and / or selling anything?" I said.

"N-o, but in the interest of full disclosure I do have a terrible memory," he said.

"Don't remember anything else?" I said.

"If I did I would have told you by now. But, may I have your business card," he said.

"Why so?" I said.

"In the unlikely event that I remember anything," he said.

"Sure, sure," I said.

Later:

(insert mule picture here)
Houston

"So? how'd it go," said Ludwig.

"Nice chap, dead end," I said.

"Well, got the family right here," he said.

"Oh, good, good," I said.

"Well, family that lived near here, more coming in from just about everywhere," he said.

"Where's the nearby family?" I said.

"Right in here," said Ludwig, opening the door.

"Hello, I'm Detective Olaf, this is assistant Detective Ludwig," I said.

"I, already introduced," he said, "Here is the victim's son, son, son, daughter, son-in-law, grandson, more coming into town."

"Hi-" I said.

"I watch true crime shows. I know that you're going to suspect one of us-" said the daughter.

"Actually I am leadless, All I know yet is he took Uber everywhere, seemed to die doing something he enjoyed, and not a lot else, but I do know that he came to America fleeing the Communist revolutionaries in China, then worked for over 60 years as a loan officer. I know he was long retired; but is it possible that someone was denied and came back much later-" I said.

"That's crazy," said a son, "I don't think his job ever got him threatened."

"I also know that his wife died nearly 20 years ago, is it possible that he was seeing someone else?" I said.

"More that probable," said another son.

"Do you have any idea how to contact her?" I said.

"Can't say that I do, never could keep up with the girlfriend desure," he replied, "Went out with nearly every single old lady at the retirement facility."

"You think that-" I said.

"No clue, never seemed to see the same one twice," he said.

"Did he have any enemies?" I said.

"No, really he was just a typical old-" said the son-in-law.

"What?" I said.

(insert mule picture here)

Houston

"His only prior," he replied," reached a plea deal on one count of vehicular assault. Was little over 2 years ago; really was just a fine example of us having should have taken his license away. That's it."

"Oh," I said, "Will have to check that out."

Later following that up:

"Mrs. Deahuex?" I said.

"Yes?" she said.

"Detective Olaf, this is Detective Ludwig. Houston Homicide, HPD" I said.

"Oh. My God, Oh My God! What happened?!?! Was it Brian? CINDY?!?!" she said.

"No, no, I can assure that they're fine, on account of I have no idea who they are in the first place," I said.

"Don't scare people like that!" she said, "And with all due respect, why then are you here?"

"Does the name Fred Wong ring any bells? And would you like an attorney?" I said.

"Now that you mention it, yes. And yes it does, broke my leg when I was pregnant!" she said.

(police siren ringtone)

Detective Ludwig went to take a call.

"This morning he was found dead in a major city park," I said.

"As I recall, he was as old, probably stroked out. Or had cancer, or, or, or" she said.

"There was a gunshot wound," I said.

"O-h-" she said.

"Wasn't her," said Detective Ludwig.

"How do you know?" I said.

"Ballistics just came in, big fat lead," he said.

Later there at the station:

"So, what's your report?" I said.

"The bullet that killed Mr. Wong also killed a John Doe, found dead on a Metro city bus few days back," said the bulistsist.

"Found, dead?" I said.

"Mostly empty, night bus, done discreetly with a high quality silencer," he said.

"Tell me more," I said.

"If HPD, rather than MPD, had handled the case, we would have figured it out sooner. According to time of death, we lowered it to a few possible suspects," he said.

"Camera also available?" I said.

"Yes, we have two teens, but kept hands visible texting, so can rule them out. Two stereotypical little old ladies, different times, and one person that didn't use a Q card; but cash," he said.

"Any idea who he is?" I said.

"Got better, his face was in the system for a double homicide, 2nd degree so made parole, 2 weeks ago," he said.

"Something tells me it's about to be revoked," I said.

"Been beaten to it," he said.

"Let's talk to him," I said.

Later there with his lawyer:

"I will preface that everything said here is hypothetical; that being said my client will tell all, seeing as he has nothing to hide," said the attorney.

"Yea, Mr. Robinson, you have been convicted of two-" I said.

"I was 16, and I snapped. I just snapped. My little sister is taking care of me. She thinks this is my chance to have a normal life now. Why would I kill him? That makes no sense! The last time I snapped and killed my parents over something that has seemed pretty petty for 20 years. I finally got parole. It honestly makes no sense. And may I note the fact that there, to the best of my knowledge, are others that could have carried it out. Assuming that you weren't wrong about anything. All you have against them is wrong place, wrong time, and priors," he said.

"Yes, yes, does the name Fred Wong ring any bells at all?" I said.

"No, why?" he said.

"Are you sure that it rings no bells at all?" I said.

"I once had a friend named Fred, and his grandmother's maiden name was Wong. Does that count?" he said.

"Is that it?" I said.

(insert mule picture here)
Houston

"Y-yes," he said.

"No, it doesn't count," I said.

"Have you spoken to anyone since your recent arrest?" I said.

"Well, there's my sister," he said.

"Already looked into that possibly, she alibied out, next," I said.

"And then there's my lawyer," he said.

I looked at the attorney and he then said "I want a lawyer."

Later with the detective that worked the first case:

"So? any idea who the John Doe is?" I said.

"Actually, we know for sure," he said.

"Then why's he classified as a John doe?!" I said.

"He's an Illegal, it's really a technicality," he said.

"Any-" I said.

"Already called family and the consulate," he said.

"Let's have the families meet, see if any bells are rung," I said.

"Already did, nothing-" he said.

"Guys, those canvasing the area finally IDed someone that was seen fleeing the scene," said Detective Ludwig.

"Can you bring him in?" I said.

"Yea, demanded a lawyer, got him in holding,-" said Detective Ludwig.

"Give him the lawyer," I said.

Later with him:

"Against my advice, my client will tell you what happened," said the lawyer.

"So, Mike, did you kill Hose Wong?" I said.

"Martha Stewart," he said.

"Say what now?" I said.

(insert mule picture here)
Houston

Contrary to popular memory, Martha Stewart was never convicted of insider trading, she was however sent to jail for lying when she said she was innocent," he said.

"O-K, I understand. But like I said; what happened," I said.

"There's no point in me telling you, you'd never believe me!" he said.

"Oh, what harm can it do?" I said.

"You said you were going to say it; so if you are going to say it, say it," said the lawyer.

"It was unprovoked, neither even said a word to each other, he didn't even notice her!" he said.

"The victim and killer?" I said.

"Yea, and that's where things, get crazy," he said.

"What kind of crazy?" I said.

"It was a stereotypical old lady!" he said, "And might I mention that if I was going to make up a story; I would have made up one far better than that! Maybe I have simply, finally gone crackers."

"Oh," I said, "Can you describe her?"

"No," he said.

"No?" I said.

"I'm bad with faces, and names, and putting the two together," he said.

"Before we proceed might I remind you that we agreed to have my client's hands tested; and there was no gun powder residue whatsoever," he said.

"It was so simple, but at the same time so rediculas we never would have even guessed!" I said, "Are you sure you cannot describe her?"

"Well, average old lady hair, average old lady clothes, average old lady walk, average old person red walker-" he said.

"WAIT! say that again," I said.

"Ok, average ol-" he said.

"No, no, just the last part," I said.

"Old person red walker?" he said.

"Yea," I said.

"That doesn't sound so average!" I said.

"Actually it is; it was one that you lean over, that is also a seat-" he said.

"Oh," I said.

"Yea, just walked up casually, pulled a gun out of the seat that's also a basket, and bang!" he said.

"Guys!" said an officer barging in.

"We're in the middle of an interrogation!" I said.

"Not anymore, the same gun behind your murders, just killed a 2 year old girl and a mounted officer in Hermann park. They would have stopped the killer, but it was just so crazy that they couldn't-" she said.

"Let me guess, little old lady killer," I said.

"How. did. you. know." she said.

"You do your thing, I have a murder to solve!" I said, "And call Metro Police! Quick!"

Later with the detective from MPD

"So, here we are, still can rule out the teens," he said.

"And I can rule out the abundantly obvious killer," I said.

"And this security video leaves us solely with crazy town," he said.

"Look, the second old lady uses a cane, so we can rule her out," I said trailing off, "WAIT! THAT'S A GENERIC RED PUSH WALKER!!!!!!"

"Yea, so?" he said.

"There's been more impossible coincidences in this case-" I said interrupting myself, "You said that Mr. Orphaned Himself was the only one that didn't use a Q-card. Find that old lady!" I said.

Later:

"So, how'd it go?" he said.

"Went as would be expected. Pulling the sweet innocent old lady retinue, so might not be convicted. But there was gun powder residue on her hands. And we did find the gun in her room that was used to carry out all 4 killings. Also no priors and the family is reacting normally. No clue why she went this way," I said.

"Thank you, so much. No jury would have ever believed me," he said.

"Hey, I'm just glad that you got to be one of the lucky ones," I said.

(insert mule picture here)
Houston

"What do you mean?" he said.

"Crayer got to you, but you're now re-beginning your life. And with your full exoneration your parole is being reinstated as was before," I said.

"Who's Crayer?" he said.

"He's one of them that sent you to jail," I said.

"No, I would remember someone who was part of those that sent me to jail," he said.

"Well, you should have seen the look on the faces of those fellow nursing home residents in that bingo hall when we arrested her for 4 counts or premeditated murder. And when I put a BOLO for a helpless little old lady with a severe danger warning," I said.

"I can only imagine," he said.

You know how I said most of this series would be flashbacks to present day. Well, this is sort of an exception.

"Hi," I said, "I'm sorry, what was your name again?"

He replied, but I could never spell it so I will just go with Hose Wong, the disobeyer equivalent of John Smith. In this part of the world, that is.

"Oh, guess I did remember correctly after all," I said.

"So, it has come to our attention that your first murder case was straight out of The 20," he said.

"Yea, that it was," I said, "But I thought that the sequel was going to be less American and more global."

"Correct, but we want one that is like one from the 20, and that is perfect," he said.

"Oh, ok, but I wonder. Is it true how disobeyer intelligence is having layoffs because of low crime rates?" I said.

"We don't have layoffs per say, but lots of our people are taking this as an opportunity to go back home, or be moved to another part of the world. What about you?" he said.

"Well, was pretty crazy, but now have just about run out of cops to arrest, so," I said.

"Think you'll make chief?" he said.

"Actually, I think I will be looking for a position similar to my current one, but in a higher place, maybe head of NYPD Internal Affairs, or something federal," I said.

"Oh, well, shall we get to this?" he said.

(insert mule picture here)
Houston

"Oh, yes, yes, I remember that it seemed like a disobeyer family with Christian parents, I can see why you'd want to interview me, but why not them?" I said.

"What on earth makes you think that we aren't?" he said.

"Oh," I said, "But seriously, I can't believe how close to disobeyer they were, back then. Even down to the books they had, emergency preparedness, a Passover-"

"Yea, yea, yea I get the picture," he said.

"Oh, sorry, where should I start?" I said.

"How about where it all began?" he said.

"Oh, good thinking," I said.

I will skip straight into where the story actually starts going:

"So, your detective skills tell you anything?" I said.

"Let's see, mostly religious books, bibles, a Book of Mormon, torah, nothing that I could see leading to murder," he said.

"You're right, that is perfectly disobeyer," he said.

I went straight back into the story:

"How did they get found?" I said.

"Pizza boy with for mentioned food," he said.

"Think killer called to have them be found?" I said.

"Who knows, if the killer did, it wasn't random," he said.

"How so?" I said.

"Pizza was ordered with an Imogi in a tweet. Either knew the vics; or was coincidental," he said.

"What about that camera?" I said.

"Fake," he said.

"Oh," I said.

"What about your detective skills newbie?" he said.

"Well, looks like a Devout Christian family that has a small interest in similar faith's-" I said.

"Very disobeyer said Hose.

(insert mule picture here)
Houston

"Um, hum, now, where was I? Oh! yes,: a large family, not a violent bone in their body. No clue how this could have happened. Just a fine example of one big happy family." I said.

Boy was I wrong!

"ME Alztimer! have you finished your initial report?!" I said / shouted across a noisy and crowded crime scene.

"Yea, looks like someone took down the family shotgun, don't know why it was loaded, but shot mom. Then when dad reacted; he was hit in the last place any man would want to be hit. Then in that state, was beaten to death-" said Alztimer.

"With the shotgun," I said.

"Yea, anyone could have done this," said Alztimer.

"CSU! What about ya'll?!" I said.

"Whoever did this knew how to get away with murder," he said.

"Well, central called. Both parents grew up in foster care, have Juvenile Records. Getting sopenas, might have been something that should have stayed buried that happened tonight," he said.

"Then, who is kin?" I said.

"Looks, like they have 8 children, had been 9, but there was an accident 2 weeks ago," said my boss, "big family."

"Well, I doubt that that is a coincidence," I said.

"Not sure where the first seven are, but looks like one is a sophomore at University of Houston," he said.

"Guess that's where we start," I said.

When we arrived:

"Mr. Smith?" he said, "I'm detective Rathbone, these are detectives Zhang and Olaf."

"Yea," he said, "What brings you here this evening?"

"It regards your parents, Mr. and Mrs. Smith," said my boss.

"Yea?" he said.

"May we come in?" he said.

"Why are you here?" he said.

"We regret to inform you that earlier this evening, your parents were attacked. They did not survive," said detective Rathbone.

And what followed quite possibly the single strangest thing I have ever seen in all my years on the force. His reaction was a blend of rapture and having a heavy weigh lifted off his chest. I know that different people handle grief differently. I've seen people that were happy to see someone go, and those that were shocked to see someone get murdered. But never again both at once at any other time.

After a moment of collective shock he said: "Hey! You'll never believe this! Mom and Dad finally bought the farm!!" he said.

Everyone reacted differently, but collectively it was the same.

"M-Mr.-" said Detective Rathbone.

"Show-show your badge," he said.

We did.

"Well-" said detective Rathbone.

"I'll be honest with you, We watch murder mysteries. The only enemies are right here," he said.

"Don't you people want a lawyer?" I said.

Detective Rathbone elbowed me.

"Nah, innocent men don't need lawyers," he said.

"Well, that's not really true," I said, "but ok,"

"Hey, who's side are you on?!" said detective Rathbone.

"The good guys, no matter whom they are," I said.

"Man, you are Internal Affair waiting to happen," he said.

"You have no idea," I said.

"Hey, I know cops are big fat liars-" said Mr. Smith.

"Oh boy tell me about it!" I said.

I got elbowed again.

"That technically is assaulting a police officer," I said.

"Oy vey," said detective Rathbone.

(insert mule picture here)
Houston

"As I was saying, I know that we will be suspects, and I know Mr. and Mrs. Smith's will also. And I know the law, I have to be physically present. Let's start the interviews in order of age," he said.

"Why?" said detective Rathbone.

"As good a way as any," he said, "Bill!"

"Yea, bro?" said Bill.

"We're all gunu get interviewed," said Mr. Smith.

"Yea, let's talk in the car," said Detective Zhang.

"As long as I don't have to get in the back seat," said Bill.

"So, when did you last hear from your parents?" I said.

"Ex-parents," said Mr. Smith.

"Ex-parents?" said detective Zhang, "Issues I presume?"

"Issues city," he said.

"MR. Smiths," I said, "When was the last time-"

"When I disowned them," he said. About 2 weeks ago."

Bill was starting to cry so I said "Sorry about your parents."

"It-It's not that," he said, "I just miss my sister, I so badly want to forget that night."

"What exactly happened?" I said.

"Yea, what happened?" said my boss.

"She, was all our favorite sibling. She was probably the favorite also; but you could never really tell for sure. She was popular with everyone, seniors, real seniors, 2nt graders. She was even a small time online celebrity. Oddly enough, she was the middle child. 2 little brothers, two big brothers, 2 little sisters, 2 big sisters," Bill rambled and trailed off.

"Yea, but what happened?" said Rathbone.

"Parents decided that she was 'addicted to her tech' or something like that," he said, "We did nothing. And I'll have that on my conscience as long as I live."

"She the one that just died?" I said putting 2 and 2 together.

"The coroner said it was an accidental injection of air. The truth couldn't have been more obvious," he said, "Most of us disowned them. I wish I was upset about this; and Lord forgive me I wish I could say that I wasn't glad to see them go."

"Sorry to hear this," I said.

We looked at the oldest brother (only one over 18) and he said "Hey! If it had been me It would have been special circumstances! Or... Was it? And! Why would I have waited 2 weeks?!?!"

I will skip giving all the details of the interviews, and say that that is basically how all the interviews went.

At the end my boss said: "Well, all of you have motive and means, you have all simply alibied each other. I believe you were all in on it-"

"What about him?" I said pointing to the man sitting in the corner using that computer.

"Oh, yea, my dorm mate. He's more like furniture than a roommate, so I often forget he's there," said Mr. Smith.

"Mr.-" I said.

"Oh, yea, the murder alibi thing, totally legit. I was here like this the whole time, from midafternoon on, and them all longer," he said, "But I really have to get back to studying."

"I believe him," said detective Zhang.

"Why so?" I said.

"While the could be bribed or blackmailed, no one in this room has priors except-" she said.

"Ok enough said!," I said, "So, if no one here did it, who did it?" I said.

"Coroner called," said detective Rathbone, "Imogi could have been sent by the parents according to accurate time of death."

"Gets better ya'll," said detective Zhang, "Canviser called. Someone was seen in the neighborhood that made a quick visit to the crime scene-"

"The killer?" said detective Rathbone.

"Maybe be, only was seen at the scene by one person, but everyone remembered her walking through the neighborhood," she said.

"Why so?" I said.

"Was wearing a hospital gown," she said.

(insert mule picture here)
Houston

I turned and said "Your parents, or Ex-parents, had 9 children, one is dead. Mr. Smith I only see you and 6, not counting you. Where's no. 9?"

"Oh!" he said, "bout to lose another one. She's only 12. Currently still at the med center. She has had her death warrant signed by the best." and then he got emotional.

"Where is she being kept?" said my boss.

I'll skip the unneeded details the interviewer wanted and say that She denied it all. Then we saw cameras and talked to staff. From well before till right before we arrived (a good time after the double homicide) she had just disappeared. You could see that she had left for a good and exhausting while just from looking at her. When I had them have me confront her:

"Miss Smith," I said.

"Isn't my brother supposed to be here? And a lawyer?" she said.

"He, um, under the circumstances, no," I said.

"Whatdaya want?" she said, "I already told you-"

"Yes, but We know that during the whole time of the murder you were gone. And with all that hate-" I said.

"I was beyond furious, but I could get along with them. Btu my siblings were trapped in hate ridden grief. It was sooner or later-" she said.

"They were going to kill them," I said.

"You'll never prove it. Even I couldn't even if I wanted to," she said, "But I didn't."

"I know that your parents were the 5th wheels of your family. And I also know that you 9 were extremely close, your sister was ya'lls link to the cool kids, but you also loved her for her. And you're going to bite the big one anyway."

"This doesn't sound legal," she said.

"It isn't, this in not adminisble an any court," I said.

"Why should I believe you?" she said.

"Because I'm the only man on the force that doesn't lie. They hate it, but that is the case," I said.

"I don't believe you, but: This way they wouldn't be guilty of murder, and thus can't he put in jail. Yes, I did It. Not trilled but I did. Now, what can you really do to me? I'm 12! And have stage 4 pancreatic cancer," she said.

I stepped out and said: "Well, can't use that in court. But still can charge her," I said.

"Now what happens?" said Mr. Smith, "We can't protect her-"

"From Crayer, a big case like this has a long pre-trial period. She'll be dead by then. And even if not, probably won't live to sentencing. She was right, she is basically untouchable," I said.

"But you'll still ignore mitigating factors and arrest her," said Mr. Smith.

"That's where you come in," I said.

"Heh?" he said.

"Yea, if she continues treatment to prolong life, but does it here at this hospital. She can die here, but will get no chemo break. We won't be able to put her into custody. Or she can die in prison. Which I doubt would be much if any worse in her condition," I said, "Up to you."

"And I'll leave that up to her," he said.

That case was weird. They then all went in and thanked her. People handle grief differently. And I went on to see a lot of different ways that I saw people handle seeing one person they love kill someone else they love, weather accidentally or on purpose. That, though I suppose that at the time they didn't love them, was the craziest.

Well, this is the story that I was most famous for till the pilot story, among others at any rate. You will then see why.

"So, as of today I am Internal Affairs," I said.

"They why are you here?" said my assistant detective.

"Well I'm not entirely Internal Affairs," I said.

"You are just flying up the latter-" he said.

"Come On!" said a panicked officer.

"What? What's going on?" I said.

"This was one of our own," he said.

"What?" I said.

"Yea," he said, "Among others."

"Among others?" I said, "Who else."

"Not sure cause of death, but 2 minors. Ages 2 and 17," she said.

later there:

(insert mule picture here)
Houston

I walked up and said "Now how does a white teenager, a black cop, and an Asian toddler end up dead in the same yard? Sounds like the starts to a racist joke that isn't even funny."

"It never is-" said the officer.

"Well, I didn't say that that make it ok," I said. Then I bent down and said "The 99th, in the Galleria, Assistant detective Cousteau, you see about Idling the Jane Doe, Detective Zhang, you know who the other teen is?"

"Lives here, parents are in the middle of the Caribbean about now, but little sis says he's Greger Mendal-" she said.

"Greger Mendal?!?!-" I said.

"Not Mr. Pea gene monk," she said.

"Not that Gregor Mendal!" I said, "Greg Mendal! THE! Greg Mendal?! How do you not know who he is?!"

"Is he the one that is the bean the department's existence?" she replied.

"That's the one!" I said, "Maybe one of his stings went wrong."

"Ok! Somebody fill in the peanut gallery," said my assistant detective.

"Have you heard the story of my very first case on the force?" I said.

"Isn't the one with the cance-" he said.

"No, that was my first homicide case," I said.

"Oh! then it was where you got that old-" he said.

"No, when I was 11-" I said.

"Oh yea! That put fear into us all," he said.

"Yes, well he took that one news story and ran with it," I said.

"Oh! This is him!" he said.

"Yes, this is him," I said.

"His non-police stings were like yours, only he busted nearly 40 abusers," he said.

"Yea and his first 'client' if you will became his assistant. Say, where's the coroner?" I said.

"Right here," she said.

(insert mule picture here)
Houston

"Got cause of death?" I said.

"Yea, homicide," she said.

"Come on," I said.

"Well, our officer looks like a fatal gunshot wound, and Greg all I saw was Taser marks, same with our Jane Doe," she said.

"Could they have come from the officer's stun gun?" I said.

"Well, Jane Doe's marks look to have done just that, and I think that his stun gun has been used. The other matches a non-police issue found in the officer's pocket," she said.

"Looks like I have the perfect transition case from Homicide to Internal Affairs," I said.

"And I haven't looked at victim no. 4," she said.

"There's another murder victim?" I said.

Zhang came up to me and said, "Not dead, but shot bad. Last I saw was flying off for Ben Taub. If he lives he might be the key to it all."

"Perhaps, Zhang, you see what you can learn about the Jane Doe, assistant, learn what you can hear about the not dead victim, I'll see what I can learn about our officer's arrests and personal life, etc..." I said.

Later:

"So, detective Olaf, you're here about that officer aren't you?" said Captain Norquest.

"Yes-" I said.

"Well, sadly usually a fallen officer is a good one, often decorated-" he said.

"And he was also-" I said.

"No, I assumed that you already knew being Internal Affairs-" he said.

"We were going to indebt him?!" I said.

"Nothing imminate, but I've seen it before, only 2 ways his career could end: a pink slip or a pair of handcuffs, or probably both," he said, "He had been in trouble before, and as if often the case it just escalated," he said.

BANGBANG BANGBANG a me-

"Detective Olaf," I said.

"Was that-" he said.

"Yes," I said, and returned to the call, "Find anything?"

"You bet! On a hunch we compared Jane Doe's DNA and blood from the old man currently under the knife-" said the forensic scientist.

"Find something juicy-" I said, "I don't think I've ever said the before."

"You bet! Appears that Jane Doe was his great granddaughter, however being extended family we can't be sure. Might want a detective on it," he said.

"Sure, I'll call about that," I said hanging up.

Boop

"Got to go," I said dialing and leaving the 99th.

"Radclif," he said.

"Yea, you need to find out what you can about-" I said.

Boopboopboop

"Got another call, the great granddaughter, got to go," I said.

"The wha-" he said as I switched calls.

"Detective O-" I said.

"GREETINGS! I am Wolfga-" he started.

"Yea, yea, yea everybody that's anything knows who you are! Just cut the steampomp and circumstance and tell me what you found," I said.

"MY Finding Include-" he started in the annoying grandiose Victorian singsong voice he always uses to make everything take forever.

"In 100 words or less," I said.

"The Policecop and the old man seem to have had some form of duel!" he said.

"Duel?!" I said.

"Yes, I have had received the bullets from both, and each one appears to have been fired from the other gentleman's firearm-" he said.

"No 4 had a gun?" I said.

"A perfectly lawful concealed-" he started on.

"A CHL? In a crime? Curious, that's virtually unheard of," I said.

"I'm rubbing off," he said finally talking normal.

"Rurrrr!" I growled into the phone as I hung up. By which point I was in an elevator.

Later:

"Find anything detectives?" I said.

"Yes, we have IDed the Jane Doe," said detective Zhang.

"Was the great granddaughter theory correct?" I said.

"The parents IDed her, and the coroner confirmed she was tazed to death with our officer's service weapon," she said.

"Bad heart to begin with? And Greg?" I said.

"It was simply that she was 2. But we do have proof of premeditation," she said.

"Oh, do tell," I said, "Well, I have similar proof, but I want to hear yours," I said.

"The stun gun that killed Greg was tampered with, nearly twice fatal. Probably to make it look like an honest accident," she said.

"I know that he was in trouble with Internal Affairs, probably wasn't going to be arrested, but was about to lose his shield, but then they decided that it was all 'bogus'" I said.

"Well, he was texting someone who knew he was in some real trouble, and if he tazed him with that stun gun, it would all go away," she said, "Was even told where to find it."

"Any clue where he got the stun gun?" I said.

"Under a park bench, other than that no clue where," she said.

"And who was he texting?" I said.

"All we know is that it was a burner, bought with cash off camera, set up with a pay phone, and only took or sent texts to our late officer," she said.

"Any idea where? And that's it?" I said.

"Well, there was message from a Nigerian prince selling life insurance, but that's it. Phone was set up at a gas station that isn't even a safe place to buy drugs, and texts were sent and received from a nearly 4 mile diameter, that includes almost all of downtown," she said.

(insert mule picture here)
Houston

"Was 1PP in there?" I said.

"Well, among a lot of other things, yea, near the edge, why?" I said.

"Talk to the bigwigs in the department, starting with the chief," I said.

"Before you go off to crazytown, we have Greg's number two in interview 2," she said.

"He lawyering up?" I said.

"Nope, says nothing to hide, and gets better," she said.

"How so?" I said.

"Greg kept great records, and he has decided to hand them all over," she said.

"Anything good?" I said.

"He brought down 3 cops, one, was the assistant Police commissioner," she said.

"Awesome! well, seriously, start with those bigwigs!" I said as I went into interview room 2.

"Finally!" he said.

"Oh, keep you waiting?" I said.

"No kidding, and let me guess, you think I did it," he said.

"What makes you say that?" I said.

"Why do you think I needed his help? Why do you think he ever had to do what the does?!" he said.

"Everyone blindly assumes you're lying because you have a record," I said.

"BINGO!" he said.

"I technically made Internal Affairs, as such I DON'T CARE!" he said.

"Funny you should mention Internal Affairs," he said.

"How so?" I said.

"Bout 2 weeks ago, he took an interview for Fox 26, here in town. Your captain, Fitzgerald, I think the name is, came up also. Greg said he'd have his job in a decade tops," he said.

"Really," I said, "When I got information from my captain, everyone acted so weird-" I said unknowingly thinking out loud.

"Before you go off to crazy theory village, you should know that he's been stepping up his game," he said.

"How so?" I said.

"The service that puts me into foster homes, he's been going after. I know he bugged their offices, other than that he said it as need to know, and he asked me for prayer about the secret mission, he said the day he died he had enough to come forward. I was E-mailing footage when it happened!" he said, but, that's where it, gets weird."

"Of what and what kind of weird?" I said.

"Don't know, but usually he has me send to footage proof into HPD the Texas Rangers, the State Troopers, CPS, FBI, metro police, HISDPD, the county Sheriff, and the Constable's office, and sometimes also some local news, but this time he had me send it to CPS, FBI, HPD, FOX, CNN, NBC, CBS, ABC, CIA, MSNBC and Interpol instead," he said, "And there was way more footage than normal!"

"How much more?" I said, "And did you see any of it."

"The difference between minutes and days, and no, that is all that I know, except," he said.

"Except what?" I said.

"Usually he works with former 'clients' as he calls them. Such as myself. But this time it was a cancer patient," he said.

"Cancer patent?" I said.

"Yea, 4 months back he was having a malignant tumor removed from his sinuses, and his roommate was having an eye removed. But, he was still going to die. He then sent him off to Ju Ve, but found no proof of anything illegal, so I was never called in. Then he sent him off again. I think he just died; but don't know that for a fact," he said.

"Off where?!" I said.

"A secret mission is all I know; but I have a strong hunch it's somewhere far from here," he said.

"Anything else you know?" I said.

"Nope, and in case you're wondering I really did give you everything and yes, he really kept everything. You should see his room," he said.

"Well, thank you sir," I said.

I stepped out and said "You know anything about this-"

"Secret mission?" she said, "Was a whole military school in Germany he busted. Local authorities did a massive raid just this morning."

"Think that was the cause?" I said.

(insert mule picture here)
Houston

"If it was then it was needle in a haystack, I don't know that anyone even knew he was behind it," she said.

"What about the informant?" I said.

"He has an alibi, he was in a German mourge," she said.

"How'd he even rat this out?" I said.

"Prosthetic eye with built in camera, ear microphone, both streaming straight to the vic's bedroom," she said.

"Bring in the informant's family," I said.

"Chief alibied out, and so did everyone else, all high ranking officers were called in an emergency conference called by Internal Affairs," he said, "So, either you're wrong, or there was no help."

"Or someone wasn't expecting things to go wrong, and wanted the perfect alibi, and new leads on that phone?" I said.

"Seems to have dropped off the face of the earth minutes before the crime-" said my assistant.

"Or just into a faraday cage," I said.

"But, the prince did call back," he said.

"Well, I don't think he's the killer, Anything else?" I said.

"Sorry," he said, "But we are bringing in those that he couldn't get convicted."

"Not Guilty? He always had them on camera!" I said.

"Proof or no, it's always hard to sell an old person beating a juvenile delinquent to a jury," she said.

"Ya'll interview them, though I think this is closer to home then we would expect," I said.

"Oh! Boss! good news!" said my assistant.

"What's that?" I said.

"The survivor's woken up, still in intensive recovery in Ben Taub, but talking," he said.

"Let's go see him," I said.

When we arrived:

"Sir?" I said.

"I under arrest?" He said.

"No, no, don't move, you've been shot pretty bad," I said, "You want a lawyer?"

"Doubt I could if I wanted to, I admit I-"

"I think it was self-defense," I said.

"You're pulling my leg!" I said.

"No, We looked into phone records and forensic evidence. That cop had abandoned his beat to carry out a contract kill," I said, "Let me guess, wrong place, wrong time, saw something you weren't supposed to?"

"How's you know?" he said.

"Could you tell us what happened?" I said.

"Well, I now live with my daughter, and she was baby-sitting her granddaughter, this is something we do on a normal basis; and she asked to come along on my evening walk. Once again normal. We were almost at the turnaround back home point when I heard something, then suddenly she was getting tazered. I reached for my gun, noticed that it was a cop, assumed a fake and fired. next thing I know she's not moving and there's a hole in me," he said, "She gunu be ok?"

I then had to tell him what happened.

Later:

"How'd it go?" said my assistant.

"Wrong place at the wrong time, what a stupid reason to die! Ya'll 2 interview the 'not guilties' I will go after some more likely suspects," I said.

the first interview:

"Good morning Mr. Calzone," I said.

"Like, What's so good about it?" he said.

"Like, I think I've solved a murder, that's what," I said.

"And what does that have to do with me?" he said.

"I have just one question," I said, "How'd you do it?"

"What?!" he said.

"It was a contract kill, and an HPD officer was the mercenary. Only he was paid in making problems relating to Internal Affairs go away instead of unmarked bills," I said.

"I was in here all this time!" he said.

(insert mule picture here)
Houston

"Yes, but you are also the only high ranking officer that was caught on camera by the victim beating his son, and believed to have his wife be blackmailed into letting her daughter not dump her boyfriend," I said, "Though that part I don't think to be a bad thing"

"IT was a set up!" he said.

"A likely story Mr. Assistant Commissioner," I said.

Later:

"Ya'll turn up anything?" I said.

"None could disprove being the one that bought the phone. And we still don't know where it currently geography is either," said detective Zhang.

"Well, my other set of people have been acting so weird. And have ya'll heard what went on at that conference. Nothing! It was just first day at the academy basics. That's it!" I said.

"What're you saying?" she said.

"Let's confront them, I'm sure they have their story straight so I see no significant point in separating them," I said.

"What? Why?" she said.

"Why? what motive do you mean?" I said, "He was spitfire, on a near witch hunt, if it was a cop all the better, and completely clean and unstoppable," I said.

"Like you?" she said, "And that's not what I meant."

"I would like to think so," I said, "COME ON! And bring back up!"

Later there:

"Detective Olaf, what's with this small flock of officers, and why did you call us together in an official capacity?" said Captain Fitzgerald.

"I'm glad you asked, can you confirm that everyone in Internal Affairs is here?" I said.

"Yea, but can I use the can?" he said.

"No," I said.

"What! How!-" he said.

And so I began "I have worked this ultra-complex case for some time," I said, "And when I first saw the scene, I thought something had gone wrong. I was right."

"You would first think it pertained to that camp in Germany, but the busting data was being handed over to the authorities right during the time of death."

"Greg was killed in a plot that started at least 2, possibly more, thought unlikely, more, weeks before he died."

"You would think that the man that fatally shot the officer would be the next big lead. Wrong. There is no evidence or testimony whatsoever that would indicate anything but his story which is that he was in the wrong place at the wrong time and was simply acting in defense of himself and his now late great granddaughter."

"Then you would logically turn your attention to the corrupt but legally untouchable foster service that put most of his clients into the situation which required his help in the first place. We, the police, also understood their corruption. But when he released everything he could find about them, they would almost defenatly be, as the saying goes, sued into the ground, presuming revengeful foster children, ex-foster children, or vigilantes, didn't get to them first. But this theory also has no solid evidence to back it up. But in the interest of full disclosure I should say that I cannot be disproven. But don't get excited. If they had done it, they would have gone too far enough lengths to kill that work. Also as an FYI I will tell you that said information is being posted on the internet as we speak. But do not worry; I have someone in a different portion of the department insuring that there is no violence, whatsoever."

"Then one would turn their attention to his random busts, most were lower class abusers that ended up in jail; but some weren't convicted. None of the busts produced anyone with motive, and means to find a corrupt cop, and get the police to let him off the hook in exchange for carrying out the killing."

"Then logic takes us to his personal life. We spoke to his family, girlfriend, and what few friends he did have. No one knew of anyone that would have motive, let alone means. Also there is no evidence whatsoever of robbery, so if was random it would have to have been purely psychopathic. Almost statically impossible."

"Which leaves us with one and only one remaining suspect, or group of suspects, that would have motive, and they would also have perfect means. I've had a hunch all along, but even I had to admit it was a crazy theory. That's why I'm here," I said.

"Are you accusing me of something?" said Captain Fitzgerald.

"Yes, I am already serving sopenas and search warrants, however whoever in on it probably would not have left us enough of a trail to find him or her, let alone convict. But I can prove that that weird, pointless, all muchidy muck meeting happened," I said, "giving someone the perfect alibi. However I think that that someone is here." I said, "Also if it was done for the alleged sake of the whole department they probably would have also taken out Greg's assistant. And planned that out well enough to succeed. However they may have had to do an abort."

"You'll never prove it," he said.

(insert mule picture here)
Houston

"You're wrong; I believe I can convince a jury beyond a reasonable doubt that you did play a role. And, if you're anything like me, you would have had to have all been on it. Maybe not all willingly, but in on it nonetheless. However the victim, as well as myself, did not believe in police lying so I will be honest. We don't know who did it. It seems unlikely that anyone that was high ranking enough to have carried this out would have had enough motives. Except you captain. He said you and your department was asleep at the wheel. Inevitably he would get you sued. And he wanted your very position. And had a good shot at of getting it. But I have no proof. I am sure that ya'll have all gotten your story straight enough that I didn't even bother to separate you out," I said, "I would offer a deal in exchange for solving it, but if you actually are innocent then there is the risk that one of you might make something up in exchange for no actual jail time. Which I know is the very last thing the victim would want. But if by 'you'll never prove it', you meant that I would never prove that you killed him. You are probably right," I said.

"Come back with proof, while I look for a reason to fire you-" said Chief Fitzgerald.

"ENOUGH!" said another member of Internal Affairs, "We're supposed to be the cleanest of all! Look at us, I'll testify," he said.

Later with the chief:

"Perhaps I misjudged you, at first I thought you were some wild, ravenous dog that was on a near witch hunt for corrupt cops," said the commissioner.

"Oh, I don't know that you misjudged me so bad," I said.

"First Internal Affairs case and you end up arresting your whole department," he said.

"Yes, should have seen when I took them down to be booked," I said.

"I can only imagine," he said.

"I want to request a favor," I said.

"Really, I didn't think you were that type," he said.

"Well I'm normally not. It's about the fallen officer's memorial," I said, "for fallen officers."

"What about it?" he said.

"Greg did a lot, and when he becomes of age I will get his assistant on in Internal Affairs, which is the position Greg always wanted, well, captain thereof that is. What I want is for Greg to get an exception and be in the memorial," I said.

Thought we were done with Crayer. I wish.

"Deputy chief Brenda Lee Johnston, you are under arrest for forced entry, you have the right to remain silent, anything you say can and will be used against you in a court of law. If you cannot afford an

(insert mule picture here)
Houston

attorney one will be provided for you by the court. Do you understand these rights as they are read to you?" I said.

"Yea," she said as I handed her off.

"Last time she goes into a high school locker without permission or a warrant," I said.

"Students have no reasonable expectation of privacy in their lockers," said a collage.

"That's what I told her to tell the judge," I said, "Hopefully she'll be locked away till she learns the true meaning of the old saying 'Come Back With a Warrant!'" Then I laughed.

"Shesh, not even Internal Affairs and you're arresting your fellow officers," she replied.

"I am not Internal Affairs," I said, and then said "yet."

BANGBANG BANGBANG a meer meer a meer meer meer-

"Detective Olaf," I said.

"Yes, we've got a dead one here in a public pool," said coroner Alztimer.

"I'm on my way," I said.

When I got there:

"So, you think foul play?" I said.

"Well, in something like this I'd usually initially assume drowning, but he's wearing a school uniform, and didn't take it off. However I've seen drunks do stupid and stranger," said Alztimer.

"Same, say is he wearing short sleeves and gloves?" I said.

"In winter, I've seen Houstonians dressed even weirder," said Alztimer.

"Ditto, so, any guesses?" I said.

"Well, bruising and black eyes, along with 2 cracked ribs indicates he may have been beaten to death. But can't confirm anything till the autopsy," said Alztimer.

"Alz, this a John Doe?" I said.

"No, well, maybe, still has a school ID, but bruised and dead enough might not be him," said Alztimer.

"You think that he was beaten to death and dumped here?" I said, "Not like it's a good place to hide it," I said.

"Well, got 9 inches of rain over night. No forensic evidence will be left after that frog strangler," said Alztimer, "And don't' even get me started on choline."

Houston

Later at the station:

"Hello, I'm Houston Independent School District Police Department Lutenant John Smith, I'm looking for Detective Olaf," he said, "and you are?"

"An actual real police officer, and that's detective," I said, "Now you said you had information regarding the death of Winston Farnsworth."

"Yes, we solved it," he said.

"Oh really,-" I said.

"Yes, eyewitnesses," he said.

"So, what happened, allegedly that is," I said.

"Was a typical case of bullying, small for his age, wired name, weird voice, the list goes on," he said.

"And where were you people?" I said.

"Don't push it!" he said poking me.

"Ha! assaulting an officer!" I said, "First time arresting a school district cop!"

Later:

"So, he was beaten to death, the victim was not allowed to defend himself, and he died. And now you're trying a 15 year old as an adult for voluntary manslaughter! And where were you?" I said.

"I was having to help confiscate a cell phone used in class!" he said.

"Get up," I said.

"What!" he said.

"Get up, you're under arrest for robbery and child endangerment," I said, "You have the right to remain silent, anything you say can and will be used against you in a court of law. If you cannot afford an attorney one will be provided for you by the court. Do you understand these rights as they are read to you?" I said.

"Fine!" he said, "But I committed no crime!"

"Call it canned words, but, 'tell it to the judge'" I said, "I am just having a great day!"

"Stop!" said another HISDPD officer.

"On what grounds?" I said.

"On the grounds that this is pure wrongful arrest!" she said.

"Tell it to the judge, and I still want to know how the body slipped out from under ya'll's nose and into T. C. Jester Park Pool!" I said.

"Act-u-a-lly, we, were-" she studdered.

"Hoping that I could tell you?" I said.

"Y-yes," I said.

"Get out of my way before I have grounds to arrest you for interfering in an arrest," I said.

Later with the man slaughterer:

"I know you did it, and I you should go to jail, but you shouldn't be tried as an adult. I'm going to metaphorically bail you out, but only out of adult court. First, I want to make an example of you to judges like Crayer-" I said.

"The one that approved me to be tried as an adult?" he said.

"Bingo, and second, I'll need you as a key witness in a case that's coming up," I said.

"Like what?" he said.

"Can't say, need to know. But you have anything at all that could help me. Because I need to hold this up," I said.

"Like what?" I said.

"Like, say, if I could arrest the judge for misdemeanor assault," I said.

"Like if he had poked me once at one nebulas point?" he said.

"Yea, like that," I said.

"He did," he said.

"Ok! That's good enough for me!" I said.

"But, those charges will never stick!" he said.

"Don't care!" I said.

Later at the judge's courtroom:

"Hey you! Big, fat, and ugly in the black! Get down from there!" I shouted at the judge.

"Contempt!" he said banging his gavel.

(insert mule picture here)
Houston

"No, I'm not, because there's a new Sheriff in town, and his name is-" I said, but when I reached for my badge the bailiffs tackled me, "Owch!"

"Yea, an officer, Plancloseman Edwards, arrest these bailiffs," I said to a plaincloseman showing his badge, "As for you judge, You're honor, you're under arrest. I always wanted to say that, but seriously, you're under arrest. Your Honor you are under arrest for misdemeanor assault, you have the right to remain silent, anything you say can and will be used against you in a court of law. If you cannot afford an attorney one will be provided for you by the court. Do you understand these rights as they are read to you?" I said.

"Ugh!" he said.

"Ugh, did not answer my question," I said.

"I thought you said I had the right to remain silent!" he replied.

"Ok, good point," I said.

"WHAT TH-" said judge Crayer bursting in.

"Oh hey, you just missed the action," I said.

"This is about that little thing when you were 10! Isn't it?!" he said.

"Oh! I'd hardly call that a little thing!" I said.

"What is this officially about?!" he said.

"What it really is about is that school manslaughter case, the one where the murder charges were rejected by the grand jury, remember that one?" I said.

"Can someone please fill me in on what this is about?!" said the judge.

"NO!" said me and Crayer at once.

"Look, you two are agreeing already!" said the plaincloseman.

"Shut up!" said both of us, simultaneously again.

"What about it," he said really gritting his teeth.

"You know what I want, and that I won't give in!" I said.

"You won't even have a badge when my lawyers get through with you!" he said.

"Lawyers take time, by which point I could have made many arrests, wrecked many reputations, making enemies for you. Maybe even dig up something that will stick," I said.

He paused and then said so mad "FINE!"

(insert mule picture here)
Houston

"Does whatever that was about mean I'm free to go?" said the judge.

"Nope, still have to haul you in," I said.

Later:

"HPD, open the door," I said.

"Can't, the city school board is in the biggest meeting of the month," he said.

"Ok, officers arrest him for interfering in an arrest," I said.

"Wait? What!" he said as they hauled him off.

"HALT!" said a HISDPD officer, with 9 more behind him.

"Move, I am here to make an arrest," I said.

"Detective Olaf, If you don't leave now I will arrest you for-" he said.

"Arrest them all," I said.

By that point I was going alone seeing as all my backup was hauling guards and officers to the police vehicle.

"Open this door," I said to the last guard in my way.

"I can't," he said.

"How not?" I said.

"Don't have the combination," he said.

"Ok, I'll just get dynamite-" I said.

"You could burn the building down!" he said.

"Uh, yea, there's just one problem with that called 'I don't care'" I said.

"Ok! I'll-I'll open it," he said.

"So, you can open it, lying to the police is a crime-" I said.

"No! no! I-I-I'll-I'll-I'll go, go get someone who can," he said rushing off like his tail was on fire.

"Hurry back!" I shouted after him not expecting him to return. I didn't care. I tried the door and found that it wasn't locked "That little liar! Not even locked!" I walked in and blew my police whistle.

"Hey!" said the chairman, "This is a-"

(insert mule picture here)
Houston

"Uh, yea, don't care!" I said.

"Well, leave or-" he said.

"You're under arrest," I said.

"Excuse me, I was talking!" he said.

"Not anymore, You're all under arrest!" I said.

"This is absurd! You're the one that will be arrested. Guards!" he said as some of my backup was finally returning. By which point I was doing that talking mouth mock thing," Thank he- Wait, what'-"

"Like I said, You're all under arrest, your individual arresting officer will read you your rights," I said.

"This is crazy! On what grounds!" he said clearly getting scared. Finally.

"You're 'you can't defend yourself policy' resulted in a student's death. I'm charging every one of you, and many former members, with manslaughter," I said.

Now here's a good one, no evil judges, no corrupt cops, but also no arrests of public officials. Win some lose some.

"Morning," I said.

"Morning, hope you're in for a hard one," said detective Zhang.

"How so?" I said.

"Robbery, obvious," she said.

"Or just made to look that way," I said.

"Gets better," she said.

"How so?" I said.

"Feds involved," she said.

"Oh great!" I said, "Let's begin arresting federal agents for impeding-" I said.

"That won't be necessary," said a man.

"Oh boy! here we go!" I said.

"No, not really, you see we here as the Postal Police department are used to mail order fraud, mail theft, mail order drugs, well, you get the picture. But murder. Nope. As such we're taking a backseat," he said.

(insert mule picture here)
Houston

"Really, that's a pleasant change of pace, but, I don't understand, if you're so unequipped, I imagine you can't just let us do it. But, why not just have the FBI come in instead? Not that I'm complaining…" I said.

"I really have no clue, but I have officers canvasing the mail route, asking who might have been expecting what. Also having someone at his home post office see what could have been coming that would be worth killing for, like some package," he said.

"You think some mail was stolen. Maybe a mugging gone wrong," I said.

"We don't think, we know," said detective Zhang.

"How so?" I said.

"Mail bag was missing, and so was the mail truck, but don't look like mail was stolen out of boxes, did catch him at the start of his shift however, so a lot missing," said the Postal Police Detective.

"You're mail trucks wouldn't happen to have Lojack, would they?" I said.

"That all federal vehicles will have," he said, "Already found it; bout 2 neighborhood blocks away, and one street over."

"Great! CSU finished with their sweep?" I said.

"That we would normally handle, but our forensic science is, I hate to have to admit, inferior to your, this one time I will let you handle it," he said.

"Thanks?" I said.

"I hate to break up the pleasantries, well no not really, but CSU hasn't gotten to it yet," she said.

"How busy can they be?" I said.

"HFD still hasn't handed it over," he said.

"Oy, well there goes that, how bad was the fire?" I said.

"Well, accelerant everywhere last I heard. And all they could say for sure was that the mail had gone missing. But a little could be left. But will be pretty crispy," he said.

"Well, when the arson investigator is done telling us what we already know, have CSU come in and not find anything," I said.

"You, Postal cop,-" I said.

"Postalpoliceman Ginsburg," he said, "No connection to the Judge."

"What-ever, anything coming up in your investigation?" I said.

(insert mule picture here)
Houston

"Well, having people tell us what they're expecting as is per usual, not everyone wants to cooperate. Also packages, in any neighborhood like this, some are every expensive. But nothing special. I'll turn the haystack over to you as it comes in," he said.

"Well, thank you, isn't this the time of year when people getting stuff back from the IRS?" I said.

"Yea, but lots of people, especially these people, will most likely be doing everything through a tax service. Even I do that," he said.

"Same, but this is the Memorial neighborhood, and as nice as it gets without gates. I don't think that this was some mugging gone wrong. I think what ever happened was pre-planned and designed to target," I said.

"How so?" he said.

"Thank of all that could be gotten from that mail by an ID thief. And this is the upper crust. Zhang, have cyber-crimes put an advanced ID theft watch on all mail theft victims. Could be our best bet at cracking this," I said.

"Good thinking," he said.

"Also, I want you, Ginsburg, to see about similar crimes, might be someone really did have something go south," I said, "Where's the coroner?"

"I had a federal coroner from the FBI come in," said Ginsburg.

"Fine, where is he?" I said.

"Right there, and she," he said.

"Hi, I'm-" I said.

"Yea, the main detective, Medical Examiner Hypertension," she said, "Looks to me like he was shot with a flare gun."

"Does that help us?" I said.

"No, he was making his rounds, and was shot by something surprising quiet, unregeneratable, and there will be no ballistics to match to the murder weapon. Whoever did this is good," she said.

"Know of any MO that this matches?" I said.

"None that would take something so small," she said.

"Really?" I said.

"Yea, could make a lot from this, but not that much," she said.

"Oh!" I said.

"Zhang, we're near Crayer's house. Probably a different mail route. But still close. Have someone ask around there just in case," I said.

Later at the station:

"Ok, time to share information," said Ginsburg.

"Well, we got a witness, but said that the killer was in a full burkea, head to toe. Dead end. CSU could recover nothing after the truck was drenched in E-85 fuel. Probably the cheapest accelerant that the killer could find. Also must have been premeditated, because no one close to the crime scene sells that form of fuel. Also witness said one killer, and shot the vic with no premeditation, or conversation. Also so far no one turning up with those stolen identities," I said.

"Well, I've handed most everything over, only one case came close. It was on the coast of the Bay of Galvez-" he said.

"You mean Galveston bay?" I said.

"Right, well, just a main truck theft. No bodily harm done, and the suspect was meeting with his public defense attorney right in the time of the murder. An ankle bracelet backed up that story. Dead end," he said.

"Well, I'm sure something is bound to turn up," I said.

"Ut,-" he said.

"Oh-" I said.

Later at the scene:

"Hypertension," What've we got?" said Ginsburg.

"Same, was stopped for a stop sign and bang," said Hypertension.

"What about theft?" I said.

"Looks identical, except no fire," she said.

"CSU, what have you found?" I said.

"Squat," they said, "Killer knew how to not leave evidence behind."

"Great, any witnesses?" I said.

"Yea, but this time they got a license plate number.

"Really, run it through the system," I said.

(insert mule picture here)
Houston

"Already did," she said, "Stolen from Houston Premium Outlets."

"Any witnesses to that?" I said.

"Well, a camera seems to have witnessed that," she said.

"Then why did no one get said car back?!" I said.

"Said it wasn't worth matching the face in this report," she said.

"Let's have our people see about that," I said, "Ginsburg! You find anything?"

"It's more what I didn't find," he said, "All the mail is missing, again!"

Later:

"Found him, his name is Christian Bruther," said Zhang.

"Silly name," I said.

"Yea, but he's on probation for stealing a Chevy. And when we arrived we found an antique Triumph in his driveway. When we ran its plates it went missing from an auto show at the George R. Brown. At the time they thought it was more misplaced than stolen. I imagine if they had done a follow up, 2 and 2 would have been put together sooner," said Zhang.

"Yea, robbery division is a real joke," I said, "When does he arrive here or is he at large."

"He's in holding, but he did demand a lawyer," she said.

"Mr. Brother-" I said.

"Bruther," he said.

"Never helps to correct me. Facing some pretty serious charges. A hot expensive car in your driveway, and seen getting a 5 finger discount on an SUV, on camera," I said.

"Don't say anything," said the lawyer.

"Was admittedly smart to get a lawyer, I must admit, especially this being Texas, however, this is going to be a federal case-" I said.

"You're a very bad liar detective," said the lawyer, "These were not-"

"Oh, you really thing this is about a couple of hot cars, do you?" I said.

"Well, what else would it be bout?" he said.

"If it was, then why am I here?" said Ginsburg.

"To assist in an interrogation?" said the lawyer.

"I'm with the Postal Police," he said, "I really don't care about the car thefts."

"And with my personal and professional experience, my department apparently doesn't either," I said.

"If no one cares can I go now?" said Christian.

"Sir, stop talking," said the lawyer.

"Mr. Bruther, does this face look familiar?" I said.

"That I will let my client answer," said the lawyer.

"No, looks like just another mailman, cept a little fatter than most, why?" I said.

"What about this newer one," I said.

"Just answer it," said the lawyer.

"Got a weird scar," he said, "But nothing special."

"They have something pretty special in common, care to guess," I said.

"Go ahead," said the lawyer.

"Extra weight?" he said.

"Wrong, consoler, I'm surprised you haven't put 2 and 2 together. Not very good at our job are we," I said.

"Who is this about?" he said.

"Oh, it's about him, you're just no very good at your job," I said.

"Officer, why am I really here?" said Christian.

"You don't get a lot of local news do you?" I said.

"What do-" he replied.

"Don't answer that," said the lawyer.

"What these mailmen have in common is they were both murdered, and all the mail was stolen," I said.

"Officer, you're a really bad liar," said Christian.

"No, no, I heard a news report about this," said the lawyer.

"Did you kill them?" I said.

(insert mule picture here)
Houston

"Don't answer that," said the lawyer.

"Why? I-" he said.

"Don't drink that-" he said.

"I would never pull that old sleazy trick, however, can't always say the same for the prosecutor," I said.

"Hey! I di-" he said.

"Stop talking," said the lawyer.

"I will get a warrant for your place, and when I find all that mail-" I said.

"Don't," he said.

"Why? Don't want me to find the mail?" I said.

"It's not that that I want you to not find," he said.

"Stop talking," said the lawyer.

"Look, I'm a man who can humor the rediculas for a while-" I said.

"What if we dotle and he strikes again?!" said Ginsburg.

"We'll keep him here," I said, "As I was saying, I'm a man who can humor the rediculas for a while, and if you didn't do it, but you can lead me to whoever did kill them. Then I can make these 2 hot cars go away, and overlook whatever is inside your house. But I need a lead," I said.

"Can I speak to my lawyer in private?" said Christian.

"Sure, I'll let you know when things are private," I said.

After that:

"My client also wants you to overlook another minor offence. It will be necessary to give you the lead," said the lawyer.

"What is that consoler?" I said.

"A drag race," he said.

"I'll ignore his part of the drag race," I said, "What's the lead?"

"My client lost the vehicle in question to a man named Flamefire. Real name is Vance," said the lawyer.

"And I need a last name," I said.

"I can tell you where you can find him," he said, "But we have no last name."

(insert mule picture here)
Houston

"Fine, I'll let you off, just one more condition," I said.

"What would that be?" he said.

"Stay here till I bring in this lead, make sure that this is real," he said.

After I got that lead, Zhang was sent to stake out the next drag race. Then I got a real lead.

"Mr. Garcia, You were arrested for identity theft. Buying $30,000 of electronics, really, smart ID thieves make a small purchase, like 1 or 2 dollars, first. Care to explain?" he said, "For reasons I don't understand you don't want an attorney."

"I did nothin," he said.

"Now I can add a charge of lying to the police," I said.

"You get that card from a friend?" said Ginsburg.

"Now what is a mail cop here for?" he said.

"If you watch news, or listen for that matter, you'd know. That credit card you used was stolen in one of the 2 robberies that left a mail carrier dead, each. Tampering with the mail if a federal offence, killing a mailman is a bigger one. Two murders could get an execution, but we didn't find the car or anything else linked to the crime in your house. But we did find something," I said.

"Oh-" he said.

"We think you illegally got the car, and ditched it. But we're not sure. Tell us where you got the credit card and I'll drop the tampering with the mail charge. And I'm sure that Detective Olaf will happily go easy on those drugs," said Ginsburg, "Isn't that right?"

"Y-yes," I said taken off my A game, "Help us and we'll help you. I do not want this thing to go triple."

"And I have way too many men tied up keeping if form going triple," said Ginsburg.

"We know you got it in a Drag Race," I said, "I have one of my best in wait to sting you on that. But you can get away with that offence, if you didn't do it and can lead us to who did."

"How do you know I ever had the alleged vehicle?" he said.

"Sir, we can match tire tracks left in mud, should have parked on the street, not in the yard," I said.

"It's true, it's all true, got 2 other credit cards in my wallet right here. Got em for that car," he said.

"Who bought the car?" I said, "And how can I be sure you don't have a trick up your sleeve?"

"Was at Chevron on Pinemont, nice clean station, probably got cameras," he said.

"There is probably more than one, can you narrow it down any?" I said.

(insert mule picture here)
Houston

"It's cross from a donut shop, good one too. And very near a freeway, ya'll of all people should know" he said.

Later:

"How'd it go?" I said.

"Only one gas station meeting the description," said Ginsburg.

"And?" I said.

"Fully co-operated, we can clearly see the car buyers face, we'll put it out, see what comes up," said Ginsburg.

"Don't bother," said Zhang, "I recognize him."

"You know him?" said Ginsburg.

"Not personally, few years back was a creepy little mugger, now he'd be about 17," she said.

Later:

"Freddie Fredrickson, used to be a little robber, but at 15 went straight before things got bigger, then clean. Look, I want to believe it wasn't you. And if you give me the killer we can forget that you bought a stolen and drag raced car with hot credit cards," I said.

"Look, this case has been crazy, and maybe you didn't do it," said Ginsburg, "but if you did you're going to federal prison forever."

"You're just a kid, but I can't protect you from the feds," I said.

"Good cop, bad cop?" said his dad.

"More, good cop, dumb cop," I said.

"Hey!" said Ginsburg.

"I didn't say who was who!" I said.

"Don't care if I get a year or 3," he said, "Got to protect-"

"Stop talking," said his dad.

"Who? The killer is dangerous," I said.

"I want immunity for everyone but the killer," he said.

"SHUT UP!" said the Dad getting mad.

(insert mule picture here)
Houston

"Are they all younger than you?" I said, slowly putting 2 and 2 together.

He nodded and the dad smacked him.

"HEY! I can get you for assault," I said, "If you'd be willing to press charges."

"I won't let him," he said.

"You don't get a say in the matter," I said.

BAM BAM

"Everything ok behind that 1 way mirror that an't fooin nobody," said the kid.

I stepped out, but not before taking Ginsburg with me.

"Everything ok?" I said.

"Cyber-crimes called, they found that a bank account was drained. It was drained into an untraceable Swiss bank account. We do know however that 2 mill was taken. Nearly $300,000.00 has already vanished," said a supervisee, "But gets better."

"You have an IP?" I said.

"In some ways better," she said, "They traced it to a restaurant with free WIFI. Cash purchase, but was cameras. Got the face of the thief right in my hand."

"Anything else?" I said.

"Yea, came back later for some online gambling, same way found out. Blew money like it was Vegas and there was no tomorrow," she said.

"I saw the photo and said "YES! IT wasn't the kid. Ginsburg, we have a killer to arrest."

We walked back in and I said "Freddie, your dad is a gambling addict-"

"Slande-" he said.

"Kindly let me speak, thank you," I said, "He was behind all this, and you and your siblings were forced into it, like a child being told to do the dishes. Might be wrong, but I will grant full immunity to all who testify against the killer, and won't you do the same Ginsburg?"

"Y-y-yes, yes," he said off his A game.

"He's going away no matter what, and I hate to put children in prison. Admittedly your dad being a single dad will leave you parentless if he goes to jail, but in 11 months you turn 18. I'll get you help in getting custody of your younger siblings. It's a great deal for them, and you. But if you say 'no' then a warrant will still be served. They and you will be arrested by the feds and I'll have no way to save any of

(insert mule picture here)
Houston

you. Your dad's addiction has gotten far out of hand. It ends now. He's a lost cause but you can save yourself and get your siblings to do likewise. Be a big brother that looks out for them. Just say yes," I said.

"We're leaving," said the father.

"Yes," said Freddie.

Freddie's Dad wacked him to the floor, I instinctively took out my gun and shoved it in his face. Accidently hitting him with it. "Ginsburg, cuff him."

And they all lived happily ever after, except for Mr. Frederickson who spent the rest of his life rotting in a federal, high security prison.

I'm sure you've heard enough about Crayer. But what about my siblings? What about that part of the story?

"Hi," she said.

"Hi," I said.

"I'm-" she said.

"Please don't apologize, you were six," I said.

"And you were 10!" she said.

"meh," I said, "I have fought prosecuting as an adult for so long, you. were. six. you're forgiven. take it."

"Well, that's one thing off my conscience," she said.

"You said you knew something," I said, "Pinkerton has been working this case for months. No leads."

"I hope you're recording this," she said.

"I am, that's what you asked for on the phone," I said.

"I know why they were killed," she said.

After the shock wore off I asked "Was it Crayer?"

"No," she said.

"He just took a bribe to-" I said.

"Try and put you where no one would listen to you," she said.

"And the cops just happened to-" I said.

"Suppose that's the only place they thought the evidence led," she said, "However, I would be surprised if they didn't encourage it along. Did you know anything at all?"

"No, nothing," I said.

"Well, how you doing being an only child?" she said.

"I'm not; while I was locked up my little brother was born. Named after the late brother," I said.

"Same, after my family left we had another little brother," she said.

"How they doing?" I asked.

"Dead," she said.

"Oh, my,-"I started.

"Yea, now no reason to fear retaliation, also bout to join them. Heart cancer," she said.

"Oh, I'm so sorry. Really wish I had looked you up," I said.

"Had a pretty good life, but with really bad patches," she said.

"So, what happened?" I said.

"My siblings or yours?" she said.

"Well, our 2 families lived side by side as neighbors. We were like one family," I said, "So-"

"We were one," she said.

"How so?" I said.

"Your brother and I were married, secretly of course," she said.

"That would explain a lot," I said.

"Yea, so you have any other siblings?" she said.

"Just my brother," I said.

"I'd like to meet my little brother in law," she said.

"I can arrange that," I said.

"What should I tell him?" she said.

"What do you mean?" I said.

"How much does he know?" she said.

(insert mule picture here)
Houston

"I told him everything a long time ago," I said.

"Oh, how'd he handle it?" she said.

"Some surprised him, some made things make sense to him," I said.

"So, what're you up to?" she said.

"Just got married and I'm a cop," I said.

"Really! where's your beat?" she said.

"Whole city," I said.

"No, that's too big to have just one ma patrolling," she said.

"No, no," I said, "I'm not a beat cop, actually I run Internal Affairs."

"REALLY!" she said, "No kidding?"

"Yea, after what happened, the owed me big. But now all is well. How's your life been?" I said

"Interesting, While you were being denied bail for about a year, my family believed that you were guilty," she said, "Moved around a lot."

"Sounds rough," I said.

"When I was 8, we were in an accident. We were all hurt and dad didn't make it. my little brother, you remember him, year younger than me. Well, he went onto fall into a bad element. Got 6 weeks in jail. At 11," she said, "Really messed him up."

"At that age it always does," I said.

"And I wanted my mom to be sympathetic and supportive. I knew it was a long psychological recovery ahead. But she was planning military school. In his condition," she said.

"What happened?" I said.

"She said she wasn't. At the 11th metaphorical hour I caught Her. Saved my brother but killed her," she said.

"Say what now?" I said.

"Made it look like suicide. Police never batted an eye," she said.

"And now you're-" she said.

(insert mule picture here)
Houston

"What've I got to lose?" she said, "After that the next of kin was mom's cousin! She was not nice. The grief, the change in family structure, the bringing back of the grief from dad's death. And most of all the trauma. Was just too much."

"What happened?" I said, "Seeing her getting choked up about this,"

"Like was your family, the siblings were much closer than to the parents After my brother gave up, my baby brother wanted to go crazy and start killing cops and shooting up courthouses. I made a compromise and after getting myself and some friends, who I need not worry about, a record I concluded that nothing illegal was going on. Not right but technically no law was broken," she said, "By them at any rate".

"How did your brother -" I said.

"Yea, I still remember the words 'you can take the inmate out of the prison, but you can't take the prison out of the inmate.' Hung himself," she said.

"Saw that, that young one other time, Crayer's son actually. Case surprisingly similar to mine," I said

"Wow," she said.

"And your other brother?" I said.

"After mom died, the next of kin was mom's cousin. She was pretty bad, when she was around. And I was doing that investigation thing when she wasn't. Shortly after I ended the investigation she was arrested for identity theft. Gets out in 8 months from now, but I almost defiantly won't make it to then. So then her daughter got us. Best life I ever had since I was 6 and, well, you know." she said.

"So, she was good?" I said.

"Oh no, it was real anarchy. But I was mom to my little brother, and finally began to let there be a normality in my life. The 6 year sour note ended. I was on my own, but happy. My little brother got a girlfriend, I made friends. Finally started having a few dates, and a relationship or two, but nothing that great. Until 2 months ago," she said.

"What happened?" I said.

"Well, one would have expected an unlimited tolerance. But right after I was diagnosed, she somehow managed to die of an overdose. Never been told or cared of what exactly," she said.

"So, how long was that going on?" I said.

"Probably as long as I knew my grand cousin," she said.

"Grand cousin?" I said.

"Yea, our parents were cousins," she said.

(insert mule picture here)
Houston

"Oh, well, sorry about what happened," I said, "Sounds like life hasn't been so good to you."

"Well, 10 out of 16, or 5 out of 8, is it really that bad?" she said.

"Yes," I said, "But what've you been up to recently."

"Well, after she died, only relative left was her uncle. He was awful. Super abusive control freak. No surprise his wife disappeared mysteriously. I think he accidently beat her to death. And one of his sons was 'accidently' beaten to death in military school. The other son was allegedly kidnapped without a trace. I bet he's next to his mom," she said.

"Wow," I said.

"Yea, one day my brother had had enough. I had to kill him to save my brother. This time however the police were suspicious of me," she said.

"So, now who's taking care of you?" I said.

"Me, his girlfriend, who's somehow worse, decided I killed what meant the most to her. So she did likewise," I said.

"She killer your brother?" I said.

"Yea, got her indicted. And then ran away form a facility that was for all intended purposes an orphanage. They said they would get me a good foster home. I have met foster kids. No thank you. Not willing to die in that hell. Furthermore I don't think I would ever be placed," she said.

"Sorry to hear about that," I said.

"Yea, didn't know where to go, so had nothing to keep me attached to this world, and about to leave it anyways. So I came all the way here to H-town. And lost a lot of weight in the process," she said, "No complaints."

"Sure you aren't just nearing the end?" I said.

"What do you mean?" she said.

"You lose appetite when you're very close to the end," I said.

"Really, well, I'm felling hungry. You know it's so funny I'm almost laughing," she said.

"What is?" I said.

"What is the two big killers that people worry about?" she said.

"Heart attacks and dementia?" I said.

Houston

"No, well, those two, but heart disease and cancer, but heart cancer, never!" she said, "Well, so far, a pretty preferable way to go."

"I think I know how I'll go," I said.

"Oh no! You dying to?" she said.

"Oh! no, no, no more than everyone else on earth," I said.

"So then, how you think you'll go?" she said.

"Well, let's just say, my last words will probably be 'drop it officer'" I said.

"Oh, so I take it you're Captain Spitfire from Internal Affairs," she said.

"Well, I try, but they normally call me Captain Call letters," I said, "Sorry about your brother. Sad to hear about the other-"

"Yea, but it was nice when it was the 5 of us, that one thing has changed so much," she said.

"Yea, but you said you kne-" I said.

"Oh yea, Well. It was simply a message to me," she said.

"What?" I said.

"Yea, they're really good. And I knew after this they'd be watching and willing to retaliate if I came forward," she said.

"This is crazy!" I said.

"If they took out me, then the police could, though unlikely, put 2 and 2 together," she said.

"What? and how does Crayer fall into this?" I said.

"Probably coincidence," she said, "And was he taking bribes?"

"Right before his kids died, he was going to be arrested," I said.

"Wow, but by who?" she said.

"Not sure, probably varies," I said.

"And the police?" she said.

"I made sure that they couldn't hurt anyone else again," I said, "And got a few others appeals."

"And they just didn't want to look totally stumped and clueless?" she said.

"Yup," I said.

(insert mule picture here)
Houston

"Pathetic," she said.

"I should have looked you up, wish I could have met your younger brother," I said.

"I doubt you could have found me," she said.

"Well, who knows?" I said.

"Yea, that is true," she said.

"So, what else do you k-" I said.

BANG!

I saw a long gun of some kind sticking out the window of a city bus. There wasn't time to run out the door, so I jumped through a picture window landing in an outside seating area. I quickly jumped onto another table, but it fell over. so I went up to the surrounding rod iron fence and jumped it. I ran as fast as I could but the bus got away. When it was out of sight I went back to the restaurant.

Later:

"So, did you know the victim," said detective Rathbone.

"Yea, but don't you know me?" I said.

"No, who are you?" he said.

"I was a detective, now I'm Captain Olaf, Internal Affairs," I said.

"Detective call letters?!" he said, "I-I-well, what happened?"

"I know exactly what happened," I said, "And who the Jane doe is."

"Who and what?" he said.

"Lily Olaf, but, that's not her legal name. Don't remember her last name," I said.

"Extended relative?" he said.

"Of a sort," I said.

"What sort?" he said.

"Apparently she was my sister in law. Sure they were 4, but they stayed together 2 years till the day my brother died," I said.

"What?" he said.

"Never mind, I know why she was killed," I said.

"Why?" he said.

"There was no one left in this world that she was close to, as such she should fear retaliation," I said, "She was coming forward."

"With what?" I said.

"Key information regarding the murder of my brother and sister," I said, "10 years ago."

"Sorry to hear about that. But I need to know, what was the key information?"

"Don't know. Was shot right before she could say," I said.

"Sounds like some typical Hollywood movie to me," he said.

"It is, but somehow true," I said.

"This is a minor teen. Where are her parents?" he said.

"Where she just arrived," I said.

"You mean she's an orphan?" he said.

"Yea, only kin left was her mother's cousin. Apparently was going to get out of jail in 8 months." I said.

"Who was taking care of her?" he said.

"No one, her brothers had died, her father was killed in an accident, she killed her mom-" I said.

"She Did What Now?!?!" he said.

"She confessed, deathbed confession; I suppose," I said.

"She was dying?!" he said.

"Yea, cancer," I said.

"Oh, but someone had to be taking care of her," he said.

"Her mom's cousin got custody being next of kin. Like I said, she was in jail. The daughter had died. And the cousin's brother just died," I said.

"You remember much of what little she did say?" said Rathbone.

"Better, recording," I said.

"Oh!-" he said. "Well, the bullet shattered the craz-" he said.

"That was me, and the mess on the patio," I said.

"Oh," he said.

"Trying to catch the shooter," I said.

"You come close?" he said.

"Yes and no, surprisingly he was shooting from a city bus. Didn't catch the root, but did catch that it was bus number '14174'" I said.

"Well, I'll call METRO Police, they will have heard about this.

Later:

"Hi, I was wondering if I could get an update on the case," I said.

"Well, Looked into that murder she did, no one batted an eye. Think we can rule that out. Also her 'investigation' no one knows anything. No one knows who was in on it. Dead end-" said Detective Rathbone.

"Or that's just what they're saying," I said, "But fat chance."

"But I did make an interesting discovery. Probably a red herring, but you never know," he said.

"What is it?" I said.

"That awful uncle, the girlfriend had the charges dropped yesterday. Also he had a wife that mysteriously disappeared. Police suspected him of foul play. But just as likely there was just a runaway battered wife. So, they didn't charge him. Also one-" he said.

"Son was killed in military school and the other disappeared without a trace," I said.

"Actually one disappeared from military school; and the other is believed to have been kidnapped," he said.

"I'm sure it was just made to look that way," I said.

"Well, the Jane Doe does match the description of a girl that ran away from a foster waiting facility. And she did claim to be that girl. Calling the women's prison, the mother's cousin might be able to ID her. Maybe," he said.

"Yea, but what about the bus?" I said.

"Well, Metro police would know about that, also we're handing the information over to them," he said.

"So, do we just sit here and wait?" I said.

"Actually, I need to ask you a few questions," he said.

"Ok," I said.

(insert mule picture here)
Houston

"I confess I had to look through your trial," he said.

"I don't blame you, I would have done the same," I said.

"She accused you of having killed before," he said.

"She was 6," I said.

"Yes, I assume you know," he said.

"That was an accident," I said.

"So you were told," he said, "Because it does seem like a strange family."

"What do you mean?" I said.

"To which do you mean?" he said.

"Both," I said.

"You were told what happe-" he said.

"When I was 2 1/2 my sister and her twin brother was 3 1/2. He hid in a freezer during hide and seek. Still to this day I will not play that game. And as for weird family. Yes, my little brother was Chinese," I said. "Any my sister was one of those people from Nigeria who were truly black skinned, in her case, very much so. Yea, everyone in my family is adopted, except for my little brother. Who I stopped calling my baby brother when he was 5. He's the one still alive. But everyone in my family is adopted. Aunts, uncles, cousins, you name it," I said.

"What?" he said.

"I was seeking, I didn't tell him to hide there. I didn't look there in the freezer. I have no direct memories of him. But I had guilt for years," I said, "But it was accidental suicide through and through."

"I, didn't know," he said.

"Then what were you talking about?" I said.

"I was talking about Lily's big sister. You were 18 months. She was 35 months. She mysteriously fell down the stairs," he said, "Your sister could have seen something, and told Lily later on. Also your Chinese brother," he said.

"What Are You Saying?! That I'm behind this! Then why would she come forward to me and me shoot her?! What sense does that make?" I said.

"To make it look like something else," he said.

"That is-" I said really getting mad.

"Far-fetched and nearly impossible. But it is enough for me to keep you out of the loop," he said.

I took the rest of the day off. That really ticked me off; but in time I realize di would have done likewise. I then remembered I had hired Pinkerton to solve my sibling's murders. They might know a thing or two. And being their client; they'd share with me. Later when I arrived there:

"Ah! Mr. Olaf. One of those cases you could make a carrier out of. Well, I must admit Detective Rathbone's theory you're trying to make things bigger than they really are and you being framed and tried-" he said.

"Don't mention it, I'm still trying to forget," I said, "And actually I think he was mostly just finding a reason to throw me off the case," I said.

"Yes, yes," he said, "Well, we know Metro police have made major leads."

"How so?" I said.

"They already knew about what happened on the bus. They got calls in. Witnessed differed and no DNA or fingerprints were left," he said, "And witnesses couldn't keep things straight. But they did agree that it was a tattooed man. All they could agree on. HPD looked at thinks closer and found that your sister in law was nearly shot before it all began. But he left that bus and got on another when he found that it had cameras."

"Did you get anything?" I said.

"Yea, we're looking into street and retail cameras that may have seen something. But the police already gave us his picture from the first bus," he said, "And that was a big break."

"Do tell," I said.

"We were able to recognize him right off the bat," he said.

"How?" I said.

"Simple, we're better because we're making money off this business," he said.

"Well, that makes sense," I said, "Who is he?"

"Is believed to have been a hit man for a major Russian mob family. But, that form of business relationship can often go south. It did. Now he just works for the highest bidder." he said.

"Oh, that sounds like it may have been hired," I said.

"Yea, and he's been busy ever sense he fled from the Russian mob. The guy uses multiple aliases, at once. This is his typical MO. You see him do it. And can't prove it's him. And he's a distant memory by the time you recognize him," he said, "Got people that have been looking for him for years. We'll just be adding your name to the list."

(insert mule picture here)
Houston

BANGBANG BANGBANG a meer meer-

"Olaf," I said.

"Yea, felt bad about earlier, so I decided to let you know that the killer used a Q card," he said.

"It's hot," I said.

"How's you know?" he said.

"Because we know who pulled the trigger," I said.

You probably wondering what a normal case is for me. Well, in this one I was pretty busy so you can see an Internal Affairs case, and one with a mystery element, a normal mystery, and an interesting mystery.

"So, how's it look?" I said.

"Well, your brother in blue was beat up pretty bad. But unless he has a severe head injury; he'll be fine," said a paramedic.

"I'll be the one investigating this," I said.

"I thought you were internal affairs?" he said.

"I am, cameras show that no one that's not on the force could have been here to do this. But we've about 240 cops that could have done it. Looking into things should narrow that down," I said.

BANGBANG BANGBANG a meer meer a meer meer meer meer mc-

"Detective / Lieutenant Olaf," I said, "HPD."

"We're gunu go," said a paramedic.

I followed them out and went straight out to a crime scene

"Hi, Alztimer," I said, "Where's the crime scene?"

"Right here-" said Alztimer.

"Wait-Parkinson? Why were 2 cononers called in? Is this a doubl-" I said.

"I found the body," said Parkinson.

"Really?! That is bizarre!" I said.

"Yea, for obvious reasons I'm not the coroner," he said.

"Ok, well-" I said.

"Over here," said Alztimer.

"Ax to the face," I said, "Sounds mad, maybe a crime of passion; 2nd degree."

"Who keeps an ax around in an efficiency?" said Alztimer.

"Oh, I don't know. This is a neighborhood that you'd never actually expect to find a dead body," I said sarcastically.

"3 days ago we did," said Alztimer.

"I hadn't heard-" I said.

"Been dead sense Lincoln was in diapers, but technically still a corpse," said Alztimer.

"Oh," I said, "Guess that rules out foul play."

"No, it was the same cause of death, cept a pick ax," said Alztimer, "But this is a tad fresher."

"Time of death?" I said.

"Between 4 and 6 am," said Alztimer.

"Neigh-" I said.

"No," said Zhang, "In this neighborhood no-body ever sees anything. Except police corruption."

"Internal Affairs, tell me about it," I said.

"Is this going to be your last homicide?" she said.

"Unless cops start killing cops, or I take a second job making professional hits, yes," I said.

"Well, hate to be a kill joy, but looks like murder suicide," she said.

"Really, those are so hard to solve," I said.

"Yea, husband was bleeding out when we came. Couldn't have been bleeding long when we arrived," she said.

"Well, that doesn't sound like murder suicide," I said.

"Well, often they don't want to be remembered as a killer," she said.

BANGBANG BANGBANG a meer meer a meer meer me-

"Olaf," I said, "Really? no kidding, busy day. On my way."

Click

"Nope, not my last homicide," I said.

"Oh, I can handle this," said Zhang.

"Actually you should probably come with me. Suspects apparently don't like distance. In the same complex." I said.

Later there:

"Still securing crime scene sir," said an officer.

"No "sir", at ease. We're cops; not the army. And we need to remember that," I said.

"O-k-k" he said, really off his ball at that.

"Now, Nph, what's the cause of death?" I said.

"Was knocked out with a hard object. Probably metal. Shape appears to be something such as a tea kettle, available at any culinary supplies store, or store that sells kitchenware. But that is just a logical guess," said Nph.

"I assume neighbors heard no evil, saw no evil-" I said.

"Canvas has yet to begin sir," said the officer.

"What did I say about sir, sir?" I said.

"You sa-" he said.

"That was a rhetorical question," I said.

"Any idea what killed him?" I said.

"Doesn't look like the head injury. But can't be sure till the autopsy," said Nph.

"Stuff is missing, or so it seems," I said, "Could be poor. OR a real dummy found the killer left things ajar, and burgled my crime scene. Oh good! CSU is here."

BANGBANG BANGBANG a m-

"Hello," I said.

"Hi, we know you're investigating the beating of Officer Fannin. Well, he was under investigation for shooting a man in his 60s with a bean bag gun. Didn't survive," said my boss.

"Were we going to indibt?" I said.

"After what you did a few days back-" said new boss.

"You mean my job?" I said.

"Yes, that thing that nearly made you captain, instead of me-" he said.

"Yet," I said.

"What?" he said.

"Nothing," I said.

"You want this lead?" he said.

"Sure," I said.

"He was survived by his daughter in law. Officer Joy Houston," said the voice.

"Great! Any other leads?" I said.

"Was accused of putting habanero and lemon powder on donuts. Other than that just the usual mad suspects, tickets, and related," he said.

"And this is the only cop that, as far as we know would have had a beef with him?" I said.

"Few years back pulled a fellow officer over for a broken tail light, on a squad car," he said, "5 years back. And that officer has an alibi called death. And in case you were wondering-"

"And I was," he said.

"Made Garfield look like a fitness buff; massive heart attack," he said, "Recent"

"Well, an old ticket to a dead guy hardly seems motive to get a cop beaten to a pulp. Thanks, probably solved it." I said.

Click

"Hey detective! Found som'n," said a CSU guy.

"Perfect timing, what is it?" I said.

"See for yourself," he said.

On, or to be more accurate over, the bathroom mirror, was a flyer from when Sylvester Turner was just running for mayor.

"I think we may have an issue," I said.

"Should we call city hall?" he said.

"Not 'we' 'I'" I said.

Then I called the mayor's office:

"Mayor Turner's office, how can I direct your call?" she said.

"You tell me, I'm Detective / Lieutenant W.X.Y.Z. Olaf Houston Police Department, Homicide / Internal Affairs," I said.

"Oy boy, this can't be good. Wadaya want?" she said.

"True, but it's not what you think," I said.

"Yea, it never is, Wadaya want?" she said.

"Look, I'm here at a crime scene-" I said.

"Who's dead?" she said.

"Charles Charleston," I said.

"Who?!" she said, "Am I supposed to recognize that silly name?"

"Doubt it, but it's what we found at the crime scene that made me call," I said.

"Waja fine?" she said.

"A flyer from when His mayorness was running for his current position," I said.

"And we should be wetting our pants, why?" she said.

"Well, I doubt his campaign put devil horns on his head, a sight target over his face, and crossed out his name and replaced it with 'Neville Chamberlin'" I said.

"Please hold while I transfer you to security," she said.

Later at officer Fannin's hospital recovery room:

"I hear no serious, lasting injuries. Somebody just knocked you out, and beat you up," I said.

"Tell that to my 3 cracked ribs," he said.

"It was a cop," I said.

"What?! That's absurd!" he said.

"No, we know it for a fact. I need to know if you had any enemies on the force, anyone that you could have gotten into a fight with, and it go south?" I said.

"Hey! I was there when I was beaten, why didn't you just ask me who did it?" he said.

"Well, I understand head injuries well enough to know that you probably won't know, but, do you know who did it?" I said.

"Well, no," he said.

"I rest my case," I said.

BANGBANG BANGBANG a meer meer a meer meer meer meer m-

"What is that?" he said.

"My phone," I said answering the phone, "Olaf," I said.

"Hi, this is Postalpoliceman Ginsburg-" said Ginsburg.

"I though you we're supposed to have phones in hospitals," said Fannin.

"Not anymore," I said.

"What?" said Ginsburg.

"Oh, someone else in the room, let me step outside," I said, stepping out of the room.

"Can you hear me now?" said Ginsburg.

"Oh, yea, sure, everything ok?" I said.

"Well, actually, I was hoping you could tell me," he said.

"How so?" I said.

"Very recently, we intercepted a package that was a crude homemade bomb. Headed for Houston Barc," he said.

"Oh, bad bomb?" I said.

"FBI tecks told me that it was most likely a small threat to postal employees handling it, and no real threat to Barc. Possibly just intended to start a fire," he said, "And whoever sent it knew nothing about making bombs."

"Oh, what does that have to do with me?" I said.

"Well, as part of our investigation, we found that, while the package was addressed to the head of Barc, there was a Barc employee, a man that decided who died and when, that was murdered last night. Coincidence, I Think Not!" he said.

"Oh, and can you tell me how I fit in with all this," I said.

"You're heading up his murder investigation," said Ginsburg.

"Is his name Charles Charleston?" I said.

"Yes," said Ginsburg.

"Well, I am glad to know this. I think the next target will be, well, I won't say over the phone," I said.

Boop, Boop, Boop, Boop, Boop, Boop

"Oh, saved by the bell. Bye," I said, switching calls.

"Detective / Lieutenant W.X.Y.Z. Olaf Houston Police Department, Homicide / Internal Affairs," I said.

"You really should change that," said Zhang.

"You're probably right," I said.

"Just thought I should tell you that I just finished talking to 2 different Medical Examiners, Mr. Austin couldn't have killed his wife. Neighbors still have seen nothing, but all during the time of death Mr. Austin was at work," she said.

"Let me guess, McDonald's?" I said.

"No, that was one of his other jobs, he was cashiering at Panda Express," she said.

"Really," I said.

"Yea, having someone confirm it; but looks like it may have been a semi-failed double homicide after all," said Zhang, "Also they were too broke for it to have been hired. Unless he stole money, or blackmailed it done."

"Interesting, anything else to know?" I said.

"Yea, Mr. Charleston was bumped to the front of the line at the request of feds. That's where things, get crazy," she said, "Still waiting for the results on Mrs. Austin."

"What kind of crazy?" I said.

"He was poisoned with a drug so bizarre it nearly went totally missed by toxicology, if they hadn't done a second look," she said.

"What is it?" I said.

"Name's a little too long, and chemist, to be able to pronounce, but it's something used by city pounds to execute; now that they've banned sucking out the lungs-" she said.

"Does Barc use it?" I said.

"Took the words right out of my mouth," she said.

"CSU got anything?" I said.

(insert mule picture here)
Houston

"No, not on either of your cases," she said.

"You mean all three," he said.

"What do you mean?" she said.

"Got an Internal Affairs Mystery too, beaten officer, in 1PP!" I said.

"Wow," she said, "I'll keep my service weapon handy."

"See what you can about executions done by Mr. Charleston. I think that's what that boils down to," I said.

Boop, Boop, Boop, Boop, Boop, Boop

"I can see, err, hear you gota go," she said.

"Bye," I said hanging up.

"Olaf," I said.

"This is nurse Ratchet at Ben Taub hospital. You're suspect is awake. He wants to talk. Not interested in a lawyer," she said.

"Uncanny timing, I'm already there on an unrelated case. What room and floor?" I said.

Later there:

"Mr. Austin?" I said.

"Yea, hope things are going better for you than me," he said.

"Yea, however short trip," I said.

"Save yourself the effort, I know the news," he said.

I pulled up a chair and said, "You do?"

"Yea, hard to get that image out of your mind," he said.

"Mr. A-" I said.

"No, I didn't do it. Probably an't smart, but I'm not interested in a lawyer. I don't want to bother," I said.

"You look like a real mess, in more ways than one," I said, "Did someone try to kill you?"

"Yea, me. Lord forgive me. I walked in and acted automatically," he said.

"I take it things were good?" I said.

(insert mule picture here)
Houston

"Oh, yea. You know how people suffering a great loss often say it's so surreal that's like walking around in a bubble. Like a dream. Not real. Being with her was like that; except in the opposite way of course. Now I just feel yanked back down into awful regular reality," he said.

"Sor-" I said.

"Save the canned words," he said.

"Any idea who would-"I said.

"Yea, I know who did it," he said.

"You, do?" I said.

"Yea, what I'm about to tell you will sound crazy, but our families will confirm the story," he said trying to not cry, "We were the best of friends as far back as either of us can remember. Round 9 we became more than just friends, at first even we didn't realize it. Till we kissed in the middle of a fight. Then at 10 we no longer afraid of bullying and told our parents. They decided that they had to keep us apart for unimportant petty reasons," he said.

"Like what?" I said.

"Mostly not having told them sooner. Then they got dogmatic, you know what that means, right?" he said.

"Yea, yea I know," I said.

"By 12 they'd tried everything. By 14 we'd both been to more military schools and bootcamps trying to force us into submission. Then they were plotting together. They dicited they'd 'lay down the law'. And that was unreal. By 15 they brought us home on our birthdays; we had the same birthday. But goofed, and brought us back the same day. Our houses were catty corner to each other. That night we ran off and spent 9 months in the desert; till we got caught," he said.

"9 months?" I said.

"Yea, we're far from outdoorsy people, but it was worth it," he said, "Her dad realized that we could not be kept apart. Later even went on to apologize. But me, they just got more determined. I was sent off to a hell hole camp. Didn't come back till I was 18. That day we made our marriage official and legal. Our birthday, and our anniversary(s) all on the same day," he said.

"And your folks-" I said.

"Just got mad," he said.

"I really am sympathetic," I said.

(insert mule picture here)
Houston

"When I was locked at that camp, it was horrible, I planned to declare my parents incompetent against their will, and put them in the most hell hole 'care' facility I could find; like maybe in the slums of NE York. But, as always, when I was with her. It all melted away," he said, "6 years I endured, her about 4. Through it all, I felt sorry for her, was mad about what I knew she was enduring, which was a scam the last time. And through it all my biggest fear was losing her. Counting the time in the desert; we only got 2 years. 2 years; it was so short, went by so fast, yet, it was worth it; it was so worth it," he said.

"So, you think your parents did it?" I said.

"I don't think, I know," he said.

BANGBANG BANGBAN-

"I know, you have to go. go," he said.

"Olaf," I said, answering the phone as I stepped out the door.

"Hello, This is Medical Exa-" said Alztimer.

"Yes, yes, I have caller ID. You did the autopsy?" I said.

"No, in progress. But I think we can rule out Dementia," said Alztimer.

"Yea, I could have told you that. Why are you calling?" I said.

"Thought you'd want the findings," said Alztimer.

"But you said you weren't finished?" I said.

"Yea, yea, yea, and I've been doing this long enough to know I won't find anything. But the one time I don't look that close, I miss something," said Alztimer.

"Alztimer, whataya got?" I said.

"Well, the victim appears to have been pregnant. Probably didn't know. Only 3-4 weeks," said Alztimer.

"Oh! Boy or girl?" I said.

"Both, one of each. But the girl would likely have been miscarried," said Alztimer.

Boop, Boop, Boop, Boop, Boop, Boop

"I gota take that," I said.

"You do that, I'll go cut up a dead person," said Alztimer.

"As morbid as always," I said switching calls.

"Olaf, news came back on the ax," said Zhang.

(insert mule picture here)
Houston

"What's that?" I said.

"Appears to never have been used before, probably bought specially for the occasion," said Zhang.

"Anything else?" I said.

"Was a cheap brand, half of all major hardware stores would have it," said Zhang, "If we get suspects, then we can go to those stores. See if he, or possibly she, was there."

Boop, Boop, Boop, Boop, Boop, Boop

"Another one, gota take that," I said, by that point I was at the elevator.

"Bye," said Zhang as I switched calls.

"Olaf," I said.

"Hi, I have a major lead on your murder case," said the forensic scientist.

"Tell me about it," I said.

"Well, your robbed crime scene. It was a man and two of his friends. All are on parole for having been a B & E crew in the past. Been going on sense 18. Also sealed juvenile records, so no doubt longer. And they have restraining orders to keep the 3 goobers apart; for obvious reasons," he said.

"I'll have em picked up," I said.

Later:

"I'll take Greg, you take the others. Each should be offered the deal: tell us everything you know. And we'll let them off with only having to have ankle bracelets added to the terms of their parole. Make sure they know we don't care about the stealin' we just want to know all we can about the killin'" I said.

Each separately complied, and it did us no good. Just tried that door, ignored the dead guy, and stole till the cows came home.

"Well, that was a waste of time," I said.

"And 3 crooks, who messed up our crime scene got away with it. That's why I hate the deal making process," said Zhang.

"No, not totally for want. At least we broke up a group of burglars," I said.

"So, now what?" she said.

"You interrogate Mrs. Austin's no doubt killer. I have work to do," I said.

"Work?" I said.

"I'm also in Internal Affairs, don't you remember?" I said.

Later there:

"May I ask why I am here?" said Officer Houston.

"You can, but we both know why you're here," I said.

"Allegedly," she replied, "We're all cops here."

"Right, right" I said, "Does the name Officer Fannin, HPD, ring any bells, all?" I said.

"Yea, killed my dad," she said.

"Y-" I said.

"And before you accuse me of lying to the police. I should let you now that he was my father in law. If you'd had my life experiences, you'd think of him as your father too," she said.

"Yes, sounds like you were close," I said.

"Extremely," she said.

"I always make a habit of knowing all I can before in interrogation," I said, "Even wonder if he was just replacing his own late daughter, with you?"

"She was a baby!" she said, "My better half's only sibling. And died two years before he was born," she said.

"Yes, yes, I know from personal experience the only child that could be the favorite over one that could die, is one that already has," I said.

"What?" I said.

"Could've gotten the needle, wouldn't have wanted an appeal," I said, "Don't ask."

"I've heard that you've had quite the past," she said, "Everyone's heard of you. Never would have guessed it was true."

"I am not a liar. Unlike most, I just am not. I can't prove it was you. And I'd let this go; but I was going to prosecute him; and now I don't know if I can," I said.

"Yea, a likely story," she said.

"So, that's why you did it, because I / we would do nothing. I've seen that before," I said. (Remember Epi. 3, that hasn't happened yet.)

(insert mule picture here)
Houston

"You're assuming guilt," she said.

"But, as you remember my having said, I always know what as much as possible before going into an interview," I said, "When you were 13, your big brother was mysteriously turned up at Memorial Hermann TMC, starved to death. When you were 17, your father was found mysteriously beaten to death. They though it was you, but for lack of proof, you were not charged. At the academy that's why everyone thought you became a cop, but I don't. Before signing up at the academy, you applied to become a Child Protective Services Agent. I honestly don't know why you didn't get the job. But I have a guess," I said, "Also I see scars on you, bad ones. Now I'm no expert. But If I was to make a guess; I'd say preteen."

"When I was 13, I found the perfect guy, I knew he was the one after our first, very nerve racking, awkward date. Before then Father said he would pick me a husband. When we finally got engaged, after only 3 months of dating, we told him, and his green hair and dad's racism probably didn't help. Then it was hell. I still remember my big brother running away from home 'holding himself for ransom' refusing to eat and threatening suicide. My little brother Crocket was also in on it. Only 3 years old and he was willing to stand up to dad for me. I still remember the exact words my big brother used, begging and insisting that I just take the sacrifice, and not feel guilt; laying in a hospital bed, dying. I made myself do as he insisted. Then we were married And I went to live with the in laws, err, in law. My dad was a single father," she said.

"So was the mailman killer," I said.

"Yea, but dad was also, and I think he tried to kill my better half right after I moved out, but there was no proof. It was heaven living over there, however probably a short trip. When I was seventeen, I finally decided I'd make father let me visit Crocket. And I found him close to death. He was so happy that things had worked out well, and had missed me. He made, and still to this day does, make the same insistence Travis did," she said.

"What happened?" I said.

"Father was, every day, giving him the beating he didn't get to give me. So I grabbed old Spanky, and well-" she said.

"I-I, In exchange for helping in Mr. Syato's manslaughter trial, which I'm sure you would have anyways. I'll get you immunity. Also I'll ask the DA for a plee deal that leaves out jail time. Might not even lose your shield, though I doubt that," I said.

"I doubt you'll convict him, he was careless and it was dumb luck it hit Daddy at the base of the skull," she said.

"Well, a big trial in and of itself is some punishment, so's a pink sli-" I said.

BANGBANG BANGBANG a meer meer a meer meer meer mee

(insert mule picture here)
Houston

"Is that-" she said.

"Yes," I said answering the phone.

"Maybe he's faking it, cause he'd gone," said Zhang.

"What?!" who's gone?!" I said.

"Mr. Austin," she said, "Ben Taub called."

"What?! I though he was on watch to keep him from re-slitting his throat," I said.

"Well they did a real bang up job," she said.

"Great! Well, see if you can find him, must admit he's a great actor," she said.

Dong! Dong!

"What Now!" she said.

"He just texted," I said.

"Who is he?!" she said.

"Austin," I said.

"The killer," she said.

"He didn't do it," I said, "Not entirely sure he got my number though."

"What are you talking about?" she said.

"Mostly a lot of babbling about how he just can't go on, can't see the coming trial through, and such," I said.

"Trying again?" she said.

"Yea, also says how very few ever came close to what they had, my life is ruined, the normal," I said.

"How would you know the normal?" she said.

"I handled these, before murders, remember?" I said.

"Oh, yea, but where is he?" she said.

"Says you'll find him at a garage in TMC, aren't they all," I said.

"Whatdaya mean?" she said.

"That garage, for some reason, more than any other place, attracts dead bodies like flies, jumpers, murders, natural causes, accidents, you name it. Go figure," I said.

"Maybe someone's just that good," she said.

"Doubtful," I said.

Boop, Boop, Boop, Boop, Boop, BoopBoop, Boop, Boop, Boop, Boop, Boop

"You got another call coming in?" I said.

"Yea, you too," she said as I switched calls.

"OLAF!" shouted the commissioner.

"And do what do I owe this pleasure?" I said.

"THIS IS NO PLEASURE!" he screamed into the phone.

"Yea, I guess from the screaming," I said.

"Don't Smart OFF!" he said.

"I'm not, but I assume something to be the matter," I said.

"YEA YO-" said the commissioner.

"Stop yelling or I'll hang up," I said.

"Care to explain why the mayor is dead?!" said the commissioner.

"I'd need an M.E." I said.

"No, the bullet hole is pretty strong evidence by itself," said the commissioner.

"Guess we can rule out SIDS, hu?" I said.

"Have some respect man!" said the commissioner.

"Ok, What happened?" I said.

"You didn't! That's what," said the commissioner.

"Just tell me," I said.

"Some guy burst into city council meeting, shouted 'THIS IS FOR MY DOG' and shot him between the eyes before we could react. Also shot the Mayor Pro-tem, but I'll probably pull through," said the commissioner.

"And he?" I said.

(insert mule picture here)
Houston

"Oh, the guards shot him dead," said the commissioner.

"And he was?" I said.

"John Doe, far as I care and the world'll know if I have anything to say about it," said the commissioner.

"I gave the City Hall Security and the mayor's office a full briefing, not my fault if they stink at their job," I said.

"Well, I'll check into that, and be looking to blame YOU!" said the commissioner.

Later:

I just wrapped up 2 cases today, how about the 3rd?" I said.

"Found Mr. Austin," said Zhang.

"Did he survive?" I said.

"Not important, but showed the note to the father, and found that he cash purchased an AX meeting the description. He is showing remorse, not just for the murder, but for everything," she said.

"What now?" I said.

"Well, apparently mama is also going to jail, not sure what's going to happen to me," said a little boy.

"Oh! hasn't Child services picked you up yet?" I said.

"Good grief! the orphanage!" he said.

"Not necessarily, I think I might just know someone who'll take you in, and be better than her father was," I said.

"Who? just lost my last living sibling," he said.

"So he did die, sorry about that," I said.

"Met him only a few times, parents kept up apart," he said.

"Can't guarantee anything, but, actually, I know a nice person named Officer Joy Houston," I said.

"Good morning, Rathbone," I said, "You said it was urgent?"

"Yes, turn around," said Rathbone.

"What?" I said confused, thinking I misheard.

"Turn around, you're under arrest for the murder of Brenda Lee Johnston," I said.

"I want a lawyer," I said.

(insert mule picture here)
Houston

Later with my lawyer:

"My client has agreed to answer most any question," said my lawyer, "But has refused a polygraph."

"Did you kill Brenda Lee Johnston?" said Rathbone.

"That is the one question he will not answer," said my lawyer, "he is afraid of being convicted of lying, a loophole around double jeopardy."

"Now, I don't know what is going on, but I'm sure that whatever is going on is just some form of misunderstanding. And as long as we're all honest and civilized, we can straighten it out," I said.

"Yea," he said, "Is it not true you have been trying to nail her for quite some time?"

"Correct," I said.

"And what was she doing?" he said.

"She worked with minor suspects. She'd scare them, make them talk, keep them from lawyering up, find any possible loophole around their rights. Some may have even been innocent. However in the interest of full disclosure, her life didn't matter, she got what she deserved, and the world is better off without her. Thought I don't know if I can justify the manner of death," I said.

"Sounds like motive to me," he said.

"Look, if I was going to start killing dishonest cops, I would have started a long time ago and I wouldn't be caught," I said.

"By the looks of things, you could have fired her, why didn't you?" he said.

"If I fired her, her victims couldn't get appeals, and to make matters worse, she could just go to another department, and then I couldn't touch her," I said.

"She was going federal," he said.

"Well, I can't say I'm sad, In fact it's an effort to not be happy," I said, "This murder investigation must go over everything she did, I might just still be able to get those appeals," I said.

"You're just digging yourself in deeper," he said.

"Stop talking," said my lawyer.

"We know it was you, your DNA and fingerprints were all over the crime scene," said Rathbone.

"You're lying, this meeting just ended," I said.

Later with my lawyer:

"They gave the evidence over in such a way that they can't lie," he said, "I had a very high quality private crime lab look things over. The DNA really did match, but there was a slight difference with one print. Not enough for exoneration, but to indicate a reframing."

"I don't think the police are framing me," I said.

"You think you aren't being framed?" he said.

"Oh no, I am defiantly being framed, but not by the police, at least not defiantly be the police. Think about it. I'm adopted, everyone in my family is. Matching DNA, almost matching prints. There's only one logical explanation," he said.

"Yea, you're being framed, or you're guilty," he said.

"No Mike, I have a twin brother!" I said.

"But, why woul-" said Fred.

"That, is the million dollar question," I said, "Now, this is what we need to sopena: my adoption records. They can redact my biological parents, I really don't care. What I do want is my identical twin brother. I know he's out there."

"I'll do what I can," he said.

Later in another interview:

"We both know that you did that murder-" said Rathbone.

"Allegedly," I said.

"Blah, blah, blah," he said, "We have bigger fish to fry."

"How so?" I said.

"5 days ago, the offices of The Leader, the neighborhood newspaper for the Garden Oaks, Heights, Oak Forest and Rice Military neighborhoods were, err was shot up. 34 dead. All those that worked for the newspaper, 3 pizza delivery men, two delivering sushi, two Pollo Tropical Caterers that required 48 hours notice. 1 from Kroger on 34th street, nearby, and 1 Houston Police Officer responding to what was thought to be most likely an accidental call to 911, for the newspaper office," said Rathbone, "And there were no survivors."

"I heard about that on the 5oclock news. I was at work the whole time!" I said.

"Yes, yes, but, I think you know who did that shooting," he said.

"How so?" I said.

(insert mule picture here)
Houston

"The next day, the offices of Dr. Donald E. Lever, DDS. Same story. Dentist, hygienist, receptionist, sandwich diliveryist, Err, I mean Sandwich delivery man from Corner Bakery nearby. Pizza hut, Dominoes, 2 sushi, and one Indian restaurant. Also someone called 911 claiming a heart attack. A cop got there first. All 10 of these people were killed. And five paramedics," he said, "Killer also seems to have laid in wait for the UPS man. Grand total at the dentist: 16 dead; 0 wounded."

"Sounds like this is really bad," I said.

"Yea, no kidding. Also whomever is doing this is using only one gun, and leaves no other evidence behind. Whatsoever. The night before the day before yesterday. Hopefully the last night you'll ever enjoy freedom-" said Rathbone.

"If I am guilty, then hopefully the last night I'll ever enjoy freedom," I said.

(short pause as he stared through me)

"The Kroger that lost a deliveryman, 19 customers, most of which walked in on it, and died in the vestibule, like the others some outside also. Also lost another 19 workers. There was one teen who seems to have been delivering illegal drugs among the dead. Otherwise, by that point no one would deliver anything in this city. Putting a lot of people, who were close to the bone to begin with, out to work," he said.

"Not to mention the mourners," I said.

"Exactly. But this time, we watched it all go down on cameras," he said.

"Let me guess, you think you saw me," I said.

"Bingo, that alone, probably can't get you convicted. Whoever did this is a super professional," he said.

"And I barley passed the police standards at the academy," I said. Might I add that that is forever held over my head.

"Exactly, but yesterday, it happened again," he said.

"I have an alibi," I said.

"Exactly, paramedics called out, police just missed the killer, but it was a fast food restaurant," he said.

"Was it open?" I said.

"Yes, but drive through only, 5 fatalities, plus 9 paramedics." he said.

"Anything today?" I said.

"Actually yes, but maybe not today," he said.

"What happened?" I said.

"Was in sunny side, two different plumbers were called out. Private apartment. Single mom, 6 kids, 5 plumbers, and one poor smo working late in the lease office," said Rathbone, "He's changing up his MO. Give us your partner, and we'll go easy on you," he said.

"Well, I can tell you who's pulling the trigger, but he's not with me. Nor will you be able to find him," I said.

"Well, this should be good 'I've solved your case; I didn't do it! I was framed," said Rathbone mocking me.

"Precisely," I said, "An ultra, but private, crime lab reexamined the evidence from the first crime scene. Yes DNA did match, but there was a light print difference."

"So, they goofed up," he said.

"Or he, or she," I said, "That was enough for me to sopena my adoption records. My hunch was right; I have a twin brother; obviously Identical. I have a brother on the way, so to speak. His name is Trench Monicle," I said.

"What kind of a name is Trench?!" said Rathbone.

"No crazier than mine," I said, "I looked into him. The prints are a perfect match for him. Among other things he's a Navy Seal."

"What 'other things?!'" he said.

"Classified, don't know," I said, "But his whole family, wife, 22 kids ranging from newborn twins, probably not adopted, to 17, and himself has gone missing."

"How come no one called to report it?" he said, "And if he is your twin brother, how can he be 23 also, and have teenage children?"

"One can only assume most to be adopted, as for having had them reported missing; who worries about a Navy Seal getting kidnapped off duty? Btu we got some P.I.s on the case. Went missing 6 days ago," I said.

"How do I know what you're saying is true?" he said, obviously not believing.

"By looking into things," I said, "also, it looks more like they are just not home, can't prove it but looks like some form of knock out gas."

"Knock out gas?" he said, "And why would an American hero start killing like this?"

"The family was kidnapped, he's now a marionette. Now I know how much gas it would take to do this. One can only assume hot gas," I said, "No pun intended."

"I'll look into this," he said, seeing that the facts supported this, "Any other profiler style hints you can give us?"

"Yes, one, whoever it the puppeteer, is wanting revenge on me, and is a complete monster," I said.

Later:

"Sorry about that whole arresting you thing, at first I thing you were doing a stretched out 'my big brother made me do it' but in reality. Everything you thought checked out," said Rathbone, "Even the bunches."

"No sweat, didn't aggravate my trama much, at least considering. I guess this means that I have picked up some profiling skills," I said.

"Yea, looked into everything, it appears that your gas theory seems to be backed up, Houston Methodist hospital had a large amount of anesthetic gas just vanish," he said.

"Houston Methodist? Where my dad's an ane-" I said.

"Sthesiologist, that's the one. And I think it was him. Your Mom also rented a truck, big enough for all of it," he said.

"That cannot be right," I said.

"It is, 6 days ago, your brother stopping appearing in school," said Rathbone.

"Say what now?" I said.

Later:

"Look Dad, I'm the only one they felt was safe to send in to talk to you. We know about the missing anesthetic, the truck, and my brother. I'll see to it that you don't get charged. But I know that you know where they are. We're all on the same side; I need an address," I said.

Later:

"Captain Olaf," said Rathbone.

"Yes, don't tell me you think I did to it," I said.

"We know that it was a marionette Seal, can you please come into my office?" he said.

"Is everything ok? I heard that they found another scene." I said.

"No, and it's about that 3rd scene," he said.

"Was his family killed?" I said.

"There were 9 victims," he said, "The first was a major prosecutor, killed the same way as the cop we though you killed," he said.

"Burned to death?" I said.

"Yea, and one of the Seal's kids, only 4 years old. I think the knock out took her out-" he said.

"Forever?" I said.

"Yea, and Detective Zhang-" he said.

"Was she killed?!" I said.

"Stuffed in a closet, dehydration," he said.

"Say What?!?!" I said.

"Rural farm house, the five residents were in the attic, shot just as all other scenes. Guess wanted no attention to this one. But knew that it would be found," he said.

"What do you mean?" I said getting really scared.

"Do you remember that old lady turned deranged killer?" he said.

"Yea?" I said.

"The prosecutor, headed her case. She was released 7 days ago, just long enough for her to make the catering call to Pollo Tropical. Also the 9th victim, matched Fred Wong, similar close, shot same way, seems to have been reading Dr. Frankenstein, even stomach contents matched-" he said.

"For God's sake man! I'll learn sooner or later! Just spit it out!" I said.

"It was your little brother," he said.

I just completely broke down.

Later,

"I'm surprised you're not in there," said the chief.

"I have no business in there, she killed my brother, but what about you? Why are you behind the sidelines?!" I said.

"Killed countless Houstonians, same reason I suppose," he said.

"Uhu," I said.

"Funny, sense you were yelling in your victim's face and throwing things through these one way mirrors," he said.

(insert mule picture here)
Houston

"Hey, I was just interrogating her the way she did her interrogations," I said.

"Shhuh," he shushed.

"Zack didn't want to die, we also know that he knew it was coming; he had been crying so much before you had his brains blown out that the coroner first though that he had been choked," said Rathbone.

Later:

"Thanks for your testimony. With your help we were able to indict her for all murders. Also you'll will get a dishonorable discharge, but probably not anything else. Also I'm seeing to it that all those appeals happen also. You know it's strange. In one day I traded my little brother, who I was probably over protective of, for a twin brother I never knew I had," I said.

F.Y.I.: don't be confused. This takes place right before the last one.

"Captain, someone on the phone for you," said my assistant.

"Probably my brother, what line?" I said.

"1" she replied.

"Hey bro," I said.

"Hey," replied the caller.

"Hey! You're not my brother!" I said.

"Well, in a way I am," he said.

"Well in Ch-" I said.

"Look, I've got an emergency. I don't know who else to call, any possible chance you could come," he said.

"Maybe, who is this? A-" I said.

"Do you remember Gregor Mendal?" he said.

"Yea, but what ab-" I said.

"I was the assistant," he said.

"out 911-" I said, "Where to?"

Later there:

"What happened?" I said.

"It's my brother-" he said.

"I thought you were a foste-" I said.

"We were split at 7," he said, "After 10 years I finally found him."

"Where do I come in?" I said.

"It's that he's gone missing, this is my other brother, who's been taking care of him," he said.

"How old is he?" I said.

"Turned 12 few weeks back," said the other brother.

"And you are?" I said.

"Call me Pat," he said.

"O-k, Pat, why didn't you call the police, or is calling me your idea of calling the police," I said.

"He just got out of jail, that's the deal," said Pat.

"Whoa," I said, "Sorry to hear about that."

"You know, you're the first to have that response that I've ever met," said Pat.

"Well, um, not important," I said, "What clues do we have?"

"That's why we didn't call," said Pat.

"What's going on?" I said.

"He left this letter on the computer," said Pat pulling it up.

"Hey, don't beat yourself up. Don't bother calling the police. After losing you know who, I don't see any reason to hang around. But I will turn up, sorta. But I am going out with a bang. I don't know if I'll turn up first, or him. Either way, there will be yellow police tape. Yes, I did kill him."

"Who did he kill?" I said.

"I Don't Know?!" he said, "He was always conspiracy minded!"

"And who is you know who?!" I said.

"Once again beats me! I don't want him to go to jail. But, this reads like a suicide note!" he said.

"A weird one at that!" I said, "But not the first with a murder confession."

"What?!" he said.

"Before I was a homicide detective, I was responding to these," I said.

"Well, Find Him Fast!" he said.

"Ok, I will. But is anything missing from the house?" I said.

"Nothing! Not that I can find!" said Pat.

"You look, might be a clue to see how he's doing what," I said, and turned to the other brother said "What was he in jail for?"

"Drugs, he-" he said.

"Yea, nuf said," I said, "You wouldn't happen to know where he was locked up?"

"Yea, Lynch Juvenile Reformatory-" he said.

"What Did You Just Say?!" I said.

"Why do you ask?" he said.

"I was there," I said.

"Really, I've been trying to bust them for a while, they're good," he said.

"Could my testimony help?" I said.

"I don't know, only real offenders go there, and those whose parent have tried everything else-" he said.

"What kind of parents wou-" I said.

"They think they're at their wits end-" he said.

"There. is. no. excuse-" I said.

"As bad as my little brother described?" he said.

"P.T.S.D." I said.

"You to?" he said.

"You have him on tape describing what happened there?" I said.

"Not him, I have no proof, just the word from some that the police woul-" he said.

"Can I have it?" I said.

"Won't do you any good," he said.

"Don't care, I'll be back in 30 with a warrant," I said.

(insert mule picture here)
Houston

That evening:

"Don't have jurisdiction, so all the rigmarole took nearly 3 hours," I said, over the phone, "Also if there's anything relevant to our problem, they'll find it. Got a lot of testifying to do. Lot of really bad people going away for good. Lot of kids getting off. CPS is also investigating anyone that ever sent anyone here," I said, "Ya done good Phil, ya done good."

"Guess you're too tied up to help us," said Phil.

"No, I'm HPD Internal Affairs. Tonight, this is the Liberty County Sheriff's problem, and every Juvenile anything's worst nightmare. But I did get a personal answer," I said.

"Did you crack your siblings murders?" he said.

"No, my sister-in-law's little brother; a childhood friend of mine was locked up here, but never could have guessed that that happened so close. Guess a lot were bussed in here," I said.

ba wa wa ba wa wa wa gota 14249 wa 454 ba wa wa

"Oh, dear," I said.

"What?" he said.

Later:

"Why are we here?" said Pat.

"Yea," said Phil.

I knew I'd need Pat's help, and wasn't willing to risk him being unable to help, so I asked "We assume that the John Doe that was killed, was from that hell hole, what if we were wrong?" I said.

"Whatdaya mean?" he said.

"Well, have you had any thoughts on who 'You know who' is?" I said.

"Actually yes," he said, "After Mom and Dad died we went back into the system, and Avery was by his side, Even her folks wanted to tear them apart; but we were too scared and just let it happen," said Pat.

"And Avery is whom?" I said, "And what happened?"

"Avery, his first girlfriend. Not sure what happened," he said.

"She vanished?" I said.

"Actually, what happened was that she fell off the roof of the jail school. All that could be ruled out was natural causes," he said.

"You don't thin-" I said.

"No, I don't, but he was conspiracy minded enough to-" he said.

"How good were they?" I said.

"Instant," he said, "She was an overachieving Asian, defended herself one time, and then refused to be punished. Even tried to blackmail the school district, don't remember how," he said.

"And he was-" I said.

"He was how I always imagined Jonas the Receiver was like as a child," he said.

"Who?" I said.

"From The Giver! But I insist, why are we here?!" I said.

I turned and said "Rathbone."

Later:

"HPD, who's missing," I said.

"Does that badge say 'Internal Affairs'?" said the clerk.

"Yes, now what muckidy muck is missing from this school," I said.

"What?" she said.

"Look, I've made calls and ruled out everyone else that's logical. Which muckidy muck from here is missing?" I said.

"What?" she said.

"Please answer the question," I said.

"I don't know," she said, "Come back when we're not checking the students in."

"Let me in to see the principal," I said.

"I can't," she said.

"I'm sorry, did I include a 'if it so please your highness?'" I said.

"Security!" she said.

"You want me to dynamite my way in?" I said.

"Do you have a warrant" she said.

"Let me put it to you this way, 'the president has a pen and a phone; I have a pen, a phone, and a gun,'" she said.

"That sounds like a threat!" she said.

"Threat, smhreat. Tough!" I said.

"You called about a problem, where's the kid?" said an officer.

"Not a student, him!" she said.

I showed my badge.

"What's going on?" said the other one.

"I know there's a big wig from this school missing, Who is it?" I said.

"I beg your pardon?" he said.

"Just tell me," I said.

"How should we know?" they said.

"Then take me to the principal's office," I said.

"Look, tell ya what, leave, and that treat can be forgotten, this is our busiest time of the day," he said.

"I'm not going anywhere, imposter," I said.

"What are you saying?!" he said.

"I'm just saying, I'm a cop and you're not," I said.

"You're the imposter, now you're going down for-" he said trying to handcuff me; so I grabbed him, and slammed the other officer against the wall, using him as a weapon.

"You're under arrest for assaulting an officer," I said, walking back up to the receptionist, and then I said "Unless you'd like me to get dynamite, open the door."

She buzzed me in. Later in the principal's office:

"Sorry officer, no one is missing," he said.

"Well, that's too bad, because the little brother of a good accotiate just washed up in Greens Bayou. I think he tried to kill someone here and you were too afraid to admit who and how, for fear of people looking into things," I said.

"What kind of things?" he said.

"Do you remember an Avery Cho?" I said.

"Oh yea, don't get too many students that could amount to anything here," he said.

"Well, maybe if someone was interested in anything other than punishment-" I said.

"Look, everyone here is worthless, and if they were to all die, we'd all be better off," he said, "So don't-"

"I will do all in my power to get those very words on the nightly news," I said, trying to entrap.

"OUT! You are here completely unofficially!" he said.

"Fine," I said, "I'll be back with a warrant or my name's not Captai-" I said.

"OUT!" he shouted.

As I left I noticed that my service weapon was missing, I was going to security, assuming they stole it. Till I heard shots. I ran back to the office. I saw a kid with a gun. I wasn't sure what to expect. Then I noticed the room was full of awards. And every one of them had a bullet in it. I saw he was bruised up. I didn't know if they did it, or were just asleep at the wheel.

"Mr. Vekeo, you hurt," I asked.

"Cap-tain Olaf, you wer-" he said.

"No, I wasn't shooting," I said.

"He-he killed my brother. I defended myself, and if I do it again, I'll have my parole revoked," he said, I guess 13. I fast realized I was reliving the single most traumatic moment of my life. I couldn't let it happen twice.

"Murder?" I said.

"Sure was no honest accident," he said.

"Girl named Avery also," I said.

"He knows no one will believe us, so he lets his workers use us punching bags among other things, I think they pay him," he said.

"What kind of other things?" I said.

"Trust me, you don't want to know. No-body gets loose," he said, "And Now I won't go home at 5," starting to turn the gun on himself.

"Wait! Wait! You Won't be arrested, I promise. I don't li-" I said.

"You can't trust a cop," he said, putting his finger on the trigger.

"You're right! You're right! Y-You you can't trust a cop, so I'll give you a reason to trust me!" I said. I then picked up the principal off the floor and slammed him down onto his desk; well, more through his desk. It disintegrated. I then turned to security, their guns drawn, and said "Give me your guns NOW! I'm Captain Olaf. You can't stop me unless you put a bullet in my brain. And they will convict you." They slowly handed their guns over. "Now! This school is being shut down. Rat it out and release everyone, and I'll ask the D.A. to go easy on you. And I remind you of how bad it is when a cop is locked up," I said.

They left.

"What's your name?" I said.

"Ned, yoused to be Franswa, but had to change it when-" he said.

"Hey!" said Mr. Vekeo, "I keep the streets clean of these little urchins! And you gun-"

Zzzzzzzzzzzzzzzzzzzzzzzzzz

"Did you jus-" said Franswa, handing me the gun.

"Hey, nobody wants to hear that guilt trap," I said.

Later:

"So? no clue who my brother killed?" said Pat.

"I don't think he did, you see, I think he failed in his mission. Someone then chloroformed him, and tried to make it look like suicide. It's not yo-" I said.

"Don't. Tell. me. It's. Not. My. Fault." he said.

I tilted my head in confusion.

"He looked out for me. Didn't want he to meet the same fate our middle brother came to. He was a far better big brother to me than I ever was to him. And I couldn't-" he said getting choked up, "And now he's-"s

You have seen a lot of firsts, here's a last:

"Hello," I said.

"Yes, we need you to solve one last case," said the assistant police commissioner.

"Need as many men on that case as you can, I see," I said.

Here's where I'll cut in and let you know 'that case' was mail order, prewrapped Hanukah gifts being replaced with bombs, not that we knew that at this point.

"No, not that one," he said, "One of our own missing own duty. Doesn't look like shirking work," he said.

(insert mule picture here)
Houston

Later there:

"So, let me get this straight, you saw this man being carried off, and covered in blood?" I said.

"Yea and I think there was a hole in him, it was pretty gross," he said.

"Freddie! What have I-" said his mom.

"Lutenant/detective Olaf. HPD," I said showing my badge.

"Oh, that's a relief, sort of. 6 years old and he's already a teenager," she said.

"Well, we need to interview him further, he seems to have been the only person to witness a homicide," I said.

"Well, that would explain all the cops earlier today," she said.

"What? What cops?" I said.

"Oh, a whole flock or 3," she said, "Seemed pretty aggressive."

"Say what now!" I said, "And can you describe any of them?"

"No, they seemed to want us to stay inside and Freddie was just as happy, to skip school for video games. And I hate my hectic job. It seemed absurd. So I told them both that we were sick. Please don't spill," she said.

"Well, I'd still ask you to take a statement, you and him both," I said.

"Sure, but I have a big date tonight, so can we keep this quick?" she said.

"Excuse me, Officer Barone, HPD, I'm looking for Ms. Koin," he said.

"Here," she said.

"Um, can we speak in private," he said.

"What is this about?" she said, "A lack of coordination?!"

"Lutenant/detective Olaf. HPD," I said showing my badge.

"Say what?" he said.

"Can we speak outside?" I said to him, and then to the mother I said "We'll be back."

Later outside:

"What's going on?" I said.

"I was going to ask you the same thing!" he said.

"I'm working my first missing person's case, you?" I said.

"Didn't know he was reported missing?!" he said.

"Of course he was reported missing! That sort of thing doesn't go unnoticed," I said.

"You have any leads?" he said.

"Yea, looks like he was murdered, what've you got?" I said.

"Really! Didn't seem that suspicious to me, just a little young," he said.

"There was a bullet in him!" I said.

"How come I was never told!" he said.

"Because someone somewhere is a clueless fool!" I said.

"Really! maybe security footage will help us," he said.

"There's security footage! Must be hidden cameras," I said.

"Oh yea! what department store doesn't have security cameras?" he said.

"What! What department store!" I said.

"The one that he died in, I was there to inform the next of kin," he said.

"Who is he?" I said.

"Michael Z. Koin," he said.

"Who's-" I said, "O-k this seems to be to different deaths, but can't be a coincidence. Can however be a big plot of some form? Tell me everything you know," I said.

"19, looks 16 or 17, walks into Sears on Shepherd, there to see the door be unlocked, goes up the stairs, lays down on a mattress. As they walk through after closing, they can't wake him. Call us to get rid of him. Cop calls in a dead one. Awaiting autopsy. Took a while to ID. Was wearing work closes, probably stopped in after work. Place of employment gave us the name. DMV gave unofficial confirmation. Official confirmation pending," he said.

"That can't be a coincidence, tell them that Lutenant/detective Olaf, HPD believes foul play, linked to the probable homicide of an on duty Houston PD Officer," I said.

Later:

"Still no body," said Zhang, "But the probable deceased in question was responding to a violent home invasion. His backup was only 7 minutes away, headed to the Sawyer Heights apartment building to raid a suspected drug den," she said.

(insert mule picture here)
Houston

"And I can tell you that he was in trouble with my department, was trying to hold onto his job," I said.

"And the head of that raid is in interview 1," she said.

"You've read him his rights, right?" I said.

"Yea, though-" she said.

"In reality everyone has the right to remain silent," I said.

I walked into the interview room

"Lutenant Foulup," I said, "Remember this morning?"

"Sure, wasn't even yesterday," he said.

"You remember this man?" I said, showing the victim's picture.

"Can't say that I do," he said, "Why? Is this a matter of the homicide or Internal Affairs department?"

"I think both, I think you had a lead foot, he didn't. Admittedly not even sure, but I think you did your raid as was planned, being the same address as the home invasion, in fact probably used even more force than planned. He finally arrives. Thinks you're fakes. Procedure tells you to shoot. You do. But procedurals, smocedurals, you have a dead cop. That's bad news," I said.

"Hey man! It went nothin like that. There was never even a shot fired! At least, not by us," he said.

"What do ya mean?" I said.

"Well, when we got there, the feds had done a raid, I think that the violence had just ended when we got there. But they were unfriendly EVEN FOR FEDS! They didn't want us to see NUTIN!" he said.

"Really," I said, "Anything you can tell me about them?"

"All I saw was bullet holes, should've been arrested for pointing guns at us. I never thought I'd say this; but they scared us off good!

Later:

"Canvas still in progress, but so far story seems to check out," said Zhang.

"See what you can find about federal operations near Taylor Street, particular in that apartment building. And get a warrant for that apartment," I said, "Also have ballistics check about that whole 'no guns fired thing, anything that could have been there-"

BANGBANG BANGBANG a meer meer a meer meer meer meer m-

"Lutenant/detective Olaf. HPD," I said.

"Yes, thought you'd like the results of that autopsy," said Barone.

"You found the body?!" I said.

"What do yo-" he said, "Oh! No! the other dead guy."

"Oh! Yea, how'd he die?" I said.

"Poisoned, was such a bizarre poison, took a while to figure out what it exactly was," he said.

"So, what was it?!" I said.

"Can't pronounce the technical name, but is also known as Aricept," he said.

"Aricept?!" I said, "Any idea the time of poisoning?"

"Can't say, F.B.I. says this appears to be the first deliberate homicidal poisoning done using any drug intended primarily for dementia," he said, "DEA and FDA looking for a guess as how to determine time of poisoning."

"Do not work with the Feds, do not cooperate with the feds, if they try to force you to do anything, find an excuse to arrest them," I said.

"WHAT?!" he said, not taking me seriously, "Why?"

"Serious," I said, "And that's on a need to know basis."

I hung up and said to Zhang "That boy, and his mom. Keep them sa-"

"I'll arrange a safe house," she said packing up the phone.

I put the phone back down and said "These are the Feds, a normal safe house just won't do. Keep them in a big police station, use that as a safe house."

"A police station?" she said, not taking me seriously.

"Yea, they can sleep in my office if need be-" I said.

BANGBANG BANGBANG a meer meer a meer meer mee-

"Lutenant/detective Olaf. HPD," I said.

"Yea, You should know that I am not a detective, thus not qualified to lead this investigation. But I do have a big lead," he said.

"What is it?" I said.

"The place he worked, was a nursing home. Under investigation," he said.

Later:

"So, you're running the case?" said M.E.

"Yes, and I came here for your findings," I said.

"Well, at first I though some form of suicide for all the heart drugs in his system, but there was congenital heart defects, you know what that means?" she said.

"Yea," I said.

"Well, wasn't enough to kill him. But there was this nebulas something I was unfamiliar with," she said.

"Aricept," I said.

"Exactly, now you'd think that we'd be familiar with that-" she said.

"But most people on it do not get an autopsy," I said.

"Yea," she said, "How'd you-"

"Up until 10, family did a lot of elder care. In fact my brother later became a court appointed, paid, elder guardian," I said.

"Well, can't rule out suicide, you say this is linked to a fallen officer?" she said, "Wasn't reciv-"

"Still looking for the body," I said.

We all heard a piano rift come on.

"What is?" she said.

"One of the best rifts ever, and we need to answer his phone," I said.

"It's APS," said the coroner.

I held in a gasp and said "Well, let's answer it."

"Mr. Koin?" said a woman.

"Y-es," I said.

"Your voice sounds different," she said.

"You have the correct number," I said, "How can I help you?"

"Is that you Mr. Koin?" she said.

"May-be" I said.

"Well, the plan is going off today," she said.

"Plan?" I said.

"Alright! Who is this!" she said.

I came right out and said "Lutenant/detective Olaf. HPD."

"Oh dear, this can't be good," she said.

"Tell me what you know," I said, being very uncorrupt, "Unless you'd like a lawyer."

"Lawyer!" she said, "This is all need to know! What's going on!"

"That's need to know, but if you're just going to claim 'need to know' then you're just digging yourself in deeper," I said.

"We're going to have a raid as soon as he goes on duty, at midnight," she said.

I nodded to Zhang, she understood. And I hung up on her.

Later:

"So, you're the only person on the nightshift with Mr. Koin, right?" I said.

"Yes," she said.

"Do you want a lawyer?" I said.

"No, I confess, I did it," she said.

"Say what?" I said.

"Yea, it was impulsive and dumb," she said.

"Why'd ya do it?" I said.

"I eloped at 16, my 16th birthday to be exact, he hated that boy, I adored him; and he adored me even more," she said, "When we came back, well, Father spent most of my childhood hating mom for petty reasons, said he was, 'savin me for the same fate'. Jerk. However that don't make right burying him next to him, had nearly 60 years of freedom I didn't deserve. I'll go peacefully," she said.

"Say what now?" I said.

"Yea, they eloped under similar conditions even younger, and I was a very late life child," she said, "They never found the bodies."

"Well. While. That. Was. helpful, Mrs. Garcia. That's not what we're accusing us of. But on a related note, would you help us find them?" I said.

"Doubt I could find them. Haven't been back there in nearly 60 years," she said.

"We're serving a warrant as we speak. We'll find the elder abuse. And the missing Aricept. But you seem honorable. Is there anything you can do to help us?" I said.

"I could testify," she said, "But what about missing Aricept?"

"It was used to poison Mr. Koin," I said.

She had a little shock and then said "It was very out of character, but the boss wanted me to get him to try some of his homemade soup. Was insistant. Wanted his opinion, was fishy, but this?!" she said.

"Soup, of course!" I said, then the Feds burst in.

Later with the abusive boss:

"Sir, do you know why you're here?" I said.

"You like waking people up in the middle of the night?" he said, "Do you know what time it is?"

"Time for you to lawyer up?" I said.

"What would be the charges, I think you ruined the Feds case against me," he said.

"True, we've hijacked that, but that doesn't mean you're not going down," I said.

"Whatever for?" he said.

"You made an unknowing person poison Mr. Koin!" I said.

"Mr-Coin?" he said.

"You remember, nightshift, looked too young for the job-" I said.

"Oh yea! I remember that weirdo! Said he'd wanted to be a Ninja sense he was 6; and been working to be a Medical Examiner since he was 11," he said, "What's with that look of shock?"

"Carry on without me," I said.

I stepped outside.

"What's going on?" said Zhang.

"He had a copy of Grand Theft Auto in the raided apartment was served a warrant on when the Feds weren't looking. Same version my siblings were murdered while playing, the only witness's big brother, my little brother wanted to be a Medical Examiner, was a child prodigy and probably could've become one. My sister wanted to be a ninja. Their room was like a ninja's layer. That's where the killer got the murder weapon-" I said.

"Oh, boy, I knew this would come someday," said Zhang.

"Run that video game! If they're the slighted similarity I want to know! MY LITTLE BROTHER-" I said.

"OLAF!" she said, "I'll have teck run the game, but you're grasping at straws!" she said.

"Oh, ok, ok," I said calming down, "See what leads we have. Cases probably aren't really related. The dealers!"

"Dealers? Card dealers?" she said.

"No, there was a drug raid. You get someone to sopena, warrant, and arrest their way to that federal S.W.A.T. team. I have a plan," I said.

Later with the dealer:

"Sir, I need your help," I said.

"I would question that, but that's no crazier than what happened," he said.

"A police officer was murdered in your apartment," I said.

"And you thin-" he said.

"No, I don't. I'll get their names. But I'll need your help to convict anyone of anything. And if that's not incentive enough. If this is even the slightest bit successful, there's no way that the Feds can make any of the charges against you," I said.

"That's why you cops posted my bail!" he said.

You've heard many cases from when I was in homicide, and a few from Internal Affairs. Here's one from when I was in suicide.

"How's it look?" I said.

"Looks like suicide, but was beat up. Can't confirm cause of death until an autopsy," said the Medical Examiner.

"I'll inform the next of kin," I said.

Later:

"Hey boss," I said.

"Yea?" he said.

"About that teen," I said, "When the coroner released the cause of death, he seemed to have been in a fight before death. Also I saw a beat up 13 year old when I informed his foster home. This looks suspicious," I said.

"Look, that was a 16 year old that was either going to turn up dead, or end up in adult court when he hit 18-" he said.

"What about the 13 year old?" I said, "I looked into things, that home takes convicted foster kids, and-" I said.

"Let me guess, they have to call the police-" he said.

"One of those kids had a similar prior from a foster home later busted by Gregor Mendal" I said.

Remember Gregor Mendal? Not the monk, the murder victim. F.Y.I. he hadn't busted many yet.

"You put bad kids together and whatdaya expect?!" he said.

"Most of their priors weren't that bad, till they got to this one or a-" I said.

"You're Off the Case! Because There Is No Case!" he said.

I paused, then came up with a devious plan:

"Ok, you'll be sorry," I said leaving.

"Olaf, hope you aren't plannin' nothin stupid," he said.

"Define stupid," I said.

That night I got a cheap diploma mill style P.I.'s license. And hired myself to investigate the suspicious death. Couldn't get to talk to his foster siblings. My next move was to hire a real PI, see what he could learn about the victim's past.

"Hi, I'm here for information regarding the-" I said.

"OLAF! You're off the case bea-" said my boss.

"Correction, Officer W.X.Y.Z. Olaf is off the case. You have no jurisdiction over Private Investigator W.X.Y.Z. Olaf," I said.

"Say What!" he said.

"Yes, I've gotten a P.I.'s license-" I said.

"When did you get a P.I.'s license?" he said.

"Last night, and I have hired myself to investigate this suspicious death. Slimy, loopholeesque, dishonest, and about a half a dozen more adjectives, yes. Illegal? No," I said.

"You wana get yourself fired?" he said.

"Can't, already spoke to a lawyer, that'd be a big expensive lawsuit," I said.

(insert mule picture here)
Houston

BABGBANG BANGBANG a mee-

"Offi-" I said, "Private Investigator W.X.Y.Z. Olaf, Really, that was fast, and the address is, I'm impressed, Thanks, you too,"

"Who wha-" said my boss said.

"Sorry, I can't discuss an ongoing investigation," I said mockingly.

Later:

"Miss Dexheau?" I said.

"Yes?" she said.

"Off- Private Investigator W.X.Y.Z. Olaf, it's about your brother," I said.

"My brother died 11 years ago when I was 8," she said.

"Do tell?" I said.

"Mom, she was horrible, so manipulative, controlling. But all anyone ever saw was the good she did, which allowed her to have her favorite weapon; guilt. After Father killed himself to get away from her. My big brother, then 16. Finally decided that with his priors the police and no one else would ever believe him about the many forms of abuse we all 3 went through. Called up an old buddy in the drug business while me and my little brother were away at summer camp. Put rat poison in soup for him and mom. In the note we received at camp he said 'so that she can't hurt anyone else, especially you two," she said getting choked up, "My big brother was a selfless hero. No matter what they say. Little did he know-" she trailed off.

"And have you spoken to your little brother?" I said.

"No one believed the note, and what my brother did to be anything but evil. Little did they now. We were blamed, only 5 and 8. Then on grew up in foster care. I tried to be a similar big sister to him, but we were split up, why?" she said.

I had to tell her the news, she insisted on blaming herself.

Later with the victim's friend:

"Someone wanted to see me? This can't be good," he said.

"It isn't but it's not what you expected," I said, "Offic-"

"Oh no," he said.

"Don't worry, it has to do with your friend that just died-" I said.

(insert mule picture here)
Houston

"What about him?" he said.

"I'm not a cop toda-" I said.

"Oh God," he said terrified.

"No! no, I'm a P.I. investigating the circumstances surrounding his death," I said.

"Yea, who hired you?" he said.

"I hired me, because the police won't do anything," I said.

"Yea, why don't you tell me why you're really here?" he said.

"Because the cops won't do anything," I said.

"Yea, a likely story," he said.

"Look, I think you're up to something, and I honestly couldn't care less," I said.

"Well, so far you're keeping up the cover," he said.

"Your best friend lived a rough life, did a few mistakes in his early teens, and then could only get bad foster homes. Abusive homes. Defended himself, no one ever believed him. Spent 2 years total in jail as a minor, longer than me," I said.

"So far so good," he said.

"Why now? What was going on that made him give u-" I said.

"Was my fault. Only ally he really had. Had a fallout bout something that seems really trivial right about now," he said

Later:

"So, you're going to foster me?" he said, "I thought that the cops were out to get me," he said.

"They are, Normally. This is temporary, but I need to talk to you about the circumstances surrounding the death of-" I said.

"Really sorry to see him go, but it wasn't murder," he said.

"I never thought it was," I said.

"He was my guardian angel, but she was just so-" he said.

"Fought back one too many times," I said.

"No, just couldn't take it anymore. She broke him," he said.

"I need you to testify," I said.

"You could never get her convicted. I have priors, she does volunteer work. Couldn't get her convicted if you caught her on camera," he said.

"Gregor Mendal has, at least most of the time," I said.

"Yea, well he an't a cop," he said.

"How'd you end up in the system?" I said.

"Been in as far back as I can remember, guess nobody wanted me," he said, a little mad.

"I'm sorry about that" I said.

Later:

"Guess you just can't stay away," said my P.I.

"Yea, just not how you think," I said, "How'd it end?"

"Well, her one biological child just turned 18. Was in her 50s so was able to declare her incompetent against her will. She's in a free government memory care facility called-" he said.

Later:

"Mrs. London?" I said.

"Who wants to know?" she said.

"I am a priva-" I said.

"I know who you are and what you want-" she said.

"And I heard from your daughter 'you needed to be here; you were losing it' I think she was abused. I'd like to pull a Gregor Mendal, but don't know how to reach him, nor do I think I could do it myself to you after all that's happened. This is a pretty nasty one-" I said.

"Yea, no kidding-" she said.

"I think this is a punishment, however if it were me, I know how proud a Texan you are. I'd find the most rat infested, moldy place in the slums or New York or Chicago, and put you there. But, maybe not. I'm a very clean cop, but not such a clean P.I." I said, "I can see that you were put in memory care just to keep you in. I could able to help you, however, maybe not without a confession. You see, if you don't confess I'll leave you here, so you can't hurt anyone else. Or falsely frame and set up anyone else; and never look back I'll give you one hour to decide. You need me to get out," I said.

Here's a case that I worked on just a few days back. I guarantee this is the last one from the present, err, future.

"So? What' it look like?" I said.

"Well, it looks-

Actually for the sake of the space time continuum, I can't tell you anything. But I will let you know that there is so much about the preset day and GSSD I'd love to tell you. I just can't

Do-

Well, can't tell you that one, hummm, righters block, great. There goes my grammar. Just come back tomorrow.

Later:

Hey, you remember my sister in law? Here goes something,

BANGBANG BANGBANG a meer meer a meer meer meer meer m-

"Captain Olaf," I said, "Really! I've waited so long! I'm on my way," I said.

Later there:

"You said there was a lead? Did you find out who hired the hit man?" I said.

"No, many people are looking for him. He pops up and disappears with no surrounding events or evidence. It's like whack-a-mole, but we're yet to make a whack," he said.

"But there are people looking for him?" I said.

"Yea, besides us there's the CIA, FBI, KGB, Russian Mob, the list is endless," he said, "No one's come that close, to my knowledge."

"Well, hopefully it'll be a good guy, might help me," I said.

"But, we do have a lead," he said.

"A real lead, or an unrelated hit by the same man," I said.

"We wouldn't even bother to call you for something like that," he said, "But before we begin, you're sure your baby brother's homicide is unrelated?"

"Yea, beyond a reasonable doubt. However don't know if a jury will be, let her go once before," I said.

"Her?" he said, "The killer?"

"Yea, I was a bit overprotective, as one would expect," I said, "But not enough I guess."

"Well,-" he said.

"What've ya got?" I said.

"We were looking into that bizarre motive thing. One weird thing has appeared," he said.

"What kind of weird?" I said.

"Well, does the name Avery Timmyson ring a bell?" he said.

Here I'll cut in and say that that has no relation to Jane Timmyson.

"I don't think so? Why?" I said.

"2 nights before the incident-" he said.

"It was not an 'incident' It was a double homicide," I said.

"My appologies, 2 nights before, Your sister-in-law Lilly-" He said.

"Lily, not Lilly," I said.

"Oh, well, Lily went to a sleepover at her friend Avery's house-" he said.

"I think I vauguly remember Avery! As I recall, was the annoying friend that could never take a hint," I said.

"Well, can't confurm that, but Lily saw something at the ajacent apartment, kept babbling about it for the rest of the night," he said.

"What kind of something?" I said.

"Well, we were really hoping you could tell us, it was a sleepover for Avery's 5th birthday. So Avery doesn't remember," he said.

"My brother probably knew, but what about parents? Other people there?" I said.

"Way ahead of you," he said, "But must proceed cautiously."

"But, you will proceed? Right?" I said.

"Of course," he said, "We're just beginning to investigate what the nebulas 'something' is, err, was." he said.

A few days later:

"Good news, bad news," he said.

"Let's get the bad news over with," I said.

"First, we're looking into who may have been living ajacent at that time, but, lower end, crummier complex. Near impossible," he said.

"You're giving up?!?!" I said.

"No! no! But, it was over a decade ago, unlikely that anyone would remember anything if we even did find them! And similar situation with Avery's other friends, though probably will find them," he said.

"What about parent?! The-" I said.

"That's the other bad news, they can't say anything, and one has died," he said.

"Wha-" I said.

"They both had early onset Alztimers. Like 40s-50s. One's insane, and the other just passed. Runs in that family too, according to Avery, and what records we could find. no foul play," he said.

"Oh great, there's no witnesses, What's the Good News?!?!" I said.

"Please calm down," he said.

"Sorry, it's just that it sounds like we can't crack it just because it's a cold case," I said.

"Relax, We have a generic idea what happened," he said.

"What happened?" I said.

"In the aject apartment, as in shared a deck, there was one resident. Last seen working the day before a 3 day work weekend, but not a holiday weekend," he said.

"Oh, what do we know about him?" I said.

"Her, and that's about it, early stages and all. Do have a name. When the police reports come in, should have more," he said.

"You know, my little brother always wanted to be a detective, and he didn't live to see this, this, overdone Hollywood, reject. My sister also wanted to be a classic noir detective.

"I though she wanted to be a ninja?" he said.

"Yea, but how'ya guna make a career out of that?" I said.

Later:

"Anything turn up?" I said.

"Not a lot," he said, "Looked hard into that neighbor. Was a middle aged to senior spinster. Friends at first thought she was ditching, shirking, and ignoring. As she often did. But after no sign of her, whatsoever, for 2 months; they called the police," he said.

"Did you get the report from missing persons?" I said.

"For once, yes, did you grease some wheels?" he said.

"Probably, but not knowingly," I said.

"Well, if you did, thanks. Was very helpful," he said.

"What did you find in it?" I said.

"Well, for starters. They at first thought she had been arrested, maybe got lost in 'the system' and no one could find her. Looked hard for her there. but after nothing came up. They thought some form of kidnapping," he said.

"Kidnapping?" I said.

"Yes, one neighbor remembered seeing her being arrested. But could only give the race and gender of the arresting officers," he said.

"Because it was already 2 months old at the time of the investigation," I said.

"I'm surprised you haven't heard of this case before, maybe before your time, but while you were in court. Internal Affairs also did an internal investigation," he said.

"But nothing turned up," I said.

"Correct. Then they assumed kidnapping," he said.

"And what came up then?" I said.

"Nothing, we've looked everyone back up. Most of her friends were older than her. And many have sense died of natural causes," he said.

"Nothing looked fishy?" I said.

"We'll look into things. But unlikely to find anything 'fishy' as you put it," he said.

"And next of kin knew nothing?" I said.

"Correct. Wasn't close to her family. Friends knew no reason someone would want this to have happen. Even looked around at the Library she worked at. Nothing," he said.

"Maybe this was all about getting something from that library," I said.

"Highly doubtful That university is letting us see what records are left. But probably she saw or knew something she wasn't supposed to," he said.

"You looking back at things that happened in this grater area, and places that she was. Hoping to find something she may have seen?" I said.

"In desperation, yes. But so far looks like a dead end," he said.

"So, one almost perfect crime simply covered another perfect crime. And we have no reason why that crime happened, except whatever it was must've been huge, or connected, or both," I said.

"One last-" he said.

"Wait! What about M.O.?" I said.

"Obscure fact: a kidnapping make to look like an arrest is as common as a murder made to look like suicide or an accident," he said.

"Really, would explain why Internal Affairs found nothing," I said.

"Well, think about it. No one would bat an eye, and the victim would likely cooperate. Unless of course they knew the arresting 'officers'" he said.

"Well, any last clues?" I said.

"Sort of, most witnesses have forgotten or memories have faded. But when the time came that they could declare her dead, the police did assume foul play. They brought in a cold case team. Really they just went over and found the same dead ends, as we are now," he said.

"So, how's it look?" I said.

"Everything is old, and what remains, doesn't indicate anything. Let alone anything as big as it must be," he said.

"Is it even conceivable that they had the wrong person?" I said.

"Well, I'd think the wrong came from the mind of a 6 year old girl, ten years later. But that was ruled out by a Russian assassin," he said, "No, whoever did this is big. Many steps ahead. So far our only hope is someone coming forward, or seeing who cleaned up the one breadcrumb. We really don't even know the motive," he said.

Well, this is a little big, but otherwise normal Internal Affairs work. And no doubt what you've started reading this series for. Well, here you go:

POW!

"Whose locker is this?!?!" he shouted, "Wait, there's a note."

(insert mule picture here)
Houston

"Dear Police, On the outside of the locker it said 'DO NOT OPEN This Means You Police'- love and warmest sarcastic regards- Internal Affairs."

"Oh-" he started.

"HPD-Internal Affairs," I said.

"Wait! This is the jurisdiction of HISD Police! You have no jurisdiction. Nor did you have the right to make a dye pack go off in my face!" he said.

"Tell it to the Judge," I said handcuffing him, "And as for the dye pack, it really does help with convicting you, You have-" I said beginning the reading of the rights.

BANGBANG BANGBANG a meer meer a meer meer-

"You really do hav-" he said.

"Captain Olaf," I said, and handing officer burglar off to a lower officer to complete the arrest.

"Captain, we have a situation here at Juvenile Hall. Hurry," she said.

Later there:

"Ok, what've we got?" I said.

"Oh no! not you again! Hav-" said the warden.

"Shut up," I said.

"Was arrested for shoplifting, arrived dead," said an officer.

"Cause of death?" I said.

"Do I look like a coroner?" she said.

"No, you just smell like one," I said.

"Hey-" she said.

"Medical Examiner! What happened?" I said.

"His heart stopped beating, brain function seas-" said the coroner.

"Yea, yea, yea, why?" I said.

"Why don't you ask me later, but only clue so far is he feels a tad warm," said the coroner.

"You think a bug took him out? Fever?" I said.

"No clue, bu-" said the coroner.

(insert mule picture here)
Houston

"Is that even a teenager?" I said.

"Probably not," said the coroner.

"Well, find anything, call me," I said, then turned and said, "Where's the arresting officer?"

"Over there," said a fellow officer.

"Officer," I said, "What happened?"

"I got a call about trouble, caught him stealing candy from a candy shop," he said.

"Was there any mistakes or errors in the arrest report?" I said.

"Of course not!" he said.

"Anything he said, or anything?" I said.

"Was weird, I don't really remember anything else other than that," he said.

"Yea, don't leave town," I said, then shouted "Where was the arrest made?!?!"

Later there,

"Ms.?" I said, showing my badge.

"Follow up hu?" she said, smacking her gum, "Talk to Victoria. She was there and called you."

"Is she here now?" I said.

"Just in time, her shift ends in one minute," she said, "HEY! VIC!"

"What?" she said, "I was about to talk to you."

"There's someone here to see you, and he's cute," she said.

"Oh!" she said walking out. I showed my badge and she sighed and said "Oh, just a follow up."

"Not exactly, does this face ring a bell," I said showing the boy's picture.

"Yea, he's the thief, didn't want to get a kid arrested, so I didn't call it in till him and his buddy were getting five finger discounts in the triple digits. Don't tell my boss," she said.

"Buddy? Was they here today?" I said.

"Yea, is he ok?" she said.

"The buddy? Can't say, honestly don't know, would you be willing to come in for a statement?" I said.

"No," she said

(insert mule picture here)
Houston

"May I ask why?" I said.

"Can't stop you, but I won't' say," she said.

"O-k, can you at least tell me something about what happened? And about the 'buddy'" I said.

She snapped her fingers and said "You know what! I can do better."

"How so?" I said.

"This is a retail establishment in modern days. We've cameras everywhere," she said.

"Can I get that footage?" I said.

beep beep

"Sorry, ask the manager. My shift ended 1 1/2 seconds ago," she said leaving.

Later with the coroner:

"Got anything?" I said.

"Oh boy do I," said the coroner, "the victim appears to have been high up on-"

"He was using drugs?" I said.

"No, sugar. I'd guess hot candy. Also found 5 different gums in his mouth, none of which were sugar free. Yet, no cavities. And wasn't fat," said the coroner.

"Well, was he a diabetic that had been denied his insulin?" I said.

"Nope, pancreas was fine," she said, "And being donated along with several other organs."

"Well, a silver lining, but how'd he die?" I said.

"A way we almost always see in infants; but sometimes in the very elderly with severe heart problems," she said.

"Well? what was it?" I said.

"A hot car," she said.

"A hot car?!" I said.

"Yea, and then it gets interesting," she said.

"Do tell," I said.

"Body got some time to cool down," she said, "Probably got driven around post mortem,"

"Well, I just got back from a case in which a child died likewise, because no one saved the child after arresting the parent. Who was doing nothing but trying to get them to-" I said.

"I remember, I did the autopsy," she said.

BANGBANG BANGBANG a meer meer a

"Olaf," I said.

"Yea, found some inconsistencies in the arrest report," said my assistant, "Is this a good time?"

"Oh, yea, tell me," I said.

"Well, the arrest happened at 7:14. But he arrived at holding, when he was found dead, at 8:44. Where was he all that time? The GPS tells an interesting story," she said.

"Do tell," I said.

"He drove out of jurisdiction, to tinbuctwo, I've called the local Sheriff. They're looking for what he was doing out there," she said.

"Tell them it's a child," I said.

"A child?" she said.

"Yea, John Doe's friend," I said, "Don't know anything else."

"Got somin!," said the coroner.

"Got to go," I said.

"What've ya got?" I said.

"I didn't' bother to tell you about the scars, because they seemed a little old, but I just Idled the John Doe," she said.

"Bring in next of kin," I said.

BANGBANG BANGBANG a m

"Captain Olaf," I said.

"Got somein big," said an officer under me.

"What is it?" I said.

"Huge," he said.

"Be more specific!" I said.

"Served a warrant on the candy shop's cameras, the victim was guilty as charged. But there was an accomplice. Also the store had audio recorders," he said.

"What happened there?" I said.

"Well, your John Doe-" he said.

"We just IDed him," I said.

"Oh, what's his name?" he said.

"Not important, go on," I said.

"Well, he was going on about 'where were you'-" he said.

"When what?" I said.

"Can't tell, wasn't exactly holding a microphone, but, the cop started a counter guilt trap. So the accomplice called him a dirty word that doesn't need repeating. Got hit in the chest hard. After that the cop arrests your John Doe and orders the clerk to carry the other child to the car, at gunpoint," he said.

"Gun point? That's enough for arrest. Get an arrest warrant. We'll add more charges when we're sure what happened. Also tell my assistant to tell her Sheriff they're looking for an injured or dead child," I said.

"I'm on it," he said hanging up.

Later with the next of kin (big sister):

"In the store, he said something about 'where were you?!' Do you have any idea what he meant by that?" I said.

"Which possibility?" she said.

"How so?" I said.

"When he was 10, bout 2 years back. My brother found out that both my parents were cheating. Meanwhile I had found the perfect guy. I was forced to drop out of school and was guarded around the clock to keep me from running off with him. My other brother, 14, chloroformed them to help me escape. Then separately blackmailed them to give special permission for me to marry," she said.

"Oh," I said, wondering where this was going.

"My brothers stood up for me, and got beaten to a pulp. But my other brother, still 14, was not going quietly into the night. He had priors so no one would believe him-" she said.

"What about Gergor Mendal?" I said.

"The monk?!" she said.

"Nuf said, never mind, please go on," I said.

"He planted drugs on them, and ratted them out to the cops. They didn't get jail time, but said something, can't remember the exact words, but it goes something like this: 'it's us or her'. They both picked me. So they were sent to live with me. After 2 weeks they realized my brothers weren't relenting. So off to Grandma's house. In back water Louisiana. She was horrible. My little brother broke a plate. She beat the live rout of him. Once again, my other brother wouldn't give up. He deliberately knocked over her china case. Broke all her china, and 2 urns. Grandma snapped his neck in a homicidal rage. Got off on some half assed self-defense excuse. But my little brother then had to live with our other grandparents in Boca. And by live with, I mean care for," she said.

"Yow," I said.

"Yea, I found out. They're now in a government home. All that happened in 8, err so, months. My brother," she said.

"Came to live with you?" I said.

"Well, yes-" she said.

"Olaf, got som'n," said an officer.

I stepped out and said "Ok, what've we got?"

"2 things, first. The officer in question just boarded a flight to a non-extraditing country. Second, this was his very first day on the job-" he said.

"And his last if I have anything to say about it," I said, "Call the FAA. Have the Air Marshall arrest him before the plane lands."

"Olaf, the Sheriff called," said my assistant.

"What does he have?" I said.

"She, and they found the body. They'll do an autopsy-" said my assistant.

"Why? we're better?" I said.

"Yea, it's actually being held at a state morge-" said my assistant.

"Why?" I said.

"Was found in a dumpster in a state park, almost got picked up before we found him," said my assistant.

"Any preliminaries?" I said.

(insert mule picture here)
Houston

"Yea, was struck in the chest hard with an unknown object," said my assistant.

"Probably a fist," I said.

"Yea, unreal," said my assistant.

"Whatdaya mean?" I said.

"Recklessly kills an 11 year old, and deliberately kills a 12 year old-" she said.

"No, it was just very careless. He killed a kid in the back of a hot squad car, while he disposed of the body of another. Didn't think anyone would ever listen to the kid. Unfortunately, technically true. If he had meant to kill him. There would have been no arrest report. Nor would we have found the body; or at least no so easily," I said.

You were probably wondering what that warden was babbling on about in the last one, well, here it is:

"Olaf, we've found something," he said.

"I'll be there," I said.

Later at Pinkerton's Texas headquarters in Downtown Houston:

"We were looking into the probable murder of that spinster librarian. Finally found something. There was a student she was seen arguing with 2 days before she vanished. Took some digging, but he was in contact with a fellow student that was running a front for the CIA. He's not cooperating; and we have no way to determine what they were arguing about," he said.

"How'd you find this?" I said.

"Really old security footage, cops just didn't dig that hard," he said.

"Any way to contact the informant?" I said.

"You kidding? Have a better chance of going to Dallas and finding the second shooter," he said.

"What do we know about Mr. 'will not cooperate'?" I said.

"Doesn't seem to be a spy, but, you know what they say 'the thinner the file'" he said.

"Learn all you can, and look into CIA activity on campus, especially in the school library," I said.

"Already are," he said.

"Do we have current whereabouts?" I said.

"That we do, might even recognize the name," he said.

"How so?" I said.

(insert mule picture here)
Houston

"He's the, well, can't remember the pinkie out, drinking tea, title. But really he's warden of Juvenile Hall, here in town," he said.

"Figures," I said, "Can't ethically do anything official. But I still have my P.I.'s license-" I said.

"You have a private investigator's license? Sense when?" he said.

"While back got booted off a case. Wouldn't give up easily. Only problem is Dr. Jekyll and Mr. Hyde," I said.

"Whatdaya mean?" he said.

"I'm a clean cop; but not a very clean P.I. And I have a plan, let me just renew and then we'll get some answers," I said.

"What's your plan?" he said.

"Need to know, just meet me there, with at least a dozen other guys, at 11 pm, tomorrow evening," I said.

Later there:

"Hi, Private Investigator Olaf," I said, "Open up."

"What now?" said the clerk.

"I said open up, I'm going to look around throughout the facility. You have no reasonable expectation of piracy," I said.

"Do you have a warrant?" he said.

"I have what I call a P.I.'s warrant. I'm not here as a cop," I said.

"And just what is that?" she said.

"This building is owned by the Texas State Department of Corrections. I told them that we were investigating the premeditated murders 3 minors, 2 being young children. And it wouldn't look good if a tie was found to them. So to look good, they gave me written permission to come in and snoop to my heart's content," I said, handing them the 'P.I.'s warrant'.

"You're investigating the murder of your siblings?" she said, "I thought you went into the Ninja layer of a bedroom they shared, and grabbed a weapon, and you killed the-" he said.

"YOU! Don't Get To Say That!" I nearly shouted, shoving my face into his.

"You, need to back," he said poking me.

"HA! You assaulted me! Citizen's arrest!" I said handcuffing him, and pushing release buttons.

(insert mule picture here)
Houston

"Now, a riot will ensue, If a guard touches an inmate; arrest them. I'm sure they will happily press misdemeanor assault charges. Don't worry, I've done this before at alternative schools. How do you think that I got rid of those pesky metal detectors that kept kids from wearing a wire to school to prove what was really going on," I said.

"We're not cops-" he said.

"Citizen's arrest," I said, "I'm a very clean cop, but not such a clean P.I." I said.

"This is unethical even you ad-" he said.

"Look at this, what do you see?" I said.

"Your, Policeman's badge?" he said.

"And what does it say?" I said.

"Houston Police department-" he said.

"And?" I said.

"And it has your name," he said.

"And?" I said.

"Internal, Affairs?" he said.

"And what else, and look very, very closely," he said.

"The manufacturer was-" he said.

"No the back, no. It says 'Get in that madhouse prison and find my siblings' killer(s) before I find dirt on all you, and there is dirt on everyone, and hand this over to a very dirty P.I.!'" I said.

Later:

"What're you doing! I know you're always hunting, like the wild ravonus dog that needs to be put down that you are, for dirty cops, especially in Juvenile-" he said.

"True, all true. But do you know why I'm here today? Hint: I'm Private Investigator Call Letter, not Captain Call Letter," I said.

"I don't know!" he said, "Sturring up trouble and helping prison escapees?" he said.

"Well that too, but I could just flash my Internal Affairs badge and have all your guards shoved in the back of the patty wagon. And I will not supply cops to guard this place-" I said.

"The charges will never stick!" he said.

(insert mule picture here)
Houston

"True, I don't need them to," I said, "But you have a way out, tell me what I want to know!"

"You know, you're just like your silly sister-in-law. Digging around where you don't belong. Making trouble for everyone else, and calling it your duty-" he said.

I hissed and shouted while getting in his face "TELL ME WHAT I WANT TO KNOW!!!!!!!!!!"

"You, need to take a chill pill," he said pushing me back.

"Allergic, and, while off duty, you just assaulted an officer. But everything that happened tonight can just go away," I said.

"Fine, but you have to promise to leave and never even come back," he said.

"I won't promise not to come back, in fact I inevitably will. But before you respond I should remind you that there have been some real goof ups in booking in the past. Seems like yesterday a Juvenile Warden was put in Juvenile Hall, his Juvenile Hall. Was like seeing an invalid feed to rabid wolves, oh, wait, that hasn't happened. But, who knows, maybe someday. Right about now your inmates seem as mad as rabid dogs," I said.

"It's classified," he said.

"I'm sure it is, start talking," I said.

"I just fought with her about overdue book fines! I'm sure there's a record of that!" he said.

"And where does the CIA come in?" I said.

"What courses I took, the whole class they tried to recruit, not that they said who they were," he said.

"And the recruiters?" I said.

"I'm sure everything was a cover story with a backup cover story," he said, "I do have an apartment number, but that's it."

"And the other would have been recruits?" I said.

"I can give you their names, haven't heard from any of them in years, honest," he said.

"We'll need all that information, or Intel, along with anything else you know," I said.

"I heard about the arrest you made yesterday, do you think the charges will stick?" he said.

"Open and shut, and it was the Air Marshall that arrested him," I said.

"I've heard of rookie foul-ups, but must be the biggest example of one ever!" he said.

"Yea, yea, yea, what've ya got?" I said.

(insert mule picture here)
Houston

"Talked to everyone from that incident," he said, "No one knew anything relevant," he said.

"Do you believe them?" I said.

"They aren't CIA, just normal people that tripped over it," he said.

"So, got anything?" I said.

"Sort of," he said, "As you may remember-"

"I remember everything relevant," I said.

"Yes, well, our Librarian. There was no crime scene. First the landlord threw the stuff out to the curb. And what the thieves didn't steal, the city ordered thrown away. Then the cops got involved," he said.

"Yes, a real dead end for us, isn't it," I said.

"True, but I believe we've found the breadcrumb," he said.

"Do tell," I said.

"We've gotten a book," he said, whoever is behind this, missed it.

"What does the book tell us?" I said.

"It was found in a secret compartment of the apartment, missed until the current residents stumbled across it. Literally-" he said.

"What does the cubby tell us?" I said.

"We've swept it, all it tells us was that she wanted to keep that book secret, no real James Bond spy stuff," he said.

"What about the book?" I said.

"We can tell by who had it and what it is, is that it came to her library when the library inherited a super-rich guy's book collection. It must have been a goof that it even went to the library. No record of it, and she went through those books, logging them in, tells us she swiped it," he said.

"What is it? How'd you get it? Any forensic evidence-" I said.

"Whoa! One at a time. It's a diary of his. They tried to sell it online. We found out and were able to get it. We're looking into the bidders, all seem to be real book collectors, but could be a great cover. But one bidder was a shell corp," he said.

"Sounds like-" I said.

"Too easy, also seems unlikely that we could outbid whoever is behind this, don't worry. You're not bankrupt," he said.

(insert mule picture here)
Houston

"Wasn't thinking of it," I said.

"As for forensic science, nothing," he said.

"Anything else?" I said.

"Yea, 2 days are missing. During which the deceased rich guy was in Dubai closing a seemingly up and up business deal. He was a big international oil tycoon," he said.

"In-ter-nation-al," I said.

"Exactly," he said, "agents in the area are talking to those linked to the deal in any way, though probably coincidental, might have been told something.

"Well, sounds like fresh leads. Call me when you find anything," I said.

Later:

"All book buyers were legit, but the shell corp was owned by another shell corp, that was owned by another shell corp, that was owned by another shell corp, that was owned by another shell corp, that was owned by another shell corp, that was owned by another shell corp, that was owned by another shell corp, but that Shell corp, someone in business registry goofed up, the shell corp that owned the bidder shell corp, also owned that shell corp," he said.

"Thus, no owner," I said, maybe corruption in registry,.

"Nope, those kinds of things are easy to make happen with enough dirty paralegals. But have found who was behind all that secret silliness," he said.

"Who is it made to look like?" I said.

"Was the home I.P. of a teck addict. Made to look like he had a bad breakup and killed himself. Ex confirmed the breakup-" he said.

"But they left a crumb," I said.

"Exactly, cops and family let us sweep the scene-" he said.

"We finally have a crime scene. First was ruined by the cops, second left nothing, third was inantvertantly destroyed. Do. Not. Let.-" I said.

"We're guarding the evidence," he said, "Worry not."

Later:

"Was carried out by this kid," he said, "As you can see was pretty dangerous. Surprised he has not yet been tried as an adult-" he said.

"#ThankGod," I said.

"But, he doesn't seem like he would ever be recruited to be a part of anything near this big," he said, "Probably trying to trick us somehow."

"Are you sure the forensic scientists are right?" I said.

"Yes," he said, "Whatdaya say?"

"I say that's he's the breadcrumb. Let's see where he leads," I said.

"We need to call the police," he said.

"Yea, any way I can get you to procrastinate? At least see where he leads us first," I said.

"No,-" he said.

"Well then, lets at least make sure nothing happens to him, you dig around, see what you can learn about him, and what his link could be," I said.

Later:

"I am advising my client not to talk," said the public defense attorney.

"Well then, you can just listen to me talk," I said.

"Don't say anything," he said.

"Look, we know your past, and I see no reason to believe that you didn't to those things. But I am like a ravenous dog, no, no, don't get scared. I know you were the one that pulled the trigger, literally. But what I want to know is why. We know your M.O. has nothing to do with this. He died not because of a breakup, as the note said, but because he was connected to something bigger than either of us can imagine. Now I don't know what that is, I'd be shocked if you did either. But I do know, that the best thing that could happen to you, even with me in your corner-" I said.

"Why would you be in my corner?" he said.

"Stop talking," said the lawyer.

"Because, besides your my breadcrumb, I went to jail when I was years younger than you, and you're not even old enough to drive-" I said.

"Actually, being fifteen, he could obtain a learner's permit," said the lawyer.

"And how does that help anyone at this table counselor?" I said, " I know that this, without help, can and will bring you down for good"

"How old?" he said.

(insert mule picture here)
Houston

"Stop talking," said the lawyer.

"Oh shut up! You waste of-" he said, "I shouldn't say.

"10 and 11- you're trying to be a better man, but it's not easy," I said.

"How'd you know?" he said.

"Between your priors, and how you fussed at your lawyer, what other logical explanation is there?" I said.

"What do you want?" he said.

"See these kids?" I said, "I know you're a big brother from looking into you."

"Y-es?" he said getting nervous.

"They were my siblings, obviously adopted, but just as much family anyway. They were murdered. I was the middle child that was framed by cops that couldn't crack it. For reasons that don't need exploration, whoever was behind that murder, is also who killed them, it's long and so convoluted even I can't believe it. But I do need a lead, give me that and I will do all in my power to get your parole reinstated as was before," I said.

"Why should my client believe any of this?" said the lawyer.

"Because the most logical explanation is that he was forced into it. See this badge?" I said, showing my badge.

"Internal Affairs? What does tha-" he said.

"Long story, but without something, this is open and shut. I see nothing suggesting a contract kill. But you're my only lead to who blackmailed you, and also time is of the essence," I said, "You're the only lead left, the one you allegedly killed, nothing has turned up."

"Sounds to me like you don't even know how to lie," said the lawyer.

I told them that I didn't lie, and I told the story of why.

"Would you be willing to take a lie detector test?" said the lawyer.

"I wouldn't run a lie detector test, it's a century old piece of psytoscience," I said.

"No, I meant you officer-" he said.

"Captain," I said.

"Captain," he said.

Houston

"And same answer, and by the way, it only detects nervousness, talking about this will make me nervous, but I can provide hard evidence of what I'm saying," he said.

Later after they reviewed that evidence and believed it:

"I blame my problems on the fact that I never had a dad, no matter what they say. When I heard from in jail that mom had had another daughter, I decided that would be a new leaf. I'm going to be that figure for her, and my other brothers and sisters. I'm determined that my siblings- technically half siblings, don't go accusing me of lying, will not meet the same fate," he said.

"Sounds like you're a good brother, I'll do what I can, bu-" I said.

"I'm not perfect-" he said.

"No one is," I said, "But what do-"

"This must all be hypothetical," said the lawyer.

"But true," I said.

"Hypothetical doesn't have to be true," said the lawyer.

"Yea, but this time it needs to be," I said.

"It doesn't have to be," said the lawyer.

"True, it doesn't have to be, it just needs to be," I said.

The lawyer just looked to his client, who would have talked anyway.

"I got this weird call from my parole officer," he said.

"What kind of weird?" I said.

"They changed the parole officer, and I didn't get forewarned, but caller ID confirmed it so I believed," he said.

"What can you tell about this call?" I said.

"Said that I had-" he said.

"Your parole officer made you do it?" I said.

"Wouldn't have done it just for me, but said something I can't even remember what, about my baby sister getting to be my age," he said.

"And for good measure, what else can you tell me?" I said.

"Told me how to do it," he said.

(insert mule picture here)
Houston

"And how'd you get in? And the DA really will want to know who sold you the gun," I said.

"The key and the gun I was told to go to different points, there I found them," he said.

"You still have the key?" I said.

"Threw it off the COSWAY Bridge into Galveston," he said.

Later as Pinkerton:

"Those drop off points were dead ends," he said.

"And the call?" I said.

"Was spoofed, and very well" he said.

"Who?" I said.

"Same guy that did the shell corps," he said, "probably didn't realize was writing up his own death warrant. No doubt was promised unlimited cash, and it went south, while he got asleep at the wheel, or was never willing all along."

"Oh, and I guess the actual phon-" I said.

"WRONG!" he said, "Was an untraceable burner, until now."

"What did you get?" I said.

"Was not seen on camera buying the airtime card, or at the pay phone where it was activated-" he said.

"Any forensic evidence?" I said.

"Target's far too busy, and the cameras were on the fritz," he said.

"That can't be a coincidence, what did that turn up?" I said.

"That Target can take 18 or more months to get a security feed recorder up and running again," he said, "Probably dumb luck by the looks of it, maybe some one knew-"

"You looking for the how? Or some snitch employee that knew" I said.

"Yea, but by the looks of the other clues, it appears to be dumb luck," he said.

"What are they?" I said.

"Well, first card and phone were-" he said.

"What about the phone?" I said.

(insert mule picture here)
Houston

"Is used by far too many drunks to get a ride to be of any help," he said, "But both the card and phone were bought with the same gift card credit card," he said.

"Any cameras?" I said.

"Yes, and I'll circle back to that in a minute," he said.

"What about where-" I said.

"The gift card credit card was bought," he said, "cameras, same as the phone store," he said, "Was charged to the credit card of an Eustace John Charleston."

"Let's giv-" I said.

"Hold on, he is in memory care, unable to speak," he said.

"Oh! Come! On!" I said.

"Hold on, the card was stolen by a random addict ID thief." He said, "We actually investigated, and busted her."

"And new clews?" I said.

"Actually yes, in a plea deal, she ratted out everyone that she had worked with illegally, a great, but somewhat dangerous, deal for her. A breakthrough for us," he said.

"How so?" I said.

"We cross referenced the security footage with that list of suspects sent in by N.O.P.D.," he said.

"N.O.P.D.?" I said.

"New Orleans," he said, "We got a killer for the first time."

"REALLY!" I said, I've waited so long.

"Don't get excited, it's a John Doe, saying nothing at all. Pled guilty, and we can't find any past for him," he said.

"What do you know about him?" I said.

"Probably from modern day dark Africa, and no past," he said.

"Let's accuse him of killing the computer geek, see how he reacts," I said.

3 days later:

"He pled guilty, he's a no body. He's dedicated to whatever this is, and a dead end-" he said.

(insert mule picture here)
Houston

"So, all this for want?" I said.

"No, our agents in Dubai investigated what those missing pages may have been. Nothing fishy or out of the ordinary about the business deal, except he decided that 4 blocks was a short walk. Took a wrong turn, and ended up taking 3 1/2 hours to get to his hotel room," he said.

"And you think, what?" I said.

"Police found a pool of blood in that general area of the city. Looked like a double homicide, nothing else known, except the one person, that didn't seem random, that was seen by what few witnesses there were, met the tycoon's description. Was a back alley, so not a lot of people out on an evening stroll. But there is samples from the scene for us to analyze, to them we're free help." he said

"So, the corrections officer has been charged with disorderly conduct," said my assistant.

"Good, usually can't get them charged for yelling and being aggressive, and sometimes mildly threatening, to a suspect," I said

"You know, they should really call you Captain Spitfire," said my assistant.

"I think they do, they just not to my fac-" I said, "Umm, I think this bank is about to be robbed my cops."

"That's absur-" said my assistant.

"GET ON THE GROUND GET ON THE FLOOR HANDS WHERE I CAN SEE UM!!!!" shouted a robber.

"I was right," I said.

We all went down to the floor but they did not react as I was expected having been in uniform at the time. Many would expect that these to have been fake cops, so I would have. But quickly recognized each one individually. Each one I was currently in the process of busting. We were all pushed into the same room.

"Hey, well, we're probably going to be here a while, let's all get acquainted," said the bank manager.

"Who put you in charge?" said a customer.

"Well, I'm the manager, so-" he said.

"Yea! And look where it's gotten ya," she replied.

"This isn't a bank robbery," I said.

"Oh yea, then what is it smart guy?" she said to me.

"Look, don't you think it's a little weird that they don't have masks?" I said.

"Probably just so they could get in at all," she replied.

"Yea, and they didn't react to there being a cop in the bank?" I said.

"There are also guards, probably just planned ahead just in case," said the manager.

"And isn't a little weird that all the robbers are cops?" I said.

"You really think that they're cops?" she said.

"I don't think, I know," I said.

"You're insane? Are you really a cop?" said a 3rd person.

"Yes, and I know who the robbers are," I said.

"Oh! So they're you're buddies! Are you in on it?" said a child.

"No, in fact the opposite is true. I'm, as you can see by my badge," I said showing it around, "Internal Affairs. And I know them because each one of them I'm actively busting."

"Oh really," said a 4th person.

"Really, the woman is out on bail for a severe accident she caused while driving drunk, on duty. The Sheriff I've been trying to get to clean up his department like I've been cleaning mine for the longest time. One man had taken up embezzlement in his spare time. And the 4th took a bribe to help in a failed holding escape," I said.

"So, if all that's true. Why are they then robbing a bank? Pay for defense?" said the 4th person.

"Well, my enemies, robbing a bank, while I'm here? I think it boils down to me," I said.

"How so?" said the 3rd person.

"Well, if they killed me when they first came in, they would know it. If now, then they would have too many witnesses. Not likely they'd be willing to kill all of you," I said.

"So, then what?" said a 5th person.

"Well, there are no guards here, manager, what do you know?" I said.

"Well, I saw the lady cop distracting one guard away," he said.

"And bill and Frank were led into my office by the plaincloseman," said the loan officer.

"That only left one!" said the manager.

"And we all saw him get tazed, using the element of surprise," said I.

"What do you think happened to them?" said the manager.

"Probably not brazen enough to kill them," I said, "Probably tied up and tazed in a closet."

"Like us?" said the child.

"Not exactly, but same train of thought," I said.

"So?" if this is about you? How? And now what?" said the 1st person.

"I'm not sure, but I'm sure they're going to make it look like it went south. Cameras, so they can't make me disappear, and no logical way to make it look like an accident, or something other than murder," I said.

"How?" said the 2nt person.

"Not sure, but I must admit that it doesn't all add up," I said.

"No kidding Sherlock," said the 5th person.

"No, no, let's brainstorm. How are they doing this? How did they know I would be here?" I said.

"How will solving your murder help us?" said a 6th person.

"The more you know about an enemy, the better," I said.

"Ok, maybe it's an international superplot!" said the child.

"You know, that is a good theory," I said.

"Ok! Officer-" said a 7th person.

"Captain," I said.

"Captain," he restated, "Looney has officially gone crackers! Are you really even a cop?!?!"

"Yes, and I'll explain. Over a decade ago, my siblings were murdered. I'll save you the long and convoluted-" I said.

"No kidding," said the 5th person.

"And I've been investigating it. I've just started getting close. They must have put these officers up to this," I said.

Just then we heard shots fired, and a different officer burst in. Everyone freaked and put their hands in the air. One handed me over.

"Don't worry, he's cool. Whoever he is," I said.

"Everybody ok?" he said.

"Yea, what bout out there?" I said.

"Shot 2, other 2 surrendered," he said.

"Or escaping now," I said.

"Oh-" he said rushing out.

"Rookie," I said to everyone else.

Later at Pinkerton:

"I was surprised to hear the final results of your investigation into Justice-" he said.

"It's just Pinkerton, I mean Crayer. He doesn't deserve that title," I said.

"C-rayer," he said, "As well as those officers. You sure that these are all coincidences?"

"Yea," I said, "What're the odds?!"

"Yea, maybe Crayer is our breadcrumb," he said.

"Nope, looked hard. No clue who's bribing him," I said.

"And the cops-" he said.

"Pure coincide," I said.

"Oh, the Texas state troopers are looking for the County Sheriff. As for the plaincloseman. Caught 39 blocks away. Trying to buy a bus ticket to Maine. The DWI officer is in Ben Taub, and the 4th robber is dead," he said.

"Any leads?" I said.

"Yes, plaincloseman took a plee deal when a second offence was presented," he said.

"There was a whole nother crime?" I said.

"Yea, their guns were used in a truck robbery in which a guard was killed," he said, "But the Sheriff wasn't there for that."

"They robbed an armored car?" I said.

"That's where the bad news comes in," he said.

"Dubai," I said.

"Fraid so," he said, "Lost the evidence right after it was loaded up at Hobby airport."

"Can we get more? It was a large pool of blood?" I said.

(insert mule picture here)
Houston

"Fraid not," he said, "Disappeared right out of the police's storage."

"Any leads there?" I said.

"They rightfully expected no internal investigation. We'll call you if anything turns up," he said.

"And I'll call if the police get any robbery leads-" I said.

"Beat you to it," he said, "And you won't like the leads."

"Well, everyone on the force hates me. So, that's no real shock." I said.

"Someone got them to do all that they did, said all their problems would go away, also was blackmail applied at least to the Sheriff," he said.

"What form?" I said.

"He's a dad. Found he got weird pictures of his own kids, probably more will turn up," he said.

"And any other leads?" I said.

"Yes, we know who was behind it, it is a great cover story," he said.

"How so?" I said.

"It's your boss, the police commissioner," he said.

"Well, I've arrested him for impeding my investigations multiple times, he tried to order me to back down or off a case. For obvious reasons, he's been acquitted every time," I said.

"Yea, someone told him exactly what to do and how," he said.

"Guess I get to arrest him, again," I said.

"You've been beaten to it," he said, "And we know motive."

"Which is? And any leads?" I said.

"Got pictures of him with several of his mistresses," he said, "But no crumbs as to how."

"RATS! Guess they're getting better!" I said.

You probably thought that the pilot was my only success against prosecuting as an adult. Wrong! I did make other attempts besides that. This was my largest.

Gu-grunk!

"What was that?" said a man.

"I think we're stuck," said a woman.

(insert mule picture here)
Houston

"So, we're locked in?" said a little girl.

"Just like your brother," said an older boy.

"Wadaya'll mean?" I said.

"Frank, find the call phone, I'll deal with this meddler," said the woman.

"I'm no meddler, I'm a cop," I said.

"Cops!" said the little girl.

"What happened?" I said.

"My sister in law was murdered," said the woman.

"To protect me," said the child.

"Oh Hush Up Child!" she said.

"What happened?" I said.

"My sister in law was killed by her ungrateful son," she said, "Fortunately there was justice. Unfortunately my nephew has filled her head with lies."

"I believe him auntie," she said.

"I want to hear the lies," I said.

"Why?" she said.

"The truth can be covert," I said.

"She was awful-" said the man.

"She Did Not 'Emotionally Abuse' you as a child," said the woman.

"I'm Internal Affairs, what happened?" I said.

"They were the normal family," said the woman.

"Except for-" said the child.

"That's all lies," said the woman.

"One day his big sister was overwhelmed. She could take it no longer-" said the girl.

"She was spoiled and selfish," said the woman.

"What happened?" I said.

"She slit her wrists," she said.

"My sister didn't deserve to die," said the girl.

"And where did you hear this side of the story?" I said.

"From her big brother," she said.

"From jail," I said.

"No, that's the adult brother," said the brother.

"Oh," I said.

"Then what?" I said.

"They protected each other and my big, their little, brother," said the girl.

"They conspired against her," said the woman.

"And the dad, who was part of the 'conspiracy' was killed," said the girl.

"It was his fault, and he killed himself out of guilt," said the woman.

"That's what it was made to look like," said the girl.

"Then what happened?" I said.

"Was too much, wanted revenge and safety, but most of all wanted to protect my brother and me," she said.

"He killed her," I said.

"Tried to make it look like she did what his sister did," she said.

"How old was he?" I said.

"When his sister died, she was 16 and he was 13. When I was born he was 14. Not yet born, and he was already loving me, suffering so much for me," she said. He suffered so as to wait for me to be born for my safety.

"He was a self centered-" said the woman.

"Hello? We're stuck," said the man.

I didn't know what was and was not true, but I knew what I had to do.

Later with that judge:

"Why did you bring me in?" he said.

(insert mule picture here)
Houston

"Harvey-" I said.

"Justice Harvey," he said.

"No, it's just Harvey," I said, "Now; you declined a lawyer, right."

"Yes, however I'm beginning to wonder if it was a mistake," he said.

"Oh, it was, does this face ring a bell?" I said.

"Yea, killed his mom," he said.

"Well, I just finished talking to him, and his living siblings. And the prosecutors in that case. Prosecutors fear me. They said-" I said.

"What is this just about? Some brib-" he said.

"YOU! Don't get to say that," I said trying to hold it in.

"First amendment says-" he said.

"First amendment isn't about to arrest you," I said.

"On What Grounds?!?!" he said.

"What you did was evil," I said.

"That's absurd, you're working for that crazy lawyer, Michael W. Sackett!" he said.

Yes, that Michael W. Sackett who was a juvenile defense attorney. This was one of his very, very few failures. And I later learned the damage that it did to him

"Well, he's a personal friend, but if I'm working for anyone, it's it 4 year old sister," I said.

"So, you're working for a toddler," he said.

"Well, technically at 3 they're no longer a toddler, and she's going on 5, her big brother just turned 9," I said.

"Not really helping," he said.

"He's been locked up long enough," I said.

"You want me to release him? How?" he said.

"I don't care, but if I do indebt you, he'll get an appeal, and the prosecution's case will be dead on arrival," I said.

"Indebt?! On what charges?!" he said.

"Child cruelty," I said.

"And on what made up-" he said.

"The case here at hand," I said.

"What?! You'll never get a conviction!" he said.

"Don't need one," I said, "Think about what that case would do to your career."

"If I let you," he said.

"I'll get more powerful now or later," Then becoming a little lighter, but only momentary I said, "You know, I think that's the name of a candy," I said.

"How are you even going to get this into court?!?! Scare them into getting your way?!" he said.

"Don't need to, the prosecutors, they-" I said.

"So you wouldn't charge them. You made the-" he said.

"More like a plea bargain," I said, "And just these charges applying to this case. Your choice. And I'll settle for just Juvenile court."

Later:

Miss Samantha Maxamillion?" I said.

"It's Ms., but yes- You, you're the elevator cop," she said.

"I, I guess I am," I said.

"How'd you get in here?" she said.

"Your mother," I said, "Whatcha doing?"

"You mean my aunt?" she said.

"Yea," I said, "Looks like Hello Kitty."

"Yea, traditional, she's just 'pink ponies' if you know what I mean," she said.

"Yea," I said, "I do."

"In this day in time, no one is interested in that, even a girl my age," she said.

"So?" I said.

"So I'm making her a detective that sometimes works for the cops, but not always," she said.

"So, she's like a consultant?" I said.

"If that's what that means," she said.

"I come bringing good news," I said.

"What kind of good news?" she said.

"News you've been waiting for since the day you were born," I said, "Literally."

"What's that?" she said.

"See for yourself," I said.

"BRO!" she said, seeing him.

"Oh! I haven't been able to hold you since the day you were born!" he said.

Tearing up she said "Thank you!"

Don't think that was my only success against prosecuting as an adult, it wasn't. But I was in that elevator going to Pinkerton (other people were not; wasn't the only thing in that building), there's the information from that trip, and the results. Next one I'll tell you another success I've had.

"Olaf," he said.

"Yea, I presume our 'outside / internal investigation' In Dubai turned up dead ends," I said.

"Actually, No!" he said.

"What did you find?" I said.

"Well, was stolen by two men who blended into the cop crowd like a charm, one we have no clue who he is, but the other," he said.

"Oh! What about our John Doe in the big easy?" I said.

"No bail, total dead end, whoever is behind this, he's loyal to, probably not organized crime," he said.

"Oh," I said, "No other leads on that front?"

"Fraid not, but Dubai is a lead," he said.

"Do tell," I said.

"Well, the other guy, was an American tourist," he said.

"What do we know about him?" I said.

"A random oil worker, bachelor, only child-" he said.

(insert mule picture here)
Houston

"Always?" I said.

"Yes, moved to America as a child, became a citizen 11 months back, nothing that says 'criminal'" he said.

"Look in harder," I said.

Later:

"His fiancé' appears to have disappeared right before he made the trip to Dubai," he said.

"Details?" I said.

"No clues to disappearance, no trace, no reason. Till now," he said.

"How so?" I said.

"He walked into Mall of America, fired a shot into the floor, said, or more shouted, 'I WAS MURDERED' and shot himself dead!" he said.

"Now that sound's fishy 6 ways to Sunday," I said.

"Local Police are calling it suicide," he said.

"Any other leads?" I said.

"Yea, IDed the other man. Was a Londoner, so took harder to ID," he said.

"Any other clues?" I said.

"We'll let you know WHEN they come in," he said.

Later:

"So? What's new?" I said.

"The Englishman, his parents disappeared under the same circumstances-" he said.

"Siblings?" I said.

"Only Child," he said, "Exact same circumstances, except we have no further breadcrumbs."

"And our Alaskan Oil Worker?" I said.

"Was in contact with 3 mysterious burner phones," he said, "Wouldn't pick up, so they had to text."

"And we know everything they said," I said.

"Yea, but that's not where the real lead lies," he said.

(insert mule picture here)
Houston

"Where is the real lead?" I said.

"The phones were stolen," he said.

"Victims?" I said.

"San Francisco police calling it muggings gone wrong," he said.

"And any leads?" I said.

"Yes," he said, "While the area the calls and texts originated from were too needle in a haystack-"

"Fiancé?" I said.

"Without a trace," he said, "But, there is a clue."

"What's that?" I said.

"The gun used on all three, was from a cop that was knocked out and robbed, in LA," he said.

"And who did that?" I said.

"The man is being held on $500,000 bail, and a known felon-" he said.

"WAIT! I just remembered, what about that bank robbery? Surly must have leads on that by NOW!" I said.

"Our first red herring, was the teachers' union," he said.

"THE TEAHCER'S UNION?!?!" I said.

"Yea, you made some arrests for, let me see. Ah! Yes! Reckless manslaughter; blackmail, criminal negligence and truancy" he said; "Say, I know the first three, they put students whose parents refused medication for Attention Deficit Disorder in "alternative" schools.-" he said.

"Yea, for some it was unsafe; and one died. They have been convicted. So the teachers' union set it all up?" I said.

"Fraid so, but what I don't understand is the truancy part?" he said.

"They suspend and expel; meanwhile under all other circumstances those students would be required to attend school. But they weren't. However it was the school district's fault. Now a few days, if it was a student and they'd had a beef I'd merely tell them very specifically where they could place that beef. As such in those cases, I let it go if it was brief. But in longer cases;-" I said.

"Yeah, what I don't get is how not being able to be forced to be subjected to compulsory education for hours is punishment to a normal child?" he said.

"I agree; but what about the felon?" I said.

(insert mule picture here)
Houston

"Oh! We're talking to local authorities, seeing about a plea bargain that'll make him talk," he said.

Later:

"He told us he dropped it off spy style at this Subway station, spy style," he said.

"And the Los Angeleans have cameras out the wazoo," I said.

"And back in said wazoo, was another known but acquitted mugger who picked it up," he said.

"And where does he take us?" I said.

"To a chalk outline; was killed," he said.

"What happened?" I said.

"Must've been in on it, not sure how he was communicating, but was," he said.

"What's your best guess as to the how?" I asked.

"Don't need one, got somin' better, " he said.

"What's that?" I said.

"A hidden camera," he said, "Cops really knocked one out of the park, got THE killer, I do believe. Just a really good canvas."

"Who is he?" I said.

"John Doe, no past, no nothing, was caught boarding a flight under a well stolen identity," he said.

Let's talk to him.

"So, it was you," I said.

"Allegedly," he said.

"Did some digging, you're with the CIA, the Feds fried, I mean tried to make this all go away. But they'd have to come out of the shadows to do so," I said.

"Why would the CIA, assuming I am guilty, want to mug and kill San Franciscans?" he said.

"To get their phones, to use to call and blackmail the fiancé of an Alaskan who they kidnapped, to blackmail him," I said.

"For what?" I said.

"To work with an Englishman who never went out into the world, or mature past 14 really, to make evidence in Dubai disappear, and then themselves. While you put the kidnapping victims at the bottom of the Marianis trench, or a cremator, or or or," I said.

"Yea, and little green policeman have been secretly running the government from the basement of the pentagon," he said.

"With a little help from Kennedy, Elvis, and Jimmy Hoffa," I added, "I don't know who or why you killed in Dubai at the beginning, but it all comes back to you. What's this about?"

"A much needed hit, but they hired a snook, then they needed someone-" he said.

"To clean it up," I said.

"Look, covers will be blown to China and back if you don't release me," he said.

"These 2 kids ring a bell?" I said showing a picture of my brother and sister.

"No," who are they?

"You know who, I've finally cracked the case. I know the one honest thing the cops said was that they tried to protect each other, and they couldn't scream," I said.

"What does this have to do with anything? Or you for that matter?" he said.

"Let me give you a hint," I said showing another picture.

"Your little brother's friends? One's too young, and the other is a girl," he said.

"This picture was taken on my 10th birthday. Ever since then I've hated my birthday, and kid's birthday parties in general. To this day, that is my most recent birthday celebration," I said.

"I know about the cops and Crayer, they were honest cops," he said.

"They Framed Me!" I said, "And the hell hole-"

"Crayer was a coincidence, but the jail, couldn't blow cover to expose it. And the cops understood the importance of covering for the company," he said.

"And now I'll investigate and charge them. You know who and what I am, and we both know that. How did they really react?" I said.

"I didn't confess!" he said.

"Yea you did, a librarian stumbled across the wrong thing from the wrong person who was in the wrong place at the wrong time," I said.

"She was going to publish!" he said.

(insert mule picture here)
Houston

"And then you had one loud mouth witness, you couldn't even keep quiet with death!" I said.

"You just don't know what it's like in the intelligence community!" he said, "I'm a good guy!"

"You aren't being held here in California," I said.

"So, you're releasing me?" he said.

"No, in Texas, we can kill you back. Albeit after 20 years," I said, "But I want everyone else, more than I want the needle for you. Which I was expecting!" I said.

"Everyone's dead, I operate outside-" he said.

"And the company allowed it," I said.

"The less you know, the less you can squeal," he said, "Even if you're a director."

Later back in Houston:

"You think we'll be able to nail anyone else in this case?" asked the Pinkerton man.

"I know no. In fact even I'm not certain beyond a reasonable doubt that the company is guilty, of any particular crime. It either is guilty, looked the other way, or at the very least criminally negligent, " I said, "But, I know we'll never know which one. But the heart of it has been taken out, so. At least there will be shockwaves in the intelligence community. "

Here's another promised success against prosecuting as an adult, from my days in suicide.

"John Doe?" I said.

"Nope," said the medical examiner.

"Think he fell?" I said.

"No," said my partner, witnesses say that he climbed over the railing, shouted a warning to those below, and then went right for the ice."

"Think he was trying to make a show of it?" I said.

"You think it was forced?" said my partner.

"Well, it's weird, and he looks like he's been in some nasty fight," I said.

"FOUND IT!" said the coroner.

"Why or where he jumped onto a skating rink to his death at the Galleria?" I said.

"From where, no, why, yes," said the coroner.

(insert mule picture here)
Houston

"What happened?" I said.

"Said that he missed her, and didn't do it," said the coroner, "Maybe family can explain it. Probably was wanted."

Later there:

"Sir, I have some bad news, is Mr-" I said.

"Let guess, my son died," he said.

"You've already heard?" I said, "I assume you called the police."

"He left his sister a note to 'open when she's old enough.' Hey, when everyone involved is out on bail, you don't call the fuzz," he said.

"Bail?" I said.

"Yes, bail," he said.

"That explains it," I said, "Would you be willing to com-"

"No, he can stay a John Doe for all I care," he said.

"Oh, what happened? Or should I not pry?" I said.

"Whatever!" he said, "Get lost!"

"O-k" I said.

Later:

"Captain, somin's going or gone on. I'm not doubting the cause of death but this calls for investigating," I said.

"Olaf, I can't can you. But I hope you aren't about to do anything stupid-" he said.

"Define stupid," I said.

"Just keep your nose clean," he said.

"As I sometimes say, crime is not in my M.O." I said.

"Get out of my office and back to work!" he said.

Later at the morgue:

"Coroner-" I said.

"I already got a call from your boss, I'm not to give you anything, P.I.'s license or not," said the coroner.

(insert mule picture here)
Houston

"Guess I'll have to learn some other way," I said.

Later:

"What did I do this time principal?" she said.

"Nothing," I said.

"And you are?" she said.

"Private Investigator W.X.Y.Z. Olaf," I said.

"Yea, in that case shouldn't you be wearing a trent coat, and where's the street light?" she said.

"It's trench coat, and next to the rotary dial phones," I said, "I'm here about your brother."

"Which one?" she said.

"Your big brother," I said.

"I repeat, which one?" she said.

"The one that just died," I said.

"I repeat, which one?" she said.

I paused and said, "Recently"

"I repeat, which one?" she said, "This is getting annoying."

"How about you start from the beginning," I said.

"Dad and Ti were having a big fight, like was always the case. And like norm, punches were being thrown, mostly by dad," she said, "Except normally no one starts spurting blood."

"WHAT Happened?!?!" I said.

"Dad said Ti stabbed himself, not sure that's true. But the police bought it," she said.

"What do you believe?" I said.

"I just told you," she said.

"How far back was that?" I said.

"22 days, and about 18 1/2 hours. Give or take 90 - 120 minutes," she said.

"So, you remember this clearly," I said.

"When you're ordered to do crime scene clean up, after the cops leave. It stays with you, when you're trying to eat, when you're sleeping, the list goes on," she said.

"Sounds like you could use professional help," I said.

"Speaking of professional help, that's where my other brother comes in," she said.

"Any sisters?" I said.

"I think I may have had one many years ago. But I know I do not now, I've become an only child," she said.

"I became an only child when I was about your age. Soon I had a baby brother, but, it's hard. And what's really bad is-" I said.

"How life changes afterward," she said.

"Yea, especially in my case," I said.

"How so?" she said.

"Don't ask," I said.

"So, want to hear where my other brother comes in?" she said.

"Very much so," I said.

"He hated our parent's guts afterward," she said, "As well as his own. But feared I'd do likewise."

"Oh, ouch," I said.

"My brother was smart, he knew he couldn't just leave home, for a list of reasons as long as both our arms combined," she said.

"So, what happened?" I said.

"He decided that he'd be free and get justice at once," she said.

"How so?" I said.

"Planted drugs on mother and dad," she said, "Mama's parole was yanked. Dad was, and still is, on bail."

"Whoa," I said.

"Yea, was funny when he took the normal response he got for sneaking around and lying, and shoved in their face as they were being arrested, cops never put 2 and 2 together," she said.

"What happened then?" I said.

"Dad started beating him harder than ever," she said.

"He was beating him?" I said.

"Oh yea, beats the fool out of all 3, or now me," she said, "But, you didn't hear that from me."

I looked at the principal, he gave a small nod, and walked out, and you can guess who he called.

"That's bad," I said.

"Yea, probably would have killed him if it hadn't been for the abundantly obvious," she said, no longer able to hold back.

"Sorry for your loss," I said.

"No, you're not," she said, "You're a cop, and he had committed some crimes in the past, all my relatives have."

"Hey, I'm here as a self-hired PI, no cop I know would do that," I said.

"So you're transemployed?" she said.

Dumbstruck, I said "I-I guess I am."

"So, how'd your brother respond?" I said.

"Just hurt inside, dad was inevitably going to kill him, unless he plated more drugs," she said.

"Did he?" I said.

"No, in fact came close to doing to job himself a couple times," she said.

"Really?" I said, "Did that make your dad mad? What about your mom?"

"No, out of sight out of mind," she said.

"Are you sure that your dad didn't try to kill your brother?" I said.

"No, he told me everything, first time he was doing this thing, much to my annoyance I was sheltered to exactly what, but I do know, is he hit an artery, passed out and nearly died," she said.

"Like he was cutting himself?" I said.

"Don't know why, but don't see what kind of drugs can cause blood to gush, and my family knows its drugs," she said.

"What happened?" I said.

Houston

"Said if he was going to kill himself, would have done it a long time ago. Needed to be a big brother to me, and," she said.

"And? And what?" I said.

"Was going to turn a new leaf, I think he had a near death experience, was even coming to church after that, and married-" she said.

"MARRIED?" I said.

"Oh yea, well, sort of," she said.

"Who? What?" I said.

"Oh yea, was his girlfriend, but everyone but our brother and myself was against it," she said.

"Why so?" I said.

"Dad, and her dad were in some kind of a mistress love triangle," she said.

"What? they weren't-" I said.

"No, if they were, you could look at them and tell by race," she said.

"So? what happened?" I said.

"Came out one day, said they were married," she said.

"How'd that go over?" I said.

"Had to stab dad, mildly, to save his live. She was watched like, no beyond a hawk; tantamount to being under lock and key," she said.

"Were more drugs planted?" I said.

"No, but one night," she said.

"What happened?" I said.

"Try to not seem like, and as anxious as, a 5 year old at the end of a candy assembly line," she said, "They both snuck out. Found her dead and my brother had a failed suicide."

"Did he-" I said.

"No, absolutely not, he adored her, and she was into him, but the cops said-" she said.

"So, who did it?" I said.

(insert mule picture here)
Houston

"Not sure, but they charged my brother, was all too much. All he cared about was my forgiveness postmortem. He got it before he asked, just wish-" she said.

"It's not your fault," I said.

"I KNOW THAT! The suggestion is offensive!" she said, clearly having a bit more guilt than she knew.

Later:

"Judge?" I said.

"Yea, I've only got 7 minutes," he said.

"Does this face ring a bell?" I said

"Yea, take this up with my secretary," he said.

"Let me cut to the chase-" I said.

"With her," he said.

"I'm accusing you of a crime personally," I said.

"What crime?" he said.

"Mistreating a minor-" I said.

"Child abuse? Officer I have no kids!" he said.

"Let me explain, and F.Y.I., I'm here as a private investigator," I said.

"Please do, and fast," he said.

"You approved him to be tried as adult, a bit young don't you think?" I said.

"What does that have to do with anything?" he said.

"I think it pushed him over a cliff, quite literally," I said.

"What does that mean?" he said.

"That was the cruelty," I said.

"I'll believe it when I see it," he said.

"Ok," I said taking him by the arm.

"HEY! Where are you taking me?!?!" he said.

"To the morgue, to see the body," I said.

"I have a trial in 10 minutes!" he said.

"Not my problem," I said.

"I didn't even break the law! This is absurd!" he said.

"You're right, you did break no American law. You broke a higher law, and as such I must bust you. But, like you said, you did break no law, so I must bust you for what I can," I said.

"Am I under Arrest?!?!" he said.

"If I was going to arrest you, don't you think I would have done it by now?" I said.

"Then why are you here?!" he said.

"I was hoping to get you to confess to the crime," I said.

"Why would I do THAT?!?!" he said.

"Besides morality and conscience, not that you have either, because that way they will go easy on you," I said.

"There's something I need to tell you, so listen up, and listen good," he said.

Getting excited I said, "And what would that be?"

"GET!!!!!!!" he paused and finished screaming "OUT!!!!!!!" also.

On the way out I turned and said "I'll be back and you'll be sorry. I only leave once"

Later:

"Sir, I believe the police were wrong in your daughter's death," I said.

"How so?" he said, "You think suicide, as that horrible boy said."

"No, I think that the police were wrong about the killer," I said.

"Really? That boy was horrible, and you'll let him walk," he said.

"If he's innocent, then her killer walks, among other reasons," I said.

"Fine, but why didn't the police let me know-" he said.

"I'm not the police, I'm a cop. But now I'm here as a self-hired P.I." I said.

"Why? And you expect me-" he said.

"To believe that, no. I'm haunted by this cas-" I said.

(insert mule picture here)
Houston

"The one you couldn't let go, I can't buy that," he said.

"No, the one I can't let go of is the murder of by brother and sister, however one that I worked like this is the one that got me to get a P.I.'s license. And the one where I decided that I would never lie as a cop," I said.

"So, why don't you thi-" he said.

"As an honest cop, I feel compelled to tell you that I'm really investigating the circumstances surrounding your son in law's-" I said.

"HE WAS NOT MY SON IN LAW-" he said.

"So, did you disown him, or your daughter?" I said.

"They were too-" he said.

"And, would you like a lawyer?" I said.

"You! you think I killed him?" he said, "That SUICIDE was the only decent thing that-"

"I've worked the cases of people whose suicide was the best thing they ever did. He didn't deserve to die, he was a good kid. And for the record, I don't doubt his cause of death. I think you killed your child, then when he found her, I don't know how good a job of making it look like suicide you did, but it was good enough to fool him. Without thinking he-" I said.

"I didn't kill her!" he said, "And that boy had prior-"

"I don't care," I said, "And if that's true, maybe your house has some evidence that would indicate so-"

"I, I don't want you to look around," he said.

"Why? because you're guilty? Or because of something else in the house, like drugs?" I said.

"There may, or may not be something I don't want you to see," he said.

"Howsabout something specific?" I said, "Like a phone-"

"Oh! Phone'll prove me, that you can see!" he said.

Later:

"Whoa! look at this! I'll have teck conform it! But if this can't get that judge indebted, nothing will!" I said "He was innocent. "

"WHAT?! you think you've got proof?" he said.

"Yes, but not of you! I should've known he'd never have access to his phone!" I said, "and this is proof!"

"What?" he said, "And I knew I should have taken that phone away! I knew it!"

"Look, he normally used lots of text slang, but he got it taken away. But not in the text through which he called her to run off. He'd never run off, leave his sister to fend for herself against the dad. HIS dad! He lured her out, and killed her. She could never run off with his son if she's dead!" I said, "You didn't do it! he did!"

To Be Continued:

Remember in that last one that judge I said "I'll be back and you'll be sorry," well, here we are.

"Everything ok? I'm in the middle of something pretty big," I said.

"What?" said the detective "Can't be bigger than this?"

"Actually, they were doing a trespassing sting, only problem was they were themselves trespassing," I said, "Not that's a foul up!"

"We've bigger fish to fry, it was one of our own," he said.

"Oh, but, you think it was a cop that did it?" I said.

"Perhaps, I think you might know what caused this officer to end up shot and tossed out the 60th floor window of the J.P. Morgan Chase building's free public observation deck," he said.

"What makes you think that?" I said.

"He was one of yours" he said.

"Oh no!-" I said.

"He's the badge, you got any clues?" he said.

"Yes, I know who his is, who killed him, how, when, where, and why. I, however, cannot explain J.P. Morgan Chase," I said, "Have men canv-"

"Way ahead of you, but, who killed him?" he said.

"Come quickly, time is of the essence, and bring a working tape recorder!" I said.

Later there:

"OLAF!" he said, "I want you OUT! Again!"

"Hello to you to judge," I said.

"Sorry to bother you, your honor," said the detective leaving.

I grabbed him by the arm and said "No, we're not sorry. Judge, would you like a lawyer?"

(insert mule picture here)
Houston

"What is this about?" he said.

"I'll take that as a no. Does this face ring a bell?" I said.

"Yea, following me around, gave me 49 parking tickets, 2 speeding tickets, one of which made me late for court, 3 littering-" he said.

"Tickets, one for running a red, two for a stop sign, one for beating a train 5-" I said.

"For not signaling, yea, I know, I was there," he said, "What's this about?"

"I think you know, we're getting a warrant for your chambers and -" I said.

"That'll never work!" he said.

"That's where you're wrong," said the detective.

"Officer, I know not about you, but once you charged me with mistreatment of a minor, and later assaulting you, no charges from you will ever stick!" he said.

"That's where you're wrong. While I can't explain the 60 story fall, I think he caught you approving a minor to be tried as an adult. And since I can't get an indictment. I have to catch you in the act. But now, I think I can not only indict. I can get a conviction," I said.

"What makes you think that?" he said.

"Well, I believe he burst in to arrest you. You rang for the bailiffs, who killed him. Now you probably didn't mean for him to die, but we'll never know for sure. But what we do know is-" I said.

"Let me do the honors," said the detective, "We know nothing about the case that sparked all this, but with something like this; I doubt anythinng'll even stick in Juvenile court."

"Well, all true and great, but what I was going to say is that eventually one of the bailiffs will realize that it's in his, or her, best interest to cut a deal," I said, "Between that and proof we're acquiring as we speak. A lot of people are going away for a long time."

"And you want me to-" he said.

"Nothing, I just want to rub your nose in it," I said.

Later:

"Wow," said the detective.

"Tell me about it," I said.

"Never thought that the next fallen officer would be Internal Affairs!" he said.

"Oh, telling people with a gun on their hip that they're going to jail. Never say never," I said.

(insert mule picture here)
Houston

"I once had a man under me fall in the line of duty," he said, "This your first time?"

"No, it was stupidity meets a poor manifestation of tenacity," I said.

"How so?" he said.

"Remember how I busted the HISDPD commissioner-" I said.

"'His department wasn't doing anything about cell phone confiscations'" he said mocking me.

"Not just phones, but yes. At first we fouled up, didn't stop to prove any confiscations in particular," I said, "No charges would stick?"

"So then what?" he said.

"You can get around double jeopardy if they are committing the same crime over and over," I said, "So I, I, I thought that an elementary school would be safe-"

"Things went south?" he said.

"Yea, lot of people went away for a long time, but that don't make things hokey doey okey dokey," I said.

"Oh, and here I thought you to be a soulless, overly honest, cop hating ravonus dog," he said.

"Well, I'm not soulless, and I only hate corrupt cops," I said, "Probably the only way I was able to close my siblings' case."

"Speaking of which, you think he could ever be convicted?" he said.

"Yea, fortunately judge realized bail should simply be denied, he pretty much confessed. Hoping to get me to not press murder charges," I said.

"And the cops involved?" he said.

"Aspect of a plea bargain. They're testifying against him," I said.

You've heard stories from my work in the Suicide, Homicide, and Internal Affairs divisions. But before all that, I was just a regular beat cop. Not many stories from then that are worth retelling, but here's one.

"So, is this the set of autopsy tools that your wife started out with when she was 12?" said my brother.

"No, she was performing autopsies with more modern equipment-" I said.

"How?" he said.

"She was a child genus, still is a genus. That's why she's the head coroner, "I said.

"No, I mean-" he said.

"Provided," I said.

"Then where did these come from?" he said.

"These were my little, your big, brother's," I said.

"I thought that this mace was his?" he said.

"No, that was our sister's" I said.

"Bro, are you even hearing yourself?!" he said.

GONG!

"Oh, that must be the Chinese I ordered," he said.

"But I just put a pizza in the oven!" I said.

"Exactly," he said, "I would have liked to meet them."

"Don't change the subject please!" I said, "Our parents willn't be happy."

"Willn't?" he said.

As I opened the door I said "Don't corr-" I said, "Bro, weird stuff is happinin!"

"That is Not what I ordered! Should I call the police?" he said when he saw her.

"Can I help you?" I said.

"Yea," she said.

"Please tell me that there's not a dead body wrapped up in there," I said.

"Ok I won't tell you," she said, furious.

"Why are you covered in blood?" said my brother.

"I tried to save him, was no way," she said.

"You sure?" he said, "And should I call the police bro?"

"Yes, I am. And you can leave. I have no reason to kill you, and you don't want to see this," she said drawing a gun.

"I know from experience, it's true. And yes," I said.

"Call the police if you want. They'll just be here to pick up the body," she said.

"Why us? Why here? What's this about?" I said.

"I'm glad you asked," She said, "Was my brother. We're close; really we only have each other. Not that that means anything to you," she said, pulling out an antique gun.

"Whoa!-" I said.

"He's had a hard life, real hard. Always trying to turn things around, trying so hard. We looked out for each other. We've been to jail," she said.

"You're a teenager-" I said.

"Exactly, so was he," she said, "He's struggled, fought back hard not to do it, you were the straw that broke the camel's back-"

"I- I don't understand-" I said.

"Earlier today," she said, "Picked him up, treated him like trash. Made bail, and, and, and he just lost it; parents lost it right back. So, why should I not kill you?"

"For your sake, don't throw your life away-" I said.

"Too late, I'm fulla cyanide, like I said, why do you deserve to live?" she said.

"Well, I have a wife-" I said.

"I'm sure she can take care of herself, any kids?" she said, "Anyone depending on you?"

"We've been together in some form since shortly after I got out of jail, when I was-" I said.

"Save the guilt/sympathy," she said, "Any kids, elders, anything you're doing of good?" she said.

"I confess, the closest thing is my kid brother-" I said.

"Leave me out of this," he said, on the phone with the cops.

"I don't even have any nieces or nephews-" I said, "But! I-I will make Intern-"

Thud BANG

She dropped dead, causing a musket ball to go into the sofa.

Later:

"Sounds like you're lucky to be alive," said the officer.

"Officer, she was right. I have a request, it will sound crazy, but please," I said.

"What?" he said.

(insert mule picture here)
Houston

"I want Internal Affairs to do a thorough investigation pertaining to the arrest, I have enough issues. I need to know I didn't fowl up. I need to know 2 children aren't dead because of me," I said.

"They were 2 thugs, one of which was about to kill you!" he said.

"So? At the time, the arrest seemed good and honest; now I feel like I scolded a child for having his hand in the cookie jar, right before he blew his brains out! It should have been me. Why couldn't it have simply been me!" I said.

I later learned that it wasn't cyanide, but simply 800 doses of ibuprofen.

You probably, right about now, are wondering where is the real 'internal affairs'? Well here's a pretty normal case for me. Also some of the proceeding may have been a real up lifter, but rest assured. This is going to be just a cheery, yes, that last sentence was just full of sarcasm.

"Can I help you?" she said.

"Yes, we have a big one," I said.

"Officer, I'm sure this is bigger," she said.

"Yea, you're still under investigation for setting off the drug sniffing dogs," I said, "So be sure you can back that up."

"Yea, in fact what could be so much bigger?" she said.

"A kid, with priors. In love with his girlfriend, parents of her wouldn't let him near her. Eloped. Cops just HAD to bring him back. Now he's in ICU. Dad was charged; heart attack beat us to the scales of justice."

"Good riddance! But how does that involve internal affairs?" she said.

"Arresting officers ignored his complaints of chest pain and nausea. Holding guard found him dead," I said.

"Well, that was more than I expected. But this is still big," she said.

"What happened?" I said.

"Hit and run, 26 month old was killed, bad," she said.

"And how does that involve internal affairs?" I said.

"Only thing witnesses can agree on was it was a cop," she said.

"Any idea which one? We've got-" I said.

"Figured I should leave that up to you," she said.

"Was an officer O'Limpet," said one of my officers, "Was rushing after another high speed chase."

"Captain Ahab just doesn't know when it's time to let the whale go! How did you solve it?" I said.

"Only cop at the time within over a mile of accident scene, also was zapped by red light camera a block away," I said.

"What do we know about the crash?" I said.

"One of those that just gets better and better," he said.

"How so?" I said.

"Received a transplant as a newborn, which is much harder and rarer than most people realize at that age. Mom was hurt in the crash. The person that saved them had moths to live, and probably cut that way down. Didn't see her in the back till the fire was too far gone." he said.

"Yeish," I said.

"Yea, and just got off the phone, teen brother," he said.

"What?" I said.

"Said that she was like a child to him-" he said.

"HE DEAD?!?!-" I said.

"No but came close. Severe shock," he said.

"Let's throw the book at-" I said.

"One more," he said, "Car was combed, defiantly the right cop. And was fiddling with the laptop at the time of the crash, like texting and driving, but for cops," he said.

"Let's get an indictment," I said.

I bet you thought that you had heard the last about Crayer. Well, there is one last chapter that should make things a little less crazy and plot hole filled. Btu brace yourself, what is learned, cannot be unlearned. Here goes:

"Miss Crayer?" I said.

"Y-yes?" she said.

"I want you to deliver this to your dad," I said.

"A letter, why not the post office?" she said.

"I have my reasons, which he will understand," I said.

The next morning:

"Where've ya been?!" said Detective Rathbone.

"Sorry boss, Traffic," I said.

"Traffic, Smaffic, hurry up!" he said.

"Sorry, may I ask the rush?" I said.

"Yea, child murdered," he said.

"What?-" I said.

"Yea, some body knocked out the dad with a gavel, cut her in half horizontally," he said.

"What've we got?" I said.

"Labbies working on that, but must've been a pro, cameras were knocked out. Can only be done if you first get into the house, so a real pro," he said.

"Anything else?" I said.

"Knew when to strike, left this letter as the only clue," he said.

The letter said "I heard that you approved an 11 year old jewel thief to be tried in adult court. I understand a parent's love, and as such I'm letting you know you shall never do anything like that again, unless you'd like something to happen to her, like what happened to my siblings- You Know Who"

I blanched, suddenly I knew everything, and it all made sense. After I recollected myself I said "What about family?"

"Wife was taking her twin brother to the pediatrician; dad said something was wrong with him. It's so sad. He's talking about wanting to join her," he said, "Older and I'd worry."

"Yow, any other siblings?" I said.

"Yea, older 11 year old big brother still hasn't been picked up from karate class, doesn't know," he said, "What's up with you?"

"Well, I, I, I-" I said.

"WAIT! The dad is-, that would explain everything," he said, "However handwriting doesn't match."

"Hold your horses!-" I said.

"Go home, we'll be back with handcuffs after C.S.U. is done their sciencey tests," he said.

The next morning:

"Sorry about all those false accusations," said Rathbone, "Cracked it easily."

"How so?" I said.

"Looked through everything, they fully cooperated. Nothing fishy, except some mysterious money rolling in from investments," he said.

"WHAT!" I said.

"Calm, nothing to do with anything," he said.

"So what happened?" I said.

"Older brother wasn't there," he said, "Later found him, and he babbled some junk about doing what he was told about his dad, faked surprise at the homicide, thought it to be a joke," he said.

"HE DID IT?!?!" I said.

"Oh yea, also there had an older sister at one point, she supposedly shot herself in some dispute about, something, a grounding I think," he said.

"Yow, you really think he did it?" I said.

"Was allbut caught with the gun in his hand," he said, "Just didn't suspect an 11 year old."

"You have proof?" I said.

"Oh yea, he just grabbed stuff from his room. Just look! No wonder he became a murderer!" he said.

"This looks like my brother and sister's room," I said.

"Yea, and look where they ended up," he said.

He saw the look on my face and then said "Ok! Sorry, that was a cheap shot."

"It's ok, so, why?" I said.

"By the looks of things, psyco," he said.

"What about those bank books?" I said, "Could I review them?" I said.

"Oh yea," he said.

Much later:

"Looks like the money comes in coinciding with him approving children to be tried as adults," I said, "Lets-"

"Olaf, the twin brother just died," he said.

(insert mule picture here)
Houston

"What?" I said.

"Yea, we thought he was murdered, but he just wandered out of the house, stabbed himself, and would have survived if he had been found. Found behind a police storefront," he said.

"Where he wanted the body to be found-" I said.

"Olaf, he was six. It's a freak accident. Do Not Go Botering That Man About Your Nonsense," he said.

"O-k," I said, "How's the older brother's trial look?"

"Bad, also just got transferred from Juvie," I said.

"WAIT WHAT NOW?!?! CRAYER-" I said.

"It was his own son, he didn't. Now kindly shut up before you get yourself fired," he said.

If they were going to fire me, they would've done it a long time ago," I said.

I was stuck. So I went to speak with the other judge.

"Judge, Why did you approve Crayer's son," I said.

"Because no child could do that, he was an adult," he said.

"Ok, Why did you really do that?" I said.

"Because, Because Crayer's my friend," he said.

"Why would Crayer want his own son-" I said.

"He was NOT his son! He stopped being his son when he killed her," he said.

I was desperate; I could not let it go. You may be wondering when it is that you'll have to brace yourself, well, here it is.

Later;

"I'm desperate, I need proof. I know he's taking bribes, however I know not who from. Can you release everything? Proving everything?" I said.

"Yes," said Paydahack.

Now let that sink in, balance it with pervious (actually future) events. No, I didn't kill Jane Doe. In fact I had long lost track of Paydahack. But this is the first time I'd even come forward about this.

The next day I went to see Crayer:

"Nothing can be used against me in court, or in impeachment. Lifetime appointment," he said.

(insert mule picture here)
Houston

"True, but now everyone is looking. You flinch, and they'll have probable cause to go in and find something that can be used against you. If you do that ever again, except maybe if it's one that even I'd approve. You'll go away for good.

Soon later I requested Crayer have some seriously dangerous teenage boys to be tried in adult court. Crayer said no. I won and I won big.

You've only heard one story from my days as just a regular cop. That's in part because they don't have as good a stories, and also those days were brief. However, sometimes they get interesting; but let us not forget the old Chinese blessing-curse "May you live in interesting life / times." So here's one that comes from my first month on the job.

"Commin' right up officers" said the waiter.

"So, what about this Crayer case?" said my fellow officer.

"Teen daughter was asked to 'quit blubbering for one night, I've had a hard day on the job' end quote. Straw that broke the camel's back. Man was going to testify against him and say that he had been harassing and tormenting her for years. All that we could nail him for. But now she'd dead, and DA dropped things before anyone else got killed," I said.

"He killed-" he said.

"Made it look like a random hit-and-run. Not solved," I said.

"So, I'm surprised you could even get it into court," he said.

"Not only that, but as an unsurprising but humorous bit of irony, it was in adult court." I said.

"I'm surprised you're trying to get him thrown in jail," he said.

"Or the electric chair," I said.

"You'd-" he said.

"It's the most the law would ever allow," I said.

After a short pause he said "Then what do you really want?"

"Oubliette," I said.

"What? What does that mean?" he said.

"You don't want to know," I said.

"Oh come on!" he said, "Nothing!"

I'll give you a hint, it comes from the French word for forget," I said.

(insert mule picture here)
Houston

A teen rushed in and said "Arrest me!"

"What for?" I said.

"Just arrest me!" he said, seeming to be in a real hurry, like fearing about to be murdered.

"On what charge? What's going on?" I said.

He smacked mu upside the head and said "Assaulting an officer."

"O-k," I said, I got out my handcuffs and said "You are under arrest. Anything you say can and will be used against you in a court of law. You have the right to an attorney. If you cannot afford an attorney, one will be provided for you by the state. Do you understand these rights as read to you?"

"I thought you said that I had the right to remain silent!" he said.

"Good point," I said.

Later:

"We were able to tell who you were," I said.

"So?" he said, "Just put me away and forget about me, you've done it before."

"Yes, you were. You were barely 8 when you confessed to killing and taxidermying your 9 year old sister. No one believed you till you were proven to have strangled your baby brother-" I said.

"Wanted it to be in adult court, but I was 8," he said.

"Yea, nothing about this makes sense. Only motive for anything would have been psyco and / or acting and / or to be treated as an adult. But you were released early, because you had immense guilt. It makes no sense, till I dug deeper. Your sister was found in a drug raid on your dad's shop. Holding a gun on the cops. She was shot, pretty pathetic with all that armor, and one day I will file charges, but, she was already dead," I said.

"I didn't kill her," he said.

"I'm sure you didn't, I also don't think you killed-" I said.

"No, I did," he said.

"Why?" I said.

"Dad made me do it all, he said that if I didn't, he'd kill 5 innocent random people," he said.

"You believed him?" I said.

"I was willing to risk jail, and hope I wasn't believed, even though I was told 'how I did it'; but I wasn't willing to kill my brother," he said.

(insert mule picture here)
Houston

"So what made you change your mind?" I said.

"He did, and said he'd do it again-" he said.

"What details do you know?" I said.

"Were all run over, cops thought that some lucky drunk-" he said.

"Can you help us prove it?" I said.

"I'm a convicted killer-" he said.

"And being exonerated as we speak! Sorry about what happened, must've messed you up in so many ways-" I said.

"Just not willing to let history repeat itself," he said.

"What! what's happening?!?!" I said.

"Dad didn't like hearing my brother, actually half-brother, crying and driving everyone nuts. He's moved in with another woman, same case, and same sireario. I just got out, I know this time it will be adult court-" he said.

"It won't be you at all, one last thing, why did he kill your sister?" I said.

"Wanted to 'make the cops stop following him by flying a UFO over'" he said, "Can I have my call now?"

"Why? And did it work?" I said.

"Yea, was crazy enough for a reasonable doubt," he said.

"Who you gunu call?" I said.

"Ghost busters," he said.

"What?" I said.

"The correct answer is always Ghost Busters," he said, "and I'd rather not say."

"We'll know," I said.

"You won't get there in time," he said.

Not this is before I fully realized that many things police did were corrupt (we need not regenerate that trauma), so I said "If you don't, I'll drop the charges."

"My parents," he said, "Expose a lot of things, cross my fingers and hope I get lucky."

"And?" I said.

"Hope they kill each other," he said.

"Leave them to me," I said.

Later:

"Bad news, your dad's girlfriend is dead, and we have no proof of anything." I said.

"Big surprise, what's so bad about this?" he said.

"Your dad however, is going away for good," I said.

"I repeat, 'what's so bad about this?'" he said.

"Your sister, we, I regre-" I said.

"Cut the canned sympathy, what happened?" he said.

"She could only be I'd by your DNA on file," I said.

"What happened?!?!" he said.

"Your father truly was a sick and evil psychopath," I said.

"I'm gunu find out sooner or later!" he said.

"She was microwaved," I said.

You remember how I said I could tell you no more about the future / my present. Well, now I have to. Jane Doe's murder, instead of all the abundly obvious evidence, was enough to get them to stop persecuting us. Nor do we have to worry about police corruption and cops wholly looking the other way with crimes against us, however often we need to call in Disobeyer Intelligence because the police are ignoring it. It's a comparative heaven, but society has united against us so hard that they just can't stop coming against us. We'll never go away, nor can they try to make us, but they can and are calling us crazy "communicable mental illness", as an excuse to forcibly unsinize us. That's what's about to happen to me. In the last word of Jane Doe "Sure there's regrets, there always is," But I'm one of the lucky ones. I am truly able to say I did as much good with my life as possible. In the last words of Admiral Lord Nelson "Thank God I've done my duty." I'd so love to tell you so much more about so much more; especially God's people in present day and how they've (and everyone else) have changed, but cest le ve, le ve. Now I'm being called crazy for the last time. And just for the record I don't think I'm personally being singled out. Bye, I will be going gently into that good night.

We've all read Captain WXYZ Olaf's "Internal Affairs." An excellent book series that was cut short when he was usinized for his religious beliefs. Well this is a book that I have been putting off writing for some time. But no longer; my memories are beginning to fade. I always wanted to write this in defense of

(insert mule picture here)
Houston

my little sister/ half sister/ half brother's half sister/ relative person. Also I wish to tell untold stories from "Internal Affairs."

I have received inspiration for this from several different classic novels. I nearly called this - A gothic novel for the 21st century - But, don't be confused; I assure you that all these stories, which you have all heard the other side of, are true. Admittedly there could be some minor misrememberings-primarilly in wording and / or dialog. First of all the long back story / first half involving Captain Call letters, or as we called him "The Viking cop" was encouraged by Mary Shelly's "*Frankenstein*". F.Y.I. the monster was made by a collage student, who was called Victor Frankenstein, the monster was just The Monster (or occasionally The Demon). Also some perspective / perspectives were encouraged by said book as well. The next most influential book was Bram Stoker's "*Dracula*". Which encouraged different perspectives, this, and including different writings. This part was however more encouraged by Gaston Leroux's preface and afterward to his own book "*The phantom of the Opera*". Another influential book would be Robert Lewis Stevenson's "*The Strange Case of Dr. Jekyll and Mr. Hyde*" Which encouraged the police report esque nature of how some things are revealed. Also I'm sure they have encouraged me in other ways as well as the ways listed. And I'm sure I've got some of my tounge in cheek from Lemony Snicket's A Series of unfortunate Events. Speaking of which you should at least think twice before reading this book as well. I'm sure lots of other books, and other things as well have encouraged me as well, but I don't which ones and to what degree. Also I have brought some of myself in. You will note that this book has this preface and 2 parts; but no chapters. I never like to stop in a chapter, but this way you can and will just stop wherever; like was in *Fahrenheit 451*. Also you will have to forgive some poorly written parts in the second half; thanks to Trademaster my editor was eaten by a hollow and can't seem to get anything done in the after room (just kidding).

It may seem wild what is included and what is not; but I want you to have the same perspective as my little sister/ half-sister/ half-brother's half-sister/ relative person had, despite my being mostly a secretive person. I just want you to have her perspective. Also again I want to reemphasize there could be some minor misrememberings-primarilly in wording of dialog; in fact I'm sure there will be a few.

And one last thing to prevent confusion. The events enumerated in this Novella are in no way alluded to in Epi. 1

Part 02: Slay

I have read many a back story; as such I can assure you that none have had a stranger childhood than I. First of all we've all we've all heard the stereotype of delivering a baby in the back of a cab; well if time traveling literature is possible; which Olaf proved it is. I then can assure that that started with me, my bad. It got weirder from there. My parents and sister were the only relatives of mine I ever knew before I turned 18, and to this day my half siblings relatives, my in laws, and so on, are the only relatives I've ever known, no other metaphorical blood whatsoever. If you even come across any clue as to why I've never known anything of my parents' families of origin,

Houston

please let me know. Also if you can ever determine which aliens built Stonehenge, please, let me know. (Just joking) (I'll explain my siblings' backstory at the end of this half of the book.)

My sister had other siblings, but that was before my time. My sister was 12 years older than me, but we were about as close as siblings can ever be, without it being creepy that is. As was once briefly the case with my half siblings, but no need to further mention that. She was older than either of my half siblings, or Uncle Pierre (will explain later) ever got to be. Most people have had at least one date that their parents didn't like. I did, will explain later. Well, my sister had had a childhood boyfriend, who I never knew. I think most of my siblings had had one such person. However I will circle around to that later. He died, at least we assume. She never knew what really happened, or at least so I thought. I was on the scene by the time she got back out there. Eventually she had a new boyfriend. But my parents didn't like him; I know why. Don't agree with what they did, but I grock it. He got her to be a Goth, along with some other such things her got her involved. I liked him. I was going to help her run off. We got caught. Many a father has wanted to kill his daughter's boyfriend, mine did. Well, not really. She jumped in front of the shotgun. She was 16, I was 4. He then needed me and Father Dracula's (I'll explain later) help to keep this under wraps. I really mourned her. But I was able to use that as a means of blackmailing my parents. Sounds like a bad thing, wrong. As I recall (however but you must remember the 3 year old perspective) they were bad enough. But they were unreal control freaks afterwards. I suppose that it was they blamed themselves for not having been stricter; however the opposite was true; they were too strict. They say "guns kill people but nowadays people often also say laws kill people. I say; bad in-laws kill people. Like I said, my parents were bad enough, but thank God, and I mean that, I only got a flavor for the amount of control that they wanted over me; No human being should ever have that much control over another human being under any circumstances. Ever. No exceptions.

Well, to circle back to that part about "I think most of my siblings had had one such person." It must have run in the family. Her name was Sam, sometimes went by Sammy. Knew each other far back as either of us could remember, and coming from me that's really saying something. At a very early age (my sister may have been still alive) we became a bit more than friends. As time went on, maybe months you know how slow time goes at that age, we realized we were more than friends. Eventually those around us had figured it out. Once again, I used blackmail to be able for us to be together, soon afterwards we were engaged. After some time, when her last living arrangement fell through; her family was so weird and complex that I won't even bother describing it to you, that way you will also be able to keep your lunch down. As I was saying: when her last living arrangement fell through she finally came to live with me. That's where the blackmail came in in one major event, rather than how I was treated day to day. We considered ourselves to be married, even called in Father Dracula, who was still getting the collar at the time (like I said I'll explain later). Were like that for nearly a year. Only other similar case was Michal W. Sackett, Captain W.X.Y.Z. Olaf's best friend, who I held as an acquaintance, even then they were older. And like attorney Sackett, died all too soon. Rather than a bizarre accidental suicide, it was 2nt degree murder. We were so great together, but; that's where Father Dracula's backstory comes in.

First of all you're probably wondering why He has such an oxymoronic name, emphasis on the "moron" part. Well, as I mentioned he was into Goth, and other such things, hence the "Dracula" part. And the "Father" part is that he went on to be a Catholic priest, and to answer the question in your head, no, not the kind of priest you hear about on the news. He was also referred to as "The Gothic Priest"; but, you can guess what assumptions could be made. As another portion of where the blackmail came into play, we stayed in contact. In the course of his life he crossed paths with Gregor Mendal and company; you remember Greg, not the monk who worked with peas and genetics. No, he was the one that went around entrapping child abusers and dirty cops. But he was killed by the Internal Affairs Division of the Houston Police Department, well, that part we will come back to. Just not so fast. As I was saying Father Dracula got involved with Greg's crew. And we were brought in in turn. We being me and Sam(my). We worked different cases and things got down to a regular protocol. We really cleaned things up, as such we had to go farther to find people to entrap. Also we dried up the Foster home supply, by shutting down the bad ones; so Sam didn't have to go to foster care. She was working a case in Austin. Drac was the one that popped out and stopped it. The abuser dictated that she would just kill them and hide it all. Father Dracula pulled through, and so did the client. Samy wasn't so fortunate. We were pushing 9. After that the organization made a strict minimum 13 age policy. All that was shortly after Greg's tazing. So I then dropped off of their radar; but not Dracula's. Months later they had to have a reunion. They needed all that they had. That evening is remembered much the same as my sister's death. So I think I will instead include these Houston Chronicle® front page headline stories.

Drive by Slaughter in Hedwig Village

About 8:50 pm The Mason Jar fern bar went from antique to horrific. A police squad car pulled up into the parking lot firing a spray of bullets all up and down the window side of the Cafe. The restaurant is rectangular in shape and the sides facing parking lot were all windows. Witnesses believe there to have been one person riding shotgun and a second shooter in the backseat both firing fully automatic assault weapons constantly into the restaurant. Fortunately the restaurant was mostly empty, except for one large party. 29 people were killed instantly, 6 were rushed to

Memorial Hermann Memorial City. 2 Are expected to almost fully recover. One is expected to not survive, and one died in transit. 2 others were also killed. In the neighboring Memorial Village of Sunnyside USA police officers Frankie Frazer, and Winston Thomas were found murdered for their car. One block from the massacre the vehicle in question was found engulfed in fire. One witness said they were "Driving past in a spray of bullets; lengthwise"...

The next day:

Justice in Fern Bar Massacre

Two Juveniles were arrested in the horrific Mason Jar Cafe Massacre. Ages 14, and 15; they are said to be part of drug operations in the neighborhood. They are being held without bail. They have been charged as adults for 32 counts of premeditated, 2 aggravated counts of premeditated murder of police officers, and 6 counts of premeditated attempted murder. Juvenile court has also pressed charges of grand theft auto, arson, and weapons violations. The district attorney has affirmed that they will be convicted and will never be free again.....It is not known if this will be later made a federal case...

Chill your palpitations, I know I had them. They were innocent; While I cannot speak on the drug allegations, I can assure you that they were framed. Sounds crazy; but let me tell you what Captain W.X.Y.Z. Olaf told me. I know you're a little confused, I'll explain when I come into play.

"I have seen cops caught by a trunk cam planting drugs; and I have seen cops caught by a trunk cam stealing, but he's the first do to both to the same perso-" I said.

I'll cut in now to let you know that this part of the story is being narrated by The Viking Cop; as he relayed it to me so don't be confused.

(insert mule picture here)
Houston

"'Ex-excuse me, I just heard about you, and, And I'd like to file a victim statement,' said the stranger."

"'Oh, hello, I'm-' I said."

"'Even taller that I heard,' he said."

"'Oh, yea, 7' 6",' I said."

"'And more muscular than I heard,' he said."

"'What?" I said."

"'Noth-nothing,' he said, 'So, where's the interview room?'"

"'Right here,' I said, setting up the recorder."

"'Oh! So the victims get the good quarters,' he said."

"'Oh, I'm sorry,' I said."

"'Don't be,' he said,"

"'Who are you?' I said."

"'My friends call me Littie-nuthin,' he said."

"'Oh, I take you were in jail, I'-' I said."

"'Don't be, I was framed,' he said."

"'So what happened?' I said."

"'My late, girlfriend, Fiancé, Wife, hard to say. Well, we, and, Well her dad walked in on something, she got scared,' he said."

"'Do you need a minute?' I said."

"'No! no,' he said, 'And to explain the first part, we were going to be together, we were probably engaged, we may have even said vows to each other, but, we were 13, so-'"

"'Know a guy widowed at that age,' I said."

"'How? did they have to? and she then-' he said,"

"'No, no, that's just what everybody thinks,' I said, 'So, then what?'"

(insert mule picture here)
Houston

"'At first I was mad at her, but I soon realized that she was just a victim as well,' he said,"

"'Then what?' I said."

"'20 years; denied it because I was I was innocent, so never got parole,' he said."

"'As an adult?,' I said."

"'Yea, I believe so,' he said."

"'Heard from her recently?' I asked."

"'No, while my family was trying to put bail together, she was killed,' he said, 'Haven't heard from her sense.'"

"'And you-,' I asked."

"'Prison releases are made at 8 am. And the walk to here takes however much time has sense passed,' he said."

"'I would like to apologize for what happened to you, and to offer my sympathies,' I said."

"'You know, you're the first law enforcement I've met sense before I was a teen that treated me like I was a human,' he said."

"'And as such I'm sure you've seen plenty enough of people with badges and guns, why don't you go enjoy your freedom. We'll call you if we need anything,' I said."

"'Sure, just one last thing,' he said."

"'Anything, sure,' I said."

"'Can I get a ride to a shelter, my feet hurt,' he said."

"'Certainly,' I said."

"I looked into the case. I don't see how he had been convicted, probably was that he never lawyered up till days before trial. Blindly trusted. His lady friend probably would have given in and told the truth on the stand; she truly was the 2nd victim. A murder victim. It was believed that his parents wanted to help him so they took her out. But it could have been her own vengeful parents that knew and buried the truth. Probably why they didn't try to build a circumstantial case. Once in suicide I myself saw someone that used a turnaquate, so that possibility also couldn't be disproven, but there was strong evidence of having been handcuffs, so. I also think the prosecution may have killed her, help get a conviction. Also some much milder priors along the same general

(insert mule picture here)
Houston

lines he had had some time back before then, also probably hurt his defense. First I wanted to speak to their families. Turned out they met by their parents being friends, bout a year into the sentence they were carpooling together to dinner and a tire blew out on a bridge to the restaurant, over the Houston Ship Channel (not a TV station). He was an only child that came from a long line of only children. His next of kin was his father's father's little sister. And his lady friend had only cousins, no help at all. I then turned to those on the case. His low-end-even-as-a-public-defender lawyer had had one too many quadruple bacon, triple fried, double beef burgers. And was now working taking up room temperature in an extra-extra-large coffin. As for the prosecutor, she was dumped by her, well, whatever you call the other man when a wife cheats, and had jumped in front of a HFD engine. I then looked at the cops. 2 Detective partners worked the case alone. One had sense been eaten by a crocodile (or alligator I was never sure, or cared). Here is my interview with the judge."

"'I assume you've been ready your rights Mr. Taylor,' I said."

"'Yes,' he said, 'And it's Justice Taylor'"

"I paused and said 'Mr. Taylor, you have waved your right to an attorney. Right?'"

"'Don't even see why I'd be offered one. What is the reason I'm here?' he said getting annoyed."

"'Just trying to make sure everything is ethical,' I said."

"'What are you talking about?' he said."

"I decided to just go for it and said 'Why, killing you, of course.' He reacted about as you would expect. I then showed a picture of the victim. 'Does this face ring a bell to you'"

"'Why are you trying to kill me?!?! And for Pete's sake! We're in a police station! You could never get away with murder!' he shouted."

"'Ah! No, no I would not shoot you, no. You're not worth the indictment, or the gunpowder' I said."

"'Copper! Make since!' he said."

"'Here in America it's just cop, or officer. Not Copper. But, to answer your question, ' I said, 'And there is more than one way to kill someone, besides murder. '"

"'So, what're you going to do? Manslaughter me?!?! ' he said. "

"'Closer, You are aware that, while very rarely done, kidnapping can carry the death penalty?' I said calmly."

(insert mule picture here)
Houston

"'KIDNAPPING?!!? Who'd I allegedly kidnap?!!?' he shouted."

"'First of all, you spit when you scream, second, please remove yourself from my face. And turtiarally, You'd probably remember him to look more like this,' I said; showing his mugshot."

"'Who is tha-' he said, 'no, wait, he, I think I remember, him-'"

"'20 years ago, 2 decades, the majority of his life. You had him tried as an adult-' I said."

"'But! But! There were prosecutors and jurors and-' he said."

"'Yes, and the average kidnapping victim is held such a short period of time it's measured in hours. I've been measuring in decades,' I said."

"'This! This! This is is Absurd! This is absolutely absurd! I I Want to speak to the police corruption department!-' he said."

"'It's called "The Internal Affairs Division." Being in criminal justice; you should know-' I said, 'and you are, well, it's more shoutin-'"

"'HOW! How could you even do this! What'd you do! threaten the prosecutor as being charged as an accomplice!-' he cried out."

"'Yes, I often do,' I said still remaining calm."

"'You know, I think I will take you up on that lawyer offer. But first, one question,' he said."

"'Fair enough, I said."

"'How on earth is this JUSTICE!?!? I mea-' he said, still mad."

"'It's not so much a matter of justice as responsibility,' I said."

"Five minutes later we had him booked for kidnapping. While my underlings went to look for him for a more formal victim statement I was talking to the surviving detective:"

"'Captain, you've opted not to have an attorney present. Correct?' I said."

"'It's my understanding is that procedures say that Internal Affairs can and should fire you if you demand a lawyer,' she said."

"'Procedure is wrong, it just is,' I said."

"'Really, I always thought that-' she said."

"'I was one of those "do as I say, not as I do"ites?' I said."

"'Yea,' she said."

"'I try very hard not to be. But I am human,' I said."

"'So, is this about that thing with the dye pack. I just am tired of seeing my imported Japanese sodas growing legs and walking,' she said."

"'No, no you did nothing wrong. Hard to believe you have to worry about things getting stolen by cops in a police station. No, that matter is trivial compared to this issue that has come to light,' I said."

"'What's that?' she said."

"'It involves a case you worked with this man,' I said, showing a picture of her former partner."

"She blanched and said 'Oh, I-I,'"

"I didn't know how to react to this so I said, 'What?'"

"'I, well, There is a saying "If you can't defeat an enemy; consider joining up,"' She was getting really emotional and said 'even if something is planted on you,'"

"'What? by who?' I said."

"'You Know Who!,' she said."

"'What do you mean?' I said."

"'Back then, it was stoppable. But now that you've-' she said."

"'I don't know what you're saying. But I'm sure I'm innocent of whatever I'm accused of,' I said."

"'Well, if that be true I'll you tell this. You must really be stupid and wholly incompetent,' she said."

"'How so?!' I said, 'And how does this, no longer a boy, boy fit in?'"

"'Oh! I remember him. You know he was actually innocent,' she said."

"'Then why was he con-' I said."

(insert mule picture here)
Houston

"'Look, I don't know what things I'm accused of but, yea,' she said, 'And to answer your question, I think it was he just wasn't fit to be on trial; age.'"

"'Then why didn't-' I said."

"'Look, you're walking into a world of things you could never even imagine,' she said."

"'How so?' I said."

"'How so, It's like this, Integral Affairs is designed to go after dirty cops. It can't go after, after-' she said."

"'What is this? You're talking crazy?!" I said.

"'You can go after dirty cops, all the dirty cops you want. But this you can't go after,' she said."

"'You're just making this up as you go along?!' I said."

"'Oh how I wish,' she said."

"'If this is real, then I can give you immunity,' I said."

"'No, You've cast out 1 demon. And 7 more, more evil than the first have filled that void,' she said, 'I give you a name, I might as well just shoot you. I know you-'"

"As I arrested her she cried about how I was killing her son. Also said something about 'Bigger than I could ever Imagine. As a precaution I sent a couple of underlings to check things out. He was dead. It was seen as and ruled that he simply left the car running in the attached garage. CSU found nothing. I then got the news. The victim was found in Memorial park, knocked out, drowned, and washed up. I took the lead investigating his murder. His next of kin was his great aunt:

"'Mrs. Babcock, I assume you heard the news about your great nephew?' I said."

"'No, I believe he was killed in jail. I was told he had been murdered,' she said."

"'No, he was released and then murdered afterward,' I said, 'How well did you know him,'"

"'Oh, I hadn't heard from him sense he was a child,' she said."

"'Before he went to jail?' I said."

"'Yea,' she said."

"'Why so?' I said."

(insert mule picture here)

Houston

"'Family's better than that, after what he did,' she said."

"'Seriously?' I said."

"'What?,' she said."

"Later,"

"'That was a lot of help,' I said, 'What about old jail friends. Bout all he had-'"

"'If you looked up "Dead lead" in the dictionary; it would say "See old jail friends-'" said a subordinate officer.

"'What about Judge Whatshisface?' I said."

"'Taylor?' said another officer."

"'Yea, not like he's worth learning the name,' I said."

"'Prepping him for death row,' said a 3rd officer."

"He's gotten his call. Right?' I said."

"Later with his wife:"

"'Ms. Taylor. you've been informed of your rights. Correct?' I said.

"'Yea,' she said, 'Let me guess. You think I killed him in dumped him in the bayou. Correct?' she said."

"'Of course I do. Did you?,' I said."

"'I want to cut a deal,' she said, panicking."

"'Life, no daylight? Talk to the DA-,' I said."

"'Manslaughter," she said."

"'Now why should I take a plea of manslaughter?' I said.

"'Because of the mitigating factor,' she said."

"'What mitigating factor?' I said."

"'My husband delivered justice. He gets out. And my husband is now needle bound! I don't think he'll avoid it!' she said."

"'Nor do I-' I said."

"'And you can't prove it,' she said."

"'Oh come on, the officers found a meat hammer-' I said."

"'Gavel,' she said."

"'What?' I said."

"'It's called a meat gavel,' she said."

"'Either way. The side with the points has blood on it. And while you could point out that it is meant to be used on meat; I'd point out that it matches the victim's wound. Just have to wait for crime techs to come back with a DNA match. The time line works great. Your husband used his call to tell you everything. You hunted him down. I for one would hesitate to use the death penalty when it's only one victim, and nothing makes it super heinous, like how it was done, or who the victim was. But for you; I'd do it. As for any alleged mitigating factor; take it up with the jury,' I said."

"Then a fellow officer burst in. I could tell by his look they had gotten to the dirty officer's other child. I said 'Oh no! they got to her daughter first.'"

"He shook his head and said. No, she's fine. And probably always will be. No, it's the officer. She's dead,'"

"A definitive cause of death was never determined. I ruled it an untraceable poison."

That was the end of that story. Far from the end of THE story. Captain W.X.Y.Z. Olaf looked into things, just in case that whole "bigger than you could ever imagine" thing was real. He only found 2 things. First of all he found an uptick in murders, especially murders committed by those very young. (young teens and tweens as well as a few pretween). His first conclusion was the logical "When the cat's away; the mice will play." But they were solving an almost suspiciously high amount of all major crimes, and even getting convictions. It didn't add up. He also found something else. Before the misalaineous memorial villages were absorbed by force into the City of Houston; they seemed to have had 2 gangs within Memorial Villages Police Department (MVPD). And they went to gang war with each other. Illogical. More strange; the Feds who investigated cooperated fully. If something is too good to be true; it probably is. And there was one hole; besides the gang war. What did the gangs do? No one knew. Logical guesses were made, but there was never anything to support it. They were logical because that's what gangs usually do. But this was a Black Swan event; gangs are not normally made up of cops! So all bets were all off.

(insert mule picture here)
Houston

Captain Olaf also (sorta) found a 3rd thing. A lot of the old Internal Affairs' documents were gone. Clean gone. Not like they were missing. But more like they rectoractivly ceased to exist. He make news reports; all that turned up was one MVPD Officer now in HPD. And he was believed to be a member of one of the gangs. But he alone they could never build a case against. Here is his interview with Captain W.X.Y.Z. Olaf:

"Thank you for coming in Officer Thomas," said Captain W.X.Y.Z. Olaf.

"Sure," he said, "I assume that this is about the Gang war."

"Yes," said Captain W.X.Y.Z. Olaf.

"You know it was phony," he said.

"I was never sure, but it sounded like a cover lie to me-" said Captain W.X.Y.Z. Olaf.

"I'll tell you the truth," he said.

"I'm all ears," he said.

"You probably shouldn't be recording this," he said.

"No, I should," said Captain W.X.Y.Z. Olaf.

"Well, let me tell you a story:-" he said.

"As long as it's true," said Captain W.X.Y.Z. Olaf.

"It all started some time back. We didn't have the capabilities to solve heinous murders. Just basic ones. We didn't want to be the scene of the next Jonbenet Ramsey. So such murders were handed over to HPD. Well one night a teenage boy was found murdered. Well, it may have been voluntary manslaughter. He died a horrific death. Seemed that someone was trying to get information out of him. He was part of Gregor Mendal's crew. Another member was arrested for it and taken into police custody as an adult by Houston police within 24 hours. But Gregor Mendal came to us. Alibied him out. Turns out the victim was his number 2. The reason I'm just telling what happened, instead of telling this as a mystery was that I wasn't on that case. We ourselves went over things and used our normal private sector crime lab; too small for our own. It proved he was innocent. We called HPD Internal Affairs. They knew that this was an ongoing situation. They said they were about to bust this all. Then Gregor Mendal turned up tazed. And you remember what you did then. No, Internal Affairs wasn't dirty. Just framed. The officer that ratted them out was blackmailed. They had his kid. All this overshadowed the fact that the accused was killed in jail before he could clear his name. No one knew who else was in that crew.

(insert mule picture here)
Houston

They, the real gang of cops, knew Internal Affairs and Gregor Mendal and Company both were after them and close. They killed two birds with one stone; no pun intended considering the victim's name was Byrd. And to make sure it all stayed buried they also took out the kidnapping victim. Framed some poor kid that had been framed before. Was in 2nd grade the first time, and had just been released. Not getting out the second time. To answer the question you're thinking, we both know what happens when cops end up in jail. But this is ridiculous. All former IA officers have sense been taken out. We then decided that we'd do a real investigation of all obvious cases of these dirty cops. But they're good. Everyone is a puppet. And when vigilante cop killers came out of the woodwork. One avenging the death of the half-sister his mom never know about. The other was, I believe avenging his son. You then charged all those that made the police protocols that caused the inciting deaths, and charged the police commission for having made the procedures that caused the inciting deaths in the first place. You mean well. But that created a void; these people are framing someone for something at least once a day; every day. All else I know is that Gergor Mendal's possy knows something else. We were secretive about step by step movements. But the overall we all knew so the truth would be told. So this gang stuff was cooked up, and I'm the only one left that wasn't killed in jail. Only one case I worked personally. A Rabbi was found dead in the parking garage after performing regular Friday night services. He had preached, or whatever the term is, a very politically incorrect message one week ago. I worked for the longest having the most uncomfortable and awkward undercover roles. And just when it had been solved; well, I'll save you the long complex murder mystery. It was THE god from the machene . A kid came out of the woodwork. Here's how the interview went:"

"'Thank you for speaking to me. Houston Police wouldn't even take a statement,' said the child."

"'Happy to. So you have knowledge relating the murder of Rabbi Asreal Somerstein,' I said."

"'That's an understatement,' he said."

"'How so?' said my partner."

"'Well for starters. I don't know who you arrested for the murder. But he, or she is innocent,' said the child."

"'What makes you think that? M. Potter more / err / less confessed-' I said."

"'Well, then it was forced. My sister found "the boy for her." I'm a boy; and I'm nine; I don't get it. But I stood up for her. How could I not? When I'm in trouble she forces my parents to let her defend me, guilty or not-' he said."

"'How is this pertinent?!' said my partner."

"'Pertinent?' he said."

"'Relevant,' I said."

"'I assure, no, I promise you that I will get to it. But let the story play out. Please,' he said."

"'Very well then,' I said."

"'Well, I helped them out. Mom was off on a carnival boat in the Atlantic, ostensibly taking care of business matters. So Dad said he'd kill an innocent person we don't know if they didn't split it off. Well, If you looked up "determined" or "strong necked" in the dictionary, you'd find our pictures. We didn't believe him. Then he told us what he'd done. Said he do it again and again unless they gave in, and gave up the blackmail. He brought home the head so we'd believe him. To answer the question you're obviously thinking, it's buried in the backyard. I'll show you where. And in case you don't believe me. Which you probably don't. He also brought home this,' he said, pulling out the victim's ID card."

First of all I'll tell you how that story ends. Yes, the dad was convicted of both murders. And yes, his sister and that boy were able to stay together. But they did get to be framies before this story ends. But don't be looking for them. They don't pop back up in my storyline.

Second, that officer was Winston Thomas. That was about 48-72 hours before the Fern Bar Massacre. Gergor Mendal's entrappers knew that they needed everyone that they could get for this current crisis. They were calling all fringes and reserves. As for the location, most, in fact almost all, of the members were simply former clients themselves. That's how Greg got started; Helping a bully from school one time. Grew from there. As such being made of Juvenile Delinquents and former Juvenile Delinquents, a fern bar was not where you'd expect them to be found. And Greg's parents stayed involved and liked the Mason Jar. We were the 'large party.' Taking up the whole, unshielded, far end. I alone survived; and only because I was in the bathroom. Probably the, for lack of a better word, cosmic reason for my water diabetes. Don't sweat it, it's no big deal. Well, as usual Captain W.X.Y.Z. Olaf rushed lights and sirens to what had happened. That's when I first met him. Here's what happened once I knew I could trust him:

"My sympathies for what happened," said Captain W.X.Y.Z. Olaf.

"You know, not the first person I lost in this movement," I said.

"What happened there?" said Captain W.X.Y.Z. Olaf.

"Oh, it's unrelated, and was time back," I said.

"What happened?" said Captain W.X.Y.Z. Olaf.

(insert mule picture here)
Houston

"Just a routine job that went south. Course the fact that we were married probally only means that you won't believe me," I said.

"No, no," said Captain W.X.Y.Z. Olaf, "I wasn't much younger when I met my wife."

"Really," I said.

"Oh yea, I remember she had just started working as a coroner," said Captain W.X.Y.Z. Olaf.

"I didn't know there was an age gap," I said.

"Oh, no, there wasn't. She is / was a child prodigy. We were twelve, she's the only one I ever went out with- Well, Enough rambling about me," said Captain W.X.Y.Z. Olaf, "Also I heard about Sam. Real loss losing an officer like that."

"She wasn't a cop," I said.

"Badge, smage," said Captain W.X.Y.Z. Olaf.

"Well, I for one," I said, "All I know is that right around the time of his death Greg was catching on to high ranking detectives that were framing. At first he / we thought that they were simply planting evidence. But soon learned that the crime lab was more of a crime lie-"

"Are You Sure?!" he said.

"As sure as I am that Father Dracula just bit the big one- I'll explain later. Then we started working on how to stop them. Soon afterward Greg ended up dead. Soon after all that Sammy died; and after that I dropped out of their atmosphere. Funny, that was the only time in my life that I had actual parents, rather than jailors, don't ask, and I wasn't able to enjoy it. Oh well enough about that. Point is that earlier tonight Father Dracula called, said for me to meet him here tonight. Not abnormal, he's a good friend. What's weird is that this organization had dropped me after Sam died-" I said.

"Thought that you would-" said Captain W.X.Y.Z. Olaf.

"Nope, then decided you had to be 13. But they called me out of the blue. All I had had the chance to learn yet was that this was them getting together all that they could, seemingly in desperation. And that they had found the mastermind, I think, an officer Sanders? I believe that was the name," I said.

"How'd you learn?" said Captain W.X.Y.Z. Olaf.

"You know, now that you mention it, I believe that I was told discretely-" I said.

"discretely by who?" said Captain W.X.Y.Z. Olaf.

"Dead, and anyone who may have been in on it as well is dead," I said.

"Everyone was here tonig-" said Captain W.X.Y.Z. Olaf.

"Actually, once, one guy got the boot. And something gang related got him killed. I forget the rest," I said.

"Well then, I think I got my next case," said Captain W.X.Y.Z. Olaf.

"Great, F.Y.I. my ride was killed. Any chance of a ride home?" I said. And as cold as that sounds; I really did mourn Father Dracula.

I called Captain W.X.Y.Z. Olaf in the morning, and then told me everything you've heard from his perspective up until this point; he said it was an active investigation; and would update as soon as he could. Same the next day. In five days he called me; he said "The case was iron clad. The only anything was that he got involved in a gang because his mom went to jail for impeding a police investigation. I was invited to sit in on the interrogation. And to answer the question you're shouting at the pages or E-reader; Officer Sanders was interrogated and denied any wrongdoing whatsoever. That was all there was.

"Officer Kraken, you've elected to not have an attorney, correct?" said Captain W.X.Y.Z. Olaf.

"I have nothing to hide," she said.

"Ok, does this face ring a bell?" said Captain W.X.Y.Z. Olaf.

"No, who is this?" she said.

"You should know; you killed him," said Captain W.X.Y.Z. Olaf.

"That officer involved shooting was years ago-" she said.

"No, no, that incident is irrelevant," said Captain W.X.Y.Z. Olaf, "You see, his mother you put in jail because you didn't get your way. He ended up in a gang, and we all know how that so often ends."

"First of all, How did I not 'get my way-'" she said.

"She," said Captain W.X.Y.Z. Olaf, then switching to a high pitched mocking voice, "impeded a police investigation-"

"She broke the law-" she said.

(insert mule picture here)
Houston

"Law, smaw, are you law enforcement; or a cop?" said Captain W.X.Y.Z. Olaf; back to his normal voice.

"First of all, same thing, second, there is no reason for me to be in chains, and third, I didn't kill him!" she said getting mad.

"Wrong, wrong, and wrong. You're a killer, that's why you're in chains; and I don't like prying nails off my face. And last but not least," said Captain W.X.Y.Z. Olaf, "You didn't have to put her in jail. But you did; and that caused his death. That, albeit not absolutely, is your fault."

"This is absurd!" she said.

"Tell it to the judge," said Captain W.X.Y.Z. Olaf.

When he went to arrest her she shouted about how he was killing her kids. Then said "Olaf, you can't chase this. It's too late-"

"How so?" said Captain W.X.Y.Z. Olaf.

She simply shook her head and said "She was innocent, I had to. Olaf; sometimes you just have to look the other way."

"You're sick," said Captain W.X.Y.Z. Olaf.

She replied as would be expected and then Olaf said "No, I mean clinically sick." She just cried out more about how he was killing her children as she was hauled to protective custody. He always did that when a cop was arrested, or someone else that might not fare well in jail.

Chillax. Captain W.X.Y.Z. Olaf thought ahead. Already had guys protecting her kids.

Captain W.X.Y.Z. Olaf walked out and a fellow officer said "Grand jury won't indibt."

Captain W.X.Y.Z. Olaf then said "Yea, but that's on their head."

Just then there was a massive explosion. My memories of what happened more resemble an "Escape from furnaces of hell or other burning building" horror movie than what actually happened. Instead I will include this USA Today front page, above the fold, headline story:

Oklahoma City Again; This Time Against Cops

The City of Houston isn't what comes to mind when you think of terrorism. But all that changed on (Mon.) (day) 20-. A fuel tanker pulled into an alley behind the Houston Police Department Central Station. Houston FD concluded the cause of its explosion was deliberate. The ATF, FBI, and HPD alike have not released anything directly regarding the vehicle in question. 102 police officers were killed in the blast; nearly doubling the number of fallen-in-line-of-duty officers in the department's history. 41 civilian employees, 29 regular civilians, and 11 suspects were also killed. Among the dead were 31 narcotics officers, 17 detectives, all on duty bilisticists, 11 Internal Affairs officers and other 2 very high ranking officers. Captain William Xavier Yolanda Zack(ery) Olaf was unharmed...

Nuff said. We had had 20 (usually 21, but Captain W.X.Y.Z. Olaf had to arrest one of his own when he didn't get permission to look in someplace, then simply held his breath) IA officers, plus The Viking Cop. 4 were injured, but recovered. Officer Kraken was among the dead suspects. I remember Captain W.X.Y.Z. Olaf saying "We all know what this is really about." Then saying no one could at all cooperate in the investigation. Everyone was dirty. Even the Feds we'd seen were dirty. And if they did cooperate; they'd be charged as accomplices to what was going on. But that doesn't mean that he was going to withhold information.

Transcript of Newsradio 740 KTRH main story:

Earlier this evening there was a shooting a KPRC Local 2 studios. 2 security guards were wounded. 2 journalists were fatally shot along with one HPD officer. One shooter was killed in the incident; police have confirmed that the other shooter was stopped.

That was an IA officer. Bringing us down to 8, and Captain W.X.Y.Z. Olaf. Then I was called back to IPP by Captain W.X.Y.Z. Olaf. Here's what happened there.

"What happened?!" I said.

"We all know what happened," said Captain W.X.Y.Z. Olaf.

"No, we don't," said an officer.

(insert mule picture here)
Houston

"We were going to tell everyone everything. The shooters were cops. We can't trust anyone," said Captain W.X.Y.Z. Olaf, "This is... unreal. No, that's not it. A veil has been removed from our eyes. We can trust no one and nothing. We can do our regular work here. But we need a special place to do this. I've got my ear to the street, helps more than you'd think-" said Captain W.X.Y.Z. Olaf.

"What does that mean?" I asked.

"The enemy of my enemy is my friend, and I imagine you all are also," said Captain W.X.Y.Z. Olaf.

"I still don't know what that means," I said.

"Most Internal Affairs bosses look amongst high ranking, highly decorated policemen-" said an officer.

"And Policewomen," said another officer.

"Yes, and policewomen. He looks in Juvenile records," said the first officer.

"I want you people to see what we can learn from the old IA division. After tonight we need to work like spies. Remember, if it's electronic, or we don't know them. It's an unnecessary risk," said Captain W.X.Y.Z. Olaf.

"What if we are defeated?" said a 3rd officer "Do we just go vigilante?"

Everyone else just looked down. We all knew the answer.

Excerpt of The Leader top story

The home invasion left a 43 year old woman and a 19 year old off duty police officer dead. A 47 year old man also died of a heart attack during the invasion. HPD caught the invaders 14 year old ... and his step brother 16 year old ... They have been charged with premeditated murder as adults...

Transcript of anonymous tip to Crime Stoppers Houston

(insert mule picture here)
Houston

"Crime Stoppers Houston how can I help you?" said the operator.

"Yes I just saw a cop get gunned dow-"

"You saw what-" said the operator.

"Yes, you heard correctly, People were swarming the scene. I know who did it."

"How do you know?" said the operator.

"He sells me my drugs. Which is why I can't give you my name; and why I am using a pay phone."

"What's the killer's name?" said the operator.

"... and yes, I'm sure. I-I have to go."

The names of the framed have been removed to protect the innocent. Both of those officers were IA officers. Bringing us down to 6, including Captain W.X.Y.Z. Olaf; 7 counting myself. Here's when we got together the next morning:

"What is this place?" said an officer, "It looks like a crack house!"

"It looks like an ordinary crack house, because it is an ordinary crack house! Not even I would suspect this for being a front for the police. You might want to wear a gas mask," Captain W.X.Y.Z. Olaf.

"Way ahead of you," I said.

"So? our new station, is a place of crime?" said a 2nt officer.

"No, our new station is the attic of a place of crime." said Captain W.X.Y.Z. Olaf.

"What if it just happens to be raided?" I said.

"We're IA, we can prevent that; at least for the time being," said Captain W.X.Y.Z. Olaf.

"So, were, like, looking the other way and even protecting crime?" said the 1st officer.

"Considering everything," said Captain W.X.Y.Z. Olaf, trailing off.

"What about last night?" said a 4th officer.

Captain W.X.Y.Z. Olaf opened up his car and said "There are," and to be honest, I have forgotten the name, other than it was just M, something, and digits, "Machine guns. I don't want to catch any of you people without one."

"So, like, were supposed to go everywhere-" said the 1st officer.

"First of all, you should be laying low as much as possible. Second the mafia hid their guns in instrument cases. I see no reason why we can't," said Captain W.X.Y.Z. Olaf.

"What about places where they would chec-" said a 5th officer.

"Avoid those places," said Captain W.X.Y.Z. Olaf.

"How do we know when-" I said.

"IF! And, I-I think if we're ever down to 3, counting me," said Captain W.X.Y.Z. Olaf.

"So, 4 more murders and-" I said.

"3," said Captain W.X.Y.Z. Olaf.

"3? I think you-" I said.

I insisted otherwise; but Captain W.X.Y.Z. Olaf told and insisted that I must be a secret and not know about me. So that if it all went sideways; at least someone would know the truth; and would exist behind the scenes pulling some strings.

"I hope you all remembered to forget your phones," said Captain W.X.Y.Z. Olaf.

I could tell by the look on everyone's faces; they hadn't Captain W.X.Y.Z. Olaf groaned and said "Oh well, this one is probally for the best if they overheard this. But BE CAREFUL! I have to go find a new secret base."

"How were you able to pull this off?" said the only officer that hasn't yet spoken.

"Like I said. Ear to the street; Enemy of my enemy is my friend," he said.

The next day at the new base:

"Sup?" I said.

"Well, I just finally busted a ring of cops taking bribes from parents wanting to punish, usually their own children; or at least in some parental capacity over them. And then planting on the for mentioned children and teens, and a few young adults," said Captain W.X.Y.Z. Olaf.

"And I'm sure you're busy thanks to the slain but not fallen cop," I said.

"Yes, yes. I was getting to that," said Captain W.X.Y.Z. Olaf.

Here I'll cut in to explain what you'll otherwise just be stuck scratching your head for the rest of the book. The officer was not alone in his dark biddings. Thought later his aides would be busted. He was doing unspeakable things to kids (8-12 mostly) and those that wouldn't cooperate would get drugs planted on their older siblings. One of the victims had a teen uncle who caught him in the act and bludgeoned him to death. Despite having been in trouble with the law before; had to let him go. Really was self-defense; you know as well as I do that it was undeniably self-defense for the police to not rule that a homicide. Cheery eh? Told you should at least think twice before reading this book.

"You didn't get much sleep last night, did you," I said.

"No, not much. But it's not that," said Captain W.X.Y.Z. Olaf.

buwanawanabawanawanawana (yea, no one can understand police blotter)

"Anything important?" I said.

"I'll say! Someone just tried to shoot one of my guys this morning!" said Captain W.X.Y.Z. Olaf.

"We now down to 6? Counting you?" I said.

"No, glad I doled out those weapons. Killed one attacker; other's in a coma. Probably gunu stay in a coma," said Captain W.X.Y.Z. Olaf.

"You got all that from that?" I said.

"Yea," he said.

Later:

"How could we ever take this down?" said an officer.

"Same way the mob was taken down. They didn't bang their head into the top. No they went after those they could catch at the bottom till someone cut a deal," said Captain W.X.Y.Z. Olaf.

"Who can we catch at the bottom? Everything is invisible!" said a 2nt officer.

(insert mule picture here)
Houston

"Were going after the wind. You can't see the wind, you can feel the wind, you can see it's affects. Sometimes you can even taste the wind. And if you have a parachute or sail; you can catch the wind." said Captain W.X.Y.Z. Olaf.

"Taste? The wind?" I said.

"Well, maybe in a sandstorm. Not the point," said Captain W.X.Y.Z. Olaf.

"I don't think I understand?" said a 3rd officer.

"Crime, closure, and conviction statistics are our tree. And public records are our parachute," said Captain W.X.Y.Z. Olaf.

"Too philosophical," I said.

"Ah! Here we are! 12 year old twins. Wanted to help their big brother get their dignity back and be a cool kid. Helped him through a wild party," said Captain W.X.Y.Z. Olaf.

"Uhhh? through?" said the 1st officer to speak.

"Misspoke. Put chloroform on their parents' pillows so they'd sleep through, and this time it mean through. When the police arrived they found them to have gotten too much. Charged as adults for 1st degree murder. Got 'gang of dirty cops' written all over it," said Captain W.X.Y.Z. Olaf.

"So? I don't groc?" said a 4th officer.

"Trial's today. We'll raid it," said Captain W.X.Y.Z. Olaf.

"I'll quietly get the warrant," said the 2nt officer.

"Don't, don't," said Captain W.X.Y.Z. Olaf.

"What?! You afraid the judge'll squeal?" replied the officer.

"Well, that too. We just need to go. What's happening is them trying to commit kidnapping. That's probable cause for us to enter without a warrant. And we both know that the judge'll say no," said Captain W.X.Y.Z. Olaf.

"Is this legal?" said a 5th officer.

"Technically, I mean this is the same thing currently putting a judge on death row," he said.

"And his wife," I said.

"No, she's charged with murder," said Captain W.X.Y.Z. Olaf.

"Is this ethical? I mean with the judge going to say no-" said the 3rd officer.

"I hope so," said Captain W.X.Y.Z. Olaf, who then shouted "Ok! Let's get the guns and go!"

I was behind the scenes and as such I had to stay back.

Later,

"How'd it go?" I said.

"South," said Captain W.X.Y.Z. Olaf.

"How so?" I said.

"Only one was twin was there. She was killed," said Captain W.X.Y.Z. Olaf, "Got someone bringing the other twin in."

"You got the judge?" I said.

"In a sense, he met a same fate, along with bailiffs-" said Captain W.X.Y.Z. Olaf.

"The prosecutor? You arrest him?" I said.

"Crossfire," said Captain W.X.Y.Z. Olaf.

"Crossfire?" I said.

"With the bailiffs," said Captain W.X.Y.Z. Olaf, "Awaiting to see what lies they'll tell. And yes now we're under investigation. But being internal affairs..."

"How we doing?" I said.

"Well, we lost an-" said Captain W.X.Y.Z. Olaf, who saw an officer hold up 2 fingers, "2?"

The officer nodded and said "Hospital called."

"2 of our own." said Captain W.X.Y.Z. Olaf.

"The rest?" I said.

"Everyone else unharmed, considering," said Captain W.X.Y.Z. Olaf.

"Now what?" I said.

(insert mule picture here)
Houston

"We continue. There's an interrogation in the morning I'm sure to be a front for corruption," said Captain W.X.Y.Z. Olaf.

"Guess we're down to 6, counting you and me," I said.

"Yea, can't even do regular-" said Captain W.X.Y.Z. Olaf.

"Any way we could get more-" I said.

"I wouldn't trust any cop, I'm even leery of my own men-" said Captain W.X.Y.Z. Olaf.

"You think?!-" I said.

"Anything this big. It's a logical conclusion," said Captain W.X.Y.Z. Olaf.

"But you got all your original-" I said.

"Yea, but under the circumstances, I'd have to have a reason to trust anyone. You sure are there are no one left from Gregor Mendal's-" said Captain W.X.Y.Z. Olaf.

"Just me; and even if I'm wrong. Have no idea who they are or how to reach them. Sorry," I said, "Maybe someone you know-"

"No, I-I wouldn't. There's no one. I don't think they'd be above an indirect attack and then anyone I'd-" said Captain W.X.Y.Z. Olaf.

"Indirect attack?" I said.

"See the officer that was bludgeoned," said Captain W.X.Y.Z. Olaf.

"Oh, I have lots of friends-" I said.

"No, No one your age," said Captain W.X.Y.Z. Olaf.

"But I thought you almost got to be a cop when you were 11-" I said.

"That was different, and, and anyone from you could lead back to you," said Captain W.X.Y.Z. Olaf.

"Fair point," I said.

The next morning:

(insert mule picture here)
Houston

I couldn't catch a word for word; but Captain W.X.Y.Z. Olaf was being shouted at. half his surviving officers had just lost someone. He calmed everyone down and then said how his parents had died. Here's his retelling of what happened:

"Captain Call Letters?" said an officer.

"Yea, what happened?" I said.

"First, can you confirm who these people are. You're listed as 'in case of emergency contact.' You knew these people?" said the officer.

"You first," I said.

"Ugh fine," said the officer.

"Tip, don't say 'ugh' to the family of a deceased. But go on," I said.

"O-key. Well some old Jewish guy found them. A route visit," said the officer.

"That must be my grandfather." I said.

"I thought he was the one that died while you were in jail; and left the window open through which your siblings' killer got in," said the officer.

"No, that was my other grandfather. Say, how'd you tell he was-" I said.

"The voice, I'm not anti-" said the officer.

"I know. What happened?" I said.

"Probally a really bad home invasion. Who are these people," said the officer.

"My parents," I said.

"How? He looks like an Indian chief; and she looks like the other kind of Indian, as in subcontinent," said the officer.

"Everyone in my family is adopted. Our family reunions are like an international festival; except more diverse," I said.

"Everyone?" said the officer.

"Except my brother that is," I said.

"So, you have both kinds of Indians in your family?" said the officer, skeptical.

"Yea, 3 if you count my cousin on the Cleveland Indians-" I said.

"I thought you killed your brother, and your sister," said the officer.

It was hard for me to control myself, but I then said "No, my siblings were murdered, I was framed. My little brother was killed by a serial killer. And my sister had a twin brother, who, while older than me died hiding in the chest freezer during hide and go seek. He was 4; I was 18 months. As such I can't remember him."

"Were any of you blood re-" said the officer.

"As I've said before. My little, not baby, though I agreed to stop calling him that when he hit 5, baby brother was Chinese. And my sister was jet black. And before you call me racist; that's what she called herself. To explain, some people from Africa are not brown skinned, but truly black skinned. She was one, so was her twin brother. I've seen pictures," I kinda smiled and said " I still remember us all at the beach and trying to get her to wear sun block. She just insisted that she was immune to sun burn. She was right."

"Ever wanted to know your real parents?" said the officer.

"I did; I assume you mean my biological parents," I said, "Are you adopted?"

"I don't see what that could have to do with anything, but no-" said the officer.

"Have you ever wanted to meet the people that would have been your parents had you been adopted?" I said.

"Well no, but-" said the officer.

"Same," said I.

"Sorry about your parents. When was the last time you talked?" said the officer.

"At the funeral of my youngest brother. I still remember right before he died; he got his first girlfriend. Her dad wanted to meet him first. It was the ultimate ultimate awesome seeing the stereotypical 'girl on her first date's father' meeting the 7' 6", super bodybuilder, as I still am, big brother of her boyfriend. She was nice, but, I ramble," I said.

"So you weren't close-" said the officer.

"They believed the cops, dumped me in jail. When I was exonerated, bail couldn't be made, I found my parents had divorced, and I had a new baby brother. Somehow losing him got those two back together where they belong. I know how this works. You think I've killed before; and always

(insert mule picture here)
Houston

assume the family. Furthermore if there hadn't been my little brother between us, probably would have been completely estranged. I'm IA; you're not. Call my lawyer," I said.

My sister had a similar experience; I'll explain later.

Just then Captain W.X.Y.Z. Olaf had to go to a briefing. The briefing was that the feds had cracked the bombing. Allegedly, it all started about 3 years ago. A kid ran from strangers, like any normal kid. Unfortunately it was cops trying to arrest him; and he was holding his baby sister; they thought he had a weapon and he was ordered to drop it. She died. Now he was 14. He was a lone wolf. He stole a gas tanker. You know the rest. After that they had to all rush over to that interview. It was an abused juvenile delinquent. His mother was so afraid of him getting in touch with the wrong crowd he was never able to call Gregor Mendal. He suffered under her as long as could. Till, one day, he just couldn't do it any longer. The police couldn't disprove it to be self-defense. And there was no father around. They went to the social worker. She said that as long as he didn't 'fess up' his little sister. Who he was determined to protect. Would be stuck in the most horrific foster home she could find. She was later found dead; suicide couldn't be ruled out. At the interview the police tried the old cop trick 'put out a glass of water'. It was another PAAA event. (That's the whitewashed abbreviation used for Prosecuting As An Adult). The police were ordered to, quote "DROP THE EVIDENCE!" Two detectives were injured. One of us died. And Dep. Chief Raider was shot clean in the forehead. Then they had to rush over to the crime lab to stop it. They just busted in. They got the evidence back; but lost one of their own. Here's what happened when they returned to me:

"You're feeling bad about having shot her. But you feel glad that she simply can't hurt anyone anymore; which makes you feel worse. Don't. You said it yourself that there are people that simply deserve to die, some that it lessens it just a little, some a bit more, and on up to the point that it shouldn't even be a crime. Raider was one such person; and you know it. She was a dirty cop, one known for intimidating-" I said.

"Captain! Just got word form crime lab," said the officer.

"What?! We know they're using clean cops as a human shield. Shoot! A whole S.W.A.T. team of 20 died-" said Captain W.X.Y.Z. Olaf.

"Worse. All evidence is gone," he said.

"Regarding what? All the dirty cases-" said Captain W.X.Y.Z. Olaf.

"No, I mean all evidence. And we were framed for it-" said the officer.

"All the evidence being process-" said Captain W.X.Y.Z. Olaf.

(insert mule picture here)
Houston

"All there is," he said.

"All HPD has ever collected?" said Captain W.X.Y.Z. Olaf, disbelieving.

"Yes, well some I'm sure had already been lost to the sands of time, but yes, and I need to discuss this situation with you alone," said the officer.

He went into another room and then relayed the following conversation to me:

"Remember when most of us lost someone? Just this morning?" said the officer.

F.Y.I., I didn't.

"How couldn't I?" I said.

"My brother was arrested. major possession / drug charges," said the officer.

"Is he guilty?" I said.

"Possibly. He's been in trouble with the law before. They clearly wanted a mole-" said the officer.

"Who's they?!" I said, overexcited.

"Tell ya if I knew," he said.

"So you want me to turn my att-" I said.

"No, I know you keep your ear to the street. Can you get us to the Maldives?" he said.

"Well, and hear me out, you're asking me to help a fugitive flee-" I said, getting cut off.

He reacted as you'd expect, complete with cussing, till I said "But, if I didn't. I'd be an accomplice to what's going on." I was thanked profusely, till I had a call to make. The kid I'd just gotten back from trying to save, had just died in prison.

End of retell.

I was later told that his big sister, who should have been guardian all along, had poisoned him and herself. Apparently jail was torture for him. And when they went to her house they found this note:

To my little sister; or whom it may concern,

(insert mule picture here)
Houston

I'm sure all this is a shock to you. I just hope you're not mad at me. It all started, as I'm sure you know, when our abusive mother one day went just too far. He told me that if he hadn't killed her, she'd have killed him. He would have given up. He'd tried talking to cops; but that was a total dead end. He needed someone to take care of you. And he thought I'd be going to jail for a long time for robbing a Jos A. Bank; and then attempting to knock over a police station. I got probation just having switched to adult court, being now, or then, 18. And as for the social worker. No one believed him that your social worker was attempting to blackmail him into confessing to murders. He was going away for good. I'm sure that this wasn't right and will help nothing. But you have no idea what he was going through. I hope you have a good life, find a good man. Maybe have some kids through whom some of me and him will live on.

In Christ,

-

After that little bit of dust settled we just looked at each other. He had no more choice. Vigilante. But against who? All we knew was 'Officer Sanders.' Captain W.X.Y.Z. Olaf then said we knew something. I had to take the back seat to that. Turns out Crayer wasn't in on this. "Why bribe someone who'll do it for free?" But he was able to look at old financial records of Crayer's. Crayer demanded such a good deal he stayed on the bench. But we caught who was bribing him. Here's what happened when Captain W.X.Y.Z. Olaf told me what happened days later.

"So, there were 19 other such judges across the country? But Crayer would have done it without the bribe?" I said.

"Yea, just seeing him," Captain W.X.Y.Z. Olaf paused emotionally, "I bled from my nose and eyes. We're going after the," he paused again to look for the word, "Damager of 100s. He damaged 1000s"

"Damaged?" I said.

"Yea, and I was only 13 months," said Captain W.X.Y.Z. Olaf, clearly it had been a hard, horrific experience.

"Why would a loving god let this happen?" I paused and skipped to, "Even if they're guilty?"

(insert mule picture here)
Houston

Captain W.X.Y.Z. Olaf paused and said "What makes you think he allows this? No, that's why we're here. Why I'm here."

"Time for me to go," said the deserter officer.

"Yea, but you've got another passenger," said Captain W.X.Y.Z. Olaf.

"Oh no," he replied thinking it was all over.

He showed the girl whose twin sister he raided the courthouse for.

"Miss?" said Captain W.X.Y.Z. Olaf, "You can walk. But there's a catch."

"I won't rat-" she said.

"No, you simply have to go to the Maldives; err, at least for the time being. You'll be safe from us there. You've even got a new dad, and a new little and a new big, brother." said Captain W.X.Y.Z. Olaf.

"This is a trap, and what's a Maldeve?" she replied.

"It's not. When some stuff gets to have a happy ending you can come back. Till then you're Jade Dragon," said Captain W.X.Y.Z. Olaf.

"Ah! A Michael Vey fan I see; but is this legal?" she said.

"Well, more my kids; and absolutely not," he said dehandcuffing her.

"But I did-" she said.

"I don't care, you're 12," said Captain W.X.Y.Z. Olaf.

Just then Captain W.X.Y.Z. Olaf had to go off. The Judges were still in jail in their local areas. But the briber had hung himself in jail after being picked up by Colorado State Troopers. Captain W.X.Y.Z. Olaf just shrugged it off. Said we got all we needed. This way we wouldn't have to release the name to the public. I asked the why? I was told "He though what he was doing was right; what was for the best. Apparently his brother committed a crime that needs not repeating, against him. Normally he would have been tried as an adult. Fortunately he wasn't. But when he got out, he did it again," I asked about the brother and I was told he was dead, long dead. I asked about the name release thing; and the how. He said "He was an obscure internet billionaire. He also was one that would do anything for name recognition. And I'll be damned alive before I let that happen. He came into this world a whole lot of nothing; and as such he will return to the dust.

We have already alerted the family and that's all anyone will ever be alerted. This man was Adolf Hitler. Least now some people will get out of jail. Some."

"So, we were fighting Besteel, and Lorac got caught in the crossfire?" I said.

"Well, Besteel's an understatement, but essentially, yes. You know I thought those books were a really original-" Captain W.X.Y.Z. Olaf said, but something too trivial to relate cut him off.

After we saw Jade Dragon and Company off we got word that the 21st IA officer had been convicted for not putting a dirty officer in protective custody. He was going to jail.

We knew that we had to go vigilante. But we knew so little.

"Would it be wrong to suggest torture?" I said.

They didn't know what to say, so I said, "I have an idea."

"What? torture him into confessing?" said Captain W.X.Y.Z. Olaf.

"Close. They do indirect attacks. Let's get someone he loves and offer him full immunity in exchange for his crew and everything. All top underlings as well get that deal as well," I said.

"Good idea, but we already did-" said Captain W.X.Y.Z. Olaf.

"But until he does, the other person gets-" I said.

"You'd really-" said the other officer.

"No! Of course not. We just make him think-" I said.

"That could work," said Captain W.X.Y.Z. Olaf's wife. We were so desperate that he had to call her in for help. Bringing our grand total up to 4.

"Wouldn't stand up in court," said Captain W.X.Y.Z. Olaf.

"Yea, but might be enough to get them to stop progressing," said Captain W.X.Y.Z. Olaf, "Also there is the paraphrased principal of it will if you don't get caught. Or at the very least expose and raise awareness."

"What if they don't help?" said the officer.

"Problem," I said.

We caught his daughter, Well, caught isn't the right word. I made the approach. She helped. Unfortunately when we brought in the Internal Affairs prosecutor; it all went south. The restraints broke. He went through a one-way mirror. The officer that had been faking the torture had to shoot him. To death. Right in front of his daughter. Captain W.X.Y.Z. Olaf saw that the restraints had been tampered with. He knew it was one of us. He thought the prosecutor, they often fought. The prosecutor thought Captain W.X.Y.Z. Olaf's wife, Captain W.X.Y.Z. Olaf's wife thought the other prosecutor, the other prosecutor thought the officer, the officer thought Captain W.X.Y.Z. Olaf and me. Captain W.X.Y.Z. Olaf' wife had to do the fingerprinting herself but there wasn't anything else she could do. The other prosecutor was right. Here's what the officer said "They said they'd kill me and frame my little siblings and kid. I've been ratting all along. It's why only myself wasn't attacked in any way." He said that Sanders was really the cover boss; and that was all he knew. He got immunity and lost his badge in exchange for a higher up. We had to give the top dog total immunity in exchange for being sure we had rooted it all out same with the top guys.

"Officer - You can totally get away with it-" said Captain W.X.Y.Z. Olaf.

"Except for losing my badge," he said.

"Well, yes. But if you leave out anything you know, it all goes out the window," said Captain W.X.Y.Z. Olaf.

"What about federal immunity?" he said.

"Fed's too scared of us," I said.

"And if I honestly forget?" he said.

"Better be able to convince a jury of that. But I wouldn't worry. We've a lot of police records to go through," said Captain W.X.Y.Z. Olaf.

Turned out the boss we had been interrogating had been a cover story just in case people started to catch on. He gave us the cop that had made him go corrupt, who we had to give immunity to get to his secret superior who gave up the true shadow commissioner. And it proved to be all, and even more, than it was cracked up to be. Here is his interrogation.

"Let's start with an overview," I said.

"Growing up, I always wanted to be a top cop," he said, "I cheated in the police academy. I wanted promotions. And those who wouldn't take bribes got stuff planted and I made them promote me; I had lots of money for bribes thanks to my family of origin. No one in all time was better at planting than me. And by making so many arrests I rose through the ranks. People looked up to me; and in time I became their shadow superior," he said.

"How so?" said Captain W.X.Y.Z. Olaf.

(insert mule picture here)
Houston

"We both know the answer to that question," he said.

"Didn't you ever feel any guilt? I mean, I doubt even Jeffery Dommer never once in his life-" I said.

"Indeed, you see for a time I tried to simply enjoy my station, but, in time I began regressing, and at first it was small, even procedural," he said.

"How so?" said Captain W.X.Y.Z. Olaf.

"At first it was small things, leaving a glass of water out by which to take DNA without a warrant, talking people out of a lawyer, etc..." he said.

"I know, I've seen that so many times, I try to build a wrongful holding case, or something related such as official oppression or abuse of power, but sometimes even I can't build the slightest case," said Captain W.X.Y.Z. Olaf.

"But they never stood up!" he said so sadistically, it was truly creepy.

"They will now," said Captain W.X.Y.Z. Olaf.

"Yea, they will now," he said.

"Then what?" said Captain W.X.Y.Z. Olaf.

"Then I decided to take it a little farther," he said.

"Bend the rules a little further?" said Captain W.X.Y.Z. Olaf.

"Well, I still wasn't bending the rules yet-" he said.

"Except for all the drugs you'd planted in the past," I said.

"Yea, except for that," he said, "I started lying, saying we had things we didn't, being deceitful, and I suppose it was gateway crimes. Within weeks we were training people to be masters of manipulation. Absolute psychological sculptors!"

"Like Dennis Hemmingway?" I said.

"Stay off the Roux," said Captain W.X.Y.Z. Olaf, "Meanwhile back at the ranch... "

"Cutting a deal, help someone that we never had even made a person of interest. 'Talk or we move you to another prison.' 'Talk or You'll be denied parole.' Put people in jail that wouldn't

(insert mule picture here)
Houston

talk when we would declare them to be only a witness with no right of silence or representation. Whatever we could think of,"

"So when *you* wouldn't make *them* a suspect, *you* could get around all most all due process-" said Captain W.X.Y.Z. Olaf.

"Olaf, we're both cops, you know that witnesses have no right to remain silent!" he said.

"Yea, but sometimes it's still good to step back and be aghast at your own evil," said Captain W.X.Y.Z. Olaf.

"So now I'm evil?" he said sarcastically.

"All throughout world history the most evil have created their own standards of right and wrong, and when they didn't come up short, they thought themselves to be good. And I suppose that everyone else is the same," said Captain W.X.Y.Z. Olaf.

"So everyone is evil?!?!" he said.

"Pretty much," said Captain W.X.Y.Z. Olaf.

"So what next?" I said.

"Oh we were master liars! We'd also make people think that, among other rights, they didn't have the right to remain silent," he said.

"Evil, but so far not criminal, What made it what it is today, err, what it was yesterday, should I say," I said.

"Yes, you should," said Captain W.X.Y.Z. Olaf.

"First time we, as WE, crossed the legal line was a lawyer that had basically exposed everything. We had to take him out, I mean it ultimately was necessary and needed to be done to protect the department, and in turn the people. I mean he was going to bankrupt us in court!- " he said.

"Tough," I said.

"Let me guess, because the family couldn't demand the murder investigation be handed over to an outside-" said Captain W.X.Y.Z. Olaf.

"BINGO! However by that point how high you were was approximately equal to how corrupt you are, " he said.

(insert mule picture here)
Houston

"And it grew from that, " said Captain W.X.Y.Z. Olaf.

"Not exactly, it's a bit of a long story," he said.

"We got all night, and all day, and unlimited coffee, " I said.

"If you want to know everything that there is to know about everything, then you're gunu need it," he said.

"Just spill it," said Captain W.X.Y.Z. Olaf.

Splash

"I meant the story! Not your coffee!" said Captain W.X.Y.Z. Olaf.

"Well, to veer off into the laboratory. When we couldn't get someone to talk. We'd simply have our crime lab tecks lie. Originally we only did it when we knew it, but just couldn't prove it-" he said.

"How can you know it? If you can't prove it?" I said.

"By court standards, we can't. But as long as at least most of those convicted are guilty, isn't that what's best-" he said.

"Our legal system is based on the principle that it is better for 100 guilty persons to walk. Than for one innocent person to be incarcerated, " said Captain W.X.Y.Z. Olaf.

"Olaf! It's 20-," he said.

"Back when those principles were laid down; there was no forensic science. It was far harder to prove someone guilty than it is nowadays," said Captain W.X.Y.Z. Olaf.

"So, that's when you officially crossed the legal line, " I said.

"You'd think. But those interviews were pretty off the wall-" he said.

"Hollywoodesque, " said Captain W.X.Y.Z. Olaf.

"In many cases, could put Hollywood to shame! " he bragged, "Why, I remember this one case in which-"

"Hey! Save if for the case by case," I said.

"We've been through the interview room-" said Captain W.X.Y.Z. Olaf.

(insert mule picture here)
Houston

"Oh no we haven't! " he said.

"What else did you do in the interviews?!" I said.

"Oh that is just so numerous! Once this one guy was wisely too afraid that we were just out the get him. Refused police protection, ended up dead. Other end of the spectrum, protection was denied; had to confess. Exchanged bullet for needle. And this one time-" he sadistically bragged.

"Like I said, save it for the case by case," Captain W.X.Y.Z. Olaf.

"So, you lied in interview rooms-" I said.

"Lied everywhere! " he said.

"Yes, but I believe his question was, how big a leap is it from lying in the interview room, to the courtroom? " said Captain W.X.Y.Z. Olaf.

"Smaller than even you'd expect," he said.

"But, going back to what you said about the, as I sometimes call them, labbies. What about defense calling for independent review?" said Captain W.X.Y.Z. Olaf.

"Often they couldn't-" he said.

"Like in DWIs?" said Captain W.X.Y.Z. Olaf.

"Well, among some more serious crimes; yes," he said.

"And the rest of the time?" I said.

"You don't really think we'd hand over the real evidence, do you?" he said.

"And that's what this superscandal boiled down to," I said.

"Oh con trerre, as this was going on, the interviews were getting even worse, " he said.

"How is that even possible?" said Captain W.X.Y.Z. Olaf.

"We would have seminars how to manipulate people. We also brought in the church of Scientology to conduct interviews. Could get people to confess to stuff not only did we not think they did; but was never accused of. But, that ended soon because it was just too expensive. After that we often went so far as to torture someone into a confession, or someone else and make them watch. Or put a gun to their head, or someone else's. They weren't interrogations; it was simply horror movies," he said, "But in time we found that it was simply easier to forge their signature on an admission of guilt."

"I read the statistics, why so many kids? Why so many 14 year olds?" asked Captain W.X.Y.Z. Olaf.

"Well, that's also a bit of a backstory, " he said.

"In order to keep your immunity-" said Captain W.X.Y.Z. Olaf.

"Yeah, yea, well, first you must understand that the department became much like The Brain in *A Swiftly Tilting Planet*. We moved effort from actual police work, of which actual investigation for anything but the most serious crimes was already nonexistent, over to the corruption. Sure we had great convection rates, but when we had no clue who did it. Didn't help. In time we were just throwing a dart in the phone book; sometimes literally; to find a person to frame. Sure when we knew-" he said.

"Thought you knew," I corrected.

(pause)

"who did it, but. Little good that does when you're completely stumped. And that was becoming more and more common. Also by this point the internal gang had formed," he said.

"Did bail have it's finger in this dark pie?" asked Captain W.X.Y.Z. Olaf.

"Oh yeah, needed it very high; same reason we liked minors," he said.

"Well that doesn't sound creepy at all," I said sarcastically.

"How so?" said Captain W.X.Y.Z. Olaf.

"In jail the authority is just like that of a parent..." he said.

"Final, with no higher power to appeal to-" I said.

"Well on both counts-" said Captain W.X.Y.Z. Olaf.

"Don't split hairs, you will never be able to it better than me," I said.

"In short, and in a word, yes," he said.

"Well I assume you don't have a love of power in and of itself so why did you-" said Captain W.X.Y.Z. Olaf.

(insert mule picture here)
Houston

"Well you would be wrong about that- but you would not be wrong," he said.

"Let me guess, you used that power however you could to ply-" said Captain W.X.Y.Z. Olaf.

"Was really great when it was both!" he said.

"Must've been cruelty to-" I said.

"Who Cares! It worked didn't it!" he said.

"Minors need bail? I mean with their parents? And you know it is never their own money, in fact what difference, barring something earth shaking or that will get them beaten will necessarily be the difference made by their-" I said.

"Spoken from the wisdom of innocence. Anything else?" asked Captain W.X.Y.Z. Olaf.

"Yeah, by this point it was totally organized crime, and spreading every everywhere like a brain tumor-" he said.

"Wouldn't want it to spill out to the real poli-" I said.

"Mostly, also, among all this, and more run of the mill police corruption, we were having to kill to cover up, first 3rd party victims of interrogation. However by the time we were just forging anything, or paying by bribe for the real thing-" he said.

"Cut to the chase!" I said.

"We were making hits! There I said it!" he said, "And I don't mean music."

"Didn't at least someone get close?" said Captain W.X.Y.Z. Olaf.

"Well, besides the old IA division,-" he said.

"Which you had a mole in!" said Captain W.X.Y.Z. Olaf.

"Yea! Did a good job at the end didn't he?!" he said.

"Blackmailed I presume" said Captain W.X.Y.Z. Olaf.

"Yea, had to kinda double cross him at the end" he said.

"But, besides Gregor Mendel, did anyone else-" said Captain W.X.Y.Z. Olaf.

"Well, the mayor was seeing this, he was planning to dissolve the police department; or at the very least disarm-" he said.

(insert mule picture here)
Houston

"I thought that Bruce simply wanted revenge for his dog! " said Captain W.X.Y.Z. Olaf.

"Oh he did! Just needed a little help-" he said.

"And you made sure he was killed by the cops at the city council meeting to make sure he didn't plee you out-" I said.

"Yep, was also a state congressman-" he said.

"Was he going to go Snowden-" I said.

"No, he didn't know too much, well literally he should have known nothing-

"Get to the point, " said Captain W.X.Y.Z. Olaf.

"He was trying to have it so that everything we said in official capacity was under oath. Among other things," he said.

"I think I remember him! Wasn't him and his staff busted for drugs by the Texas Rangers? The Texas Rangers Are Dirty!" said Captain W.X.Y.Z. Olaf.

"No need, just fell for it hook, line, and sinker. Useful idots. Pretty good job we did" he said.

"Ever do it for money?" said Captain W.X.Y.Z. Olaf.

"Remember Robin Hood and Gang?" he said.

"Yea! Those tweens that got caught trying to steal confiscated stuff from the district to give back to the right and proper owners?" said Captain W.X.Y.Z. Olaf.

"That was us. Turns out on the up and up they were about to win big bucks in class action settlement, " he said.

"You know the students really should just have their own union with all the same rights and privileges as that of the faculty unions. That would fix that," I said.

"What else?" said Captain W.X.Y.Z. Olaf.

The rest gets a little tedious. I'll let you know that they were also using tricks such as bending the rules of prosecuting as well, it started out stuff like waiting till the last possible minute to give the defense the heads up of what the prosecution was going to present which they were legally entitled to; and eventually they were sending a cop and / or a bailiff into a jury deliberation room, where they were supposed to be alone, to blackmail them whatever direction they wanted. But that took just too much cover-up; wasn't worth it. Also there was plenty of straight up violence; such

(insert mule picture here)
Houston

as leaking something, usually a lie, to get set someone up to be murdered; along with other lying such as leaking a lie to the press. Also there was also lots of other things as well, withholding or delaying a phone call, at least till some questions were answered, eavesdropping, making a verbal agreement / contract and breaking it, and let us not forget bad old fashioned coercion. I must stop that list here; the list of all forms of corruption is just too long to enumerate here. Also they got many of their ideas from the JonBenet Ramsey case; and somehow found a way to go even further! And the reason the general public or press didn't catch on was that people after the fact would often confess in jail. A few cases they were convinced they did it. But normally, they'd have parole denied along with any possible privileges in jail. They'd generally do all that they could to make it as miserable and bad till they "fessed up". I would love to go into more detail; but much more and it would be beginning to simply give details on a case by case basis. And to do so would read like a piece of reference; although quite possibly the only piece of reference ever that's really worth sitting down and reading. Also it would be about as long. You would not believe how long it took to finish that interview. And how when we went for arrest warrants; how that judge responded. Essentially had to force her to even listen to us (it took very long to go through everything) under threat of arrest for being an accomplice after the fact. Super close to being snuffed out and it being saved. But when all the arrest warrants and everything went out. You'll never know that feeling. It was beyond upsetting the apple cart. It was kicking over 1000 apple carts. About 1/3 of the force was arrested. Juvenile hall was completely empty after this bust; till we realized we had to use it as holding for the dirty cops. Once again; just too much stuff to list here.

"Almost nobody is going to serve time in jail," said Captain W.X.Y.Z. Olaf.

"How so?" I said.

"All the top dogs, and I mean dogs, got immunity; soasto make sure all of it was routed out. There's deals being made. I'll take forever because we arrested almost all the prosecutors and judges-" said Captain W.X.Y.Z. Olaf.

"Every everything in Juvenile Court," I said.

"No, no we left the court clerks, some bailiffs, and like that," said Captain W.X.Y.Z. Olaf, "And don't even get me started on how hard to convince a jury of something so crazy. Shoot; nearly half of the arrested officers are really innocent, or blackmailed. But we can't, normally, tell which ones."

"Who's watching the streets?" I said.

(insert mule picture here)
Houston

"Stretched to the brink, and calling in help everywhere we can," said Captain W.X.Y.Z. Olaf, "'cept Feds. We're arresting most of them. And a lot of those on other police forces as well."

"Are you the police commissioner?" I said.

"No, to avoid the appearance of corruption I refuse to take a higher position. For any length of time" said Captain W.X.Y.Z. Olaf, "Also despite what they say. Still need some shred of IA. And to rebuild it. All of which that remains is me. But I am the highest ranking there is, currently."

"So, mayor running the depar-" I said.

"Nope, not even appointed one. Don't you remember. No body's being appointed to anything. All of city council is awaiting bail. Problem was even *those* judges were dirty..." said Captain W.X.Y.Z. Olaf.

"Do you think anyone will ever trust the police ever again, anywhere?" I asked.

"Of course they will. When FDR rounded up the Japanese, even he himself is known to have admitted most of them were innocent; in the end however literally every single one was innocent-" said Captain W.X.Y.Z. Olaf.

"Innocent of what?" I asked, not knowing history as I should.

"Of being a spy! All they were guilty of is being the victims of racism and prejudice," said Captain W.X.Y.Z. Olaf, "Point is, that happened, yet people aren't scared to death of violating and making exceptions to due process, so no doubt this will also be filed away in the annals of history someday and forgotten."

"The cops are rioting," I said.

"WHAT! I-" said Captain W.X.Y.Z. Olaf.

"Not here! Here if a cop did anything that was the slightest bit corrupt, right about now, he'd he shot dead," I said.

"Surprised, can't say that I'm shocked," said Captain W.X.Y.Z. Olaf, "Cops just want to cover the collective-"

"That 'splains a lot. Also, naturally, the on duty cops are those that aren't part of it-" I said.

"No doubt the rioters are better armed and treated than normal," said Captain W.X.Y.Z. Olaf.

"I have a question, how is it that it's considered a war crime to use chemical weapons, yet no one bats an eye at the police using tear gas-," I said.

Knock knock

"Unless you're going to kill me, come in," said Captain W.X.Y.Z. Olaf.

"Is this a bad time?" he said.

"No, however this isn't where you go to file a victim statement," said Captain W.X.Y.Z. Olaf.

"No, I just wanted to thank you for giving me my life back," he said.

"Welcome," I said.

"Which one were you, no offence," said Captain W.X.Y.Z. Olaf.

"None taken," he said, "Just wish you could give me my sister back."

"You framed for killing her?" I said.

"No, my girlfriend, long time ago, wanted me to climb a bookcase. I was 10. I remember however totally blaming myself. And it taking hours for someone to come; but I know not it was really more like seconds, maybe minutes. But she was the one that got me up there. And I injured myself worse trying to get it off her. I confessed to everything. But the police couldn't prove I deliberately caused it, because I didn't. Put a gun to my sister's head. I thought they were bluffing. They pulled the trigger. Then did likewise to a stranger. Couldn't sacrifice his life." he said, emotionally.

"You sure the random guy wasn't really a dirty cop?" I said.

"If it was it was one great actor," he said, "Thank you. That was hell. And I thought I'd never get out," he said.

"You know, I think I have something that will help you," said Captain W.X.Y.Z. Olaf, pulling out a pamphlet.

"Police brutality victim's support group?" he said.

"As strange as it sounds; helped me. Course will now be overloaded. But," said Captain W.X.Y.Z. Olaf.

Following all this coming to light Captain W.X.Y.Z. Olaf received enough influence to be able to keep people from being forced to talk to police when they didn't want to, or anyone being denied

(insert mule picture here)
Houston

a lawyer under any circumstances. He was not however able to end PAAA. Nor was he able to take the bureaucrats that put it on the books even to a grand jury. He said "For once in the history of bill writing, it is clear as day, set in stone. Even if I could prove the politicians guilty, which I can, I could not press any charges whatsoever. Surprise surprise."

Few months after all that I hit 10. The night of the Fern Bar Massacre Father Dracula Mailed me a USB. He had written to not listen to it till I was 10. On it was a voice recording from my sister. Here is a transcript of it.

"Hey little bro. I'm sure it's a real shock for you to hear from me like this. But I want you to get to know the origin story. You came from a large family. One day one of our brothers went to jail, till his 18th birthday, for something too trivial to relate. At least I hope it was trivial. Actually it would have been better if he had been in jail. He was sentenced to a camp where in the name of straightening you out; they tried to force you to be what they wanted you to be. Even the whitewashed term for it was ominous. And to end the mystery you must be experiencing I made this recording to insure you'd know this if I didn't live to tell you. It would have been better if he had been in military school. It would have been better if he had been in boot camp. That was hell on earth if there ever was one. He soon put his foot down and they killed him. We were like Mr. and Mrs. Harker, Quency Morris, Lord Godalming, Van Helsing, and Dr. Whatshisname from Bram Stoker's Dracula. We stole some pretty serious weapons and took the place over; a pyritic victory if there was ever one. Only I survived. But we massacred them, the villains, not the captives. If you're wondering why I wasn't in jail, or were trying to remember if I was. I wasn't. A super lawyer named Michael W. Sackett worked a miracle. It was such a long case showing each and every victim, which was most of what went on there. Furthermore we even had to have the judge removed from the case just to be able to show all that. Course, what sealed it all was not the testimony of the liberated, some of which were having even their parents sent off to jail, but the testimony of two POWs. After that they had to let me go, for everything. Our parents forgot me in jail. When I got out they had become crazed control freaks. And by that point in time, you were on the scene!"

That, I listened to that for hours and hours over and over. It was a time machine. In our modern age we so often forget what miracles our modern convinces really are. For a time I was in a bubble, back in time. This is my backstory.

Part 03; Slain

Well, you have now heard my backstory. Or at least a lot of it. There is more.

Like I've already said, some of this book may seem weird the way it was written, what was included. Like in Bram Stoker's Dracula, all irrelevant matters have been removed. And I wanted you to see the story from

(insert mule picture here)
Houston

the point of view my little sister/ half-sister/ half-brother's half-sister/ relative person. And like I said, despite usually being a secretive person. I'll start off by telling you the one part I didn't tell her. At least not at first. But this whole book is done soasto allow you see things from her perspective.

At one point along in the superscandal there was a child (11-12-not sure which) that was accused. Had served time before. And it had been rough. He was interrogated. They started off with the trick of claiming to misunderstand; or thinking they heard a confession soasto force you to tell them something. He was too smart for that and quickly and wisely gave the silent treatment. He had just hours ago been through something else traumatic involving death. They were using every possible manipulation and blackmail there was. Just as you never know just what is going on in someone else's head, so you can never comprehend that, all too common, interrogation. There are simply no words in the English language...

Do you remember how Dracula (Bram Stoker) ends? (Plot spoiler) The book broke from much common (nowadays) vampire mythology. This isn't a vampire novel so I won't take the time to say anything else; but what is pertinent. Unlike in much vampire stories nowadays, when a person became a vampire, they lost their free will. They soul was trapped along for the ride, much like a zombie; and it wasn't until the vampire was slain that the true person could go into the after-life. As such when they finally slew the Count, he didn't gasp with relief, but there was a look of peace. Well with this boy it was different. One officer realized just what was happening, and saw him trying pathetically to kill himself like Christine when the Phantom was determined to marry her. He shot him. I saw the crime scene pictures from holding; he went beyond merely gasping from relief. After the superscandal broke; there was no means by which the officer could have been convicted

The other story that was left out was much like my childhood and George Orwell's 1984; not that the two can be much told apart. Right during the middle of the first half of this book a civilian, mall rat, totally unrelated. She was chasing a police officer who had just vandalized her trunk. During which he found a fellow officer that had killed herself in her squad car. When she was a young teen she found "the one." Her dad, "laid down the law." To protect her younger siblings, she could only ever see him rarely and in secret. When they finally could be together, her youngest sibling had left home, she was 43, and her father had already killed him; but homicide couldn't be totally proven. Her bad dad ended up forcing Captain W.X.Y.Z. Olaf and crew to kill him when went to tell him the news. Good night, Goodbye, Good luck, and Good riddance, don't let the universe's door hit you in the butt on the way out. However it proved wholly and totally unrelated.

Those 2 stories I left out of the first half. I only ever knew of them because they went down right in the brunt of the superscandal. Sure there's other stuff as well I know; but that was all that was worth relating.

To continue where my own personal backstory lets off: from the moment that the audio recording from by big sis (and for my fellow smart-alics; big as in older, not as in fat.) came to an end the first time I finally

(insert mule picture here)

knew what I wanted to be when I grew up. I wanted to be a super lawyer like Michael W. Sackett (Captain W.X.Y.Z. Olaf's best friend). He had a big family, mostly adopted juvenile delinquents he defended, mostly in adult court. Up until that point, I would have shrugged and guessed what Sami had wanted till she died (court appointed elder guardian) I achieved. But let's not skip ahead of ourselves. Only 2 officers served any time in jail (6 months, 2 years, paroled at 18 months) in the super scandal. I went back to normal life. Occasionally, up until his death, I would hear from Captain W.X.Y.Z. Olaf. But I mostly went back to life as was as close as ever was to as per usual. Through a series of events too unfortunate, sad, and in one case rediculas I ended having all my friends wanting nothing to do with me, moved of, or in one case dead, by the time I was 17. 9 Days before I turned 18 my parents were in a head on collision with a drunk. That was an unpleasant, complex mess. In time I was simply free. Like surf kicked off the manor I had lost everything (actually I had a house, furnished, $550,000, and 2 cars all from my parents, but that's not the point.) No friends, no family, no girlfriend fiancé or wife, and no job. At the manslaughter trial I said "Losing my parents, for reasons I'd rather not go into, has been like losing the estranged cousin you only ever met 2 or 3 times ever, and maybe had one conversation, ever. Also it was an accident, he didn't intend to hurt anyone. Sure he should go to jail, but go easy on him. It, and normally it would be a ghastly thing to say this, but my being the only kin, I think I'm entitled to be excused, it's not the end of the world. And he only killed two people."

That was like walking into a brand new world that occupies the same physical space, but everything else about it was different. 2 days after I turned 18, and was dealing with all the fun legal hoo haa, Police came to my door. To tell my parents about the death of my half-siblings' mother's death. I had never known that I had any half siblings! I soon learned that my dad, who I thought to be the last person who'd do this, had been running around. I had never had any clue. Apparently while they were at school. Their mother Shenequa had called an ambulance, she was having a baby. In our modern age it is super bizarre, we think of it as old timey, ancient. She died in childbirth. It was unreal. I had them take me to their station. But when I saw my half-brother. He looked so much like my dad I realized it was true. Seriously, walking into a brand new world that occupies the same physical space, but everything else about it was different. There was also my half-sister, who I will discuss that part later, I learned shared the same mother with my half-brother, but not the same father. So we shared no DNA, or as they used to say "Blood." But in the words of Captain W.X.Y.Z. Olaf "biological; smioligical." Then there was her formentioned brother who I rarely could keep up with what to refer to him as. He could not go more than 8 days without changing what we were to call him; and his birth name I could never spell or pronounce. Also it's too trivial to repeat. But there was a 3rd sibling, err sorta sibling, the genealogy is a little complex. Uncle Pierre, see I said I'd explain, his backstory comes about as close as anyone ever does to mine in terms of strangeness. Mostly just because of complexity. Uncle Pierre was born to a teen mom; who died in childbirth. The biological father, to me, always came across as extremely self-centered, uncaring, egotistical, and somewhat cold. Not saying that he was, just saying that he always came across that way to me. I only met him the 3 or 4 times, ever. He wanted nothing to do with anything. Uncle Pierre probably had some half siblings. Though we never knew any of them, or even for a

(insert mule picture here)
Houston

fact. Like his brother / nephew, his birth mother, who unlike Shenequa, had wanted to know the gender before the baby was born, had named him before she died in child birth. His birth name, I also could never spell or prononce. Also it's too trivial to repeat. Just like his brother / nephew. Also to further complicate things his birth mother was one of those who was raised by her grandparents. Her family was killed in a carbon monoxide accident. She had had a sleepover than night. Her parents and sister weren't so fortunate. That all happened when she was 3. Her grandmother, at that point when Uncle Pierre was born, had passed 2-3, (no one was ever sure, or cared enough to investigate in depth) months ago, and her grandfather (the widower) was found to be have been totally out of his gourd. And the other side of the family was too estranged to even bother to call. As such Uncle Pierre was raised by his great grandfather. When he was 1 the great grandfather, being an old man, did what old people do. Die. He died of natural causes. It was ruled a heart attack; but being so old they didn't bother to do an autopsy. As such all bets are off. And to answer the question you're thinking, no, no one suspected anything at all fishy I was just implying the possibly of a stroke or something; but that I suppose was a waste of Ink, being a hybrid of irrelevant and unimportant. And by now I'm sure you're shouting at the pages or E-reader, "How we were related?!?! ". Like I said. Complex genealogy. The Grandfather had been going out with my half-siblings grandmother. Not my grandmother. She took him in so that he wouldn't have to end up in "the system." He was officially adopted by her 3 weeks before she, like her late boyfriend, died of old age. (Thank God) Once again, it was ruled a heart attack; but being so old they didn't bother to do an autopsy. As such all bets are off. And to answer the question this time you're probably not thinking, no, no one suspected anything at all fishy that time either. He was 4 years old when that happened. Officially her 4 daughters took turns taking care of him. Like split custody, only 4 instead of 2 directions. In reality Shenequa was the mother, albeit adopted. And to answer the question you're thinking; I'm absolutely sure I wasn't adopted; but I hold the exact same beliefs about adoption as Captain W.X.Y.Z. Olaf; except I would want to know my biological parents and relatives. Shenequa's sisters, she had no brothers, ended up caring for Uncle Pierre little more than they ended up taking care of her other 2 kids, my half siblings (frequent baby-sitting). It was a great blessing that Shenequa's mother died when she did; by that I mean that she didn't die a little sooner. It wasn't a blessing when she did. But if it had been any sooner (well, before the 3ish weeks, that is) he (Uncle Pierre) would have found him in the same situation, only later, as if he had never even been officially adopted by Shenequa's mother in time for her death. 10 months after Shenequa took him in my half-brother was born. Up until that point Uncle Pierre had been the only male in that family; unless you count boyfriend du-sures Shenequa didn't even have any male cousins. Then 12 months later (to the day) my sister was born. Here in this 5 year time line gap (nothing worth repeating) I'll let you know that Uncle Pierre was for all intensive purposes my half siblings' big brother. But technically being their adopted uncle. He insisted on having them referring to him as Uncle Pierre. Ironically his sorta sisters, Shenequa and her 3 sisters, didn't have their nieces refer to them as Aunt this or Aunt that. I suppose when you're a child it's a major source of pride. After that it was simply force of habit. And to answer the question(s) you're thinking. Shenequa wouldn't refer to him as her brother, but she gave in soon and let him refer to her as his sister. Shenequa's sisters referred to him as their brother, and of course visa-versa. Uncle

(insert mule picture here)
Houston

Pierre was 9, my half siblings were 4 & 5 that day that I got word of them the first time. There! Can't tell you how many times over the years I've had to relate that.

I STILL don't know how we got to calling him Pierre. But it wasn't a misnomer. Despite what you've probably assumed from what you've heard; he was probably the second most masculine person I ever knew, second to Other Charlie. I'll explain later. Uncle Pierre was complicated. You've all seen the tough French mercenary with the tough French accent in some action movie, right? Yes you have. Well think in that direction and you will have begun to think in the right general direction. Honestly I full novel could have been written about his personality. As I always said Uncle Pierre was Uncle Pierre.

I'm sure you've probably given up hope of hearing about the child Shenequa died in labor of. Well, as I believe I've already typed, I was finally convinced when I saw how much my little half-brother looked like my dad. Any closer and it'd be creepy. But it was absolute, final, unneeded, and undeniable proof when I learned that the baby had the same genetic cardiac birth defect my sister had. HLRS (hypo-plastic Right Heart). I named her Lili. A few days after birth she had to have her, would have been first, open heart surgery. She died under the knife. That hurt; though I had never really known her. Uncle Pierre and my half siblings were mourning their mother. I was mourning Lili; and her loss didn't help anyone.

I then moved in to the apartment where Shenequa had lived. 2 of her sisters were in the exact same apartment building. One sharing a deck with us; and the apartment where her mother had lived, by then occupied by other people, was directly below. Her 3rd sister also lived in the same apartment complex. And my half-siblings' family became my family

Have you ever known anyone that you would simply say "he, he's Patrick, or she, she's Victoria." First of all this story has no characters named Patrick, and while Shenequa did have a niece named Victoria, that is purely coincidental and irrelevant. She never comes up. Well, it may be more of a half niece. Seeing as I believe that my half siblings' grandmother may not have had 2 children with a common (biological) father. But's not the point. Uncle Pierre was, as I have already said, one such person, from when I first met him when he was 9. Course towards the end of his life I was beginning to wonder if he was, or was totally, well, you know. This whole book is simply stories that have made the media rounds many times; just a new perspective.

After Shenequa died her sisters began to take care of Uncle Pierre as was originally planned. I got him on weekends, and when no one else was available / willing.

Fast forward 4 years. Uncle Pierre was 13, my sister was 7, and her brother was 8. Uncle Pierre had been put on trial, as an adult, for a lot of serious crimes; none of which there was any solid evidence one way or the other whatsoever. If convicted he'd never see the metaphorical light of day again. It was my summer between collage and law school 4 me. It was one of the last cases Michael W. Sackett worked before being gunned down by the angry father of an alleged victim. The alleged perpetrator he exonerated. Meanwhile back at the

(insert mule picture here)
Houston

ranch; to this day I don't know how we were able to make the high bail, I honestly don't remember. The day Uncle Pierre was finally set free is to this day a blank in my mind. My wife Charlie tells me that I confided in her that I talked him into it; or so I thought. Whatever the truth is, I found that he jumped to his death, deliberately, on a large knife from the kitchen planted upright in the ground. Carlos (he'll come up later) said I assumed poison, but knew suicide. He said that, and I also, according to him, said that he looked "released" from custody, bail, and in the Lois Lowry's The Giver's sense of the word. To me it sounds like the same look that was on the face of Count Dracula (not Father Dracula) when they slew him. I know that I was just glad that he was free, and up in heaven. Oh I grieved, I really did. He was like an uncle, son, and a nephew to me. And I called him my uncle-brother-nephew. But I was just glad that he was free; at least I was till a few months later one of the alleged victims came forward. He said that he had just been going along. You see, the whole was just a group of kids from his school pointing the metaphorical finger of accusation at Uncle Pierre. There was no physical evidence any way, one way or the other. But in the interest of full disclosure; it is possible it wasn't all trumped up. Wouldn't surprise me in the slightest. During the case, and in interviews afterwards when I was asked if I thought he was guilt, I only said "I don't care." It was totally fitting with his personality, but not with what he was. I wasn't really mad at that boy. I was just glad to have to police and PAAAsicution caught with their metaphorical pants down so much. Secondarily, a juror came forward. He said Uncle Pierre probably would have been acquitted; or it would have been a hung jury. There was no real chance of conviction. Around that time that all this came to light I first found Charlie. Also at Uncle Pierre's funeral was one of the few times I ever met his biological father. Also in all this I learned that the only child that's more likely to be the favorite than one that's deathly ill, or in this case, mortally on trial, is one that is already dead. But by half siblings understood, I didn't really kept secrets from them. Which wasn't always the best of ideas. In fact all that happened up until their adoption, I told them soon afterward, like days. I also told them days after I started taking care of them "It's dumb when teenagers run around, telling lies, and hiding stuff. No, no what you should do is plant drugs on your parents. Then rat them out to the police. Can't ground you if you're in jail. I can tell you this because you're 5 (or four in the other case) you'll have long forgotten this." On a related note never ever ever ever EVER give Espresso to preschoolers. In case you're wondering Uncle Pierre's accusers never stood trial. As I said "He was 13, the whistleblower was 12 at the time. Few of them were much older. It would be hypocritical to press charges." Also, and this admittedly would probably be the main reason, it would have been the penultimate humiliation for the police to press charges. As you may know, sometimes when a drunk driver kills someone's kid. The person can be so forgiving that the driver can be like a child to them. Similar case. The whistleblower came semi-close to taking Uncle Pierre's place in my life. In face briefly, for reasons, normal, but unneeded to be mentioned. Ok he was mildly abused, CPS stepped in. I yelled at CPS for not standing up for Uncle Pierre (though he was one of only a few that seemed to be able to handle jail; even still it was crushing what he was facing, possibly being in the last days you will ever spend as a free man! Was horrible to watch. I ended up taking him in, till his parents could have him back. But you just can't replace people, and he was very different from Uncle Pierre.

(insert mule picture here)
Houston

An uncanny thing happened 3-4 days after Uncle Pierre died. The judge over the case was found dead. He was shot in the throat in the throat with a flare gun to be exact. The police tried to pin it on me. I thought it to be the most uncanny thing ever. As I said "You obviously don't have anything on me; because if you did. A murder like this, of a judge. You'd have already arrested me." I also told everyone else, but didn't tell the police so that they couldn't recharge me with lying in the event of being charged and acquitted "They have no proof that I killed him, sure he got his comeuppance, and yes I wanted him dead. But they have no proof that I did it; and they never will. Because I didn't do that. Admittedly it's a logical conclusion. If I was them; and they were me, I'd have come to the same conclusion. But, I didn't do that." However, I questioned my own innocence. It was one of a very few things I held back from my half siblings, so far the only other thing I've held from my half siblings, that and that thing about talking Uncle Pierre into it. Those 2 things I only, till now of course, only ever told Charlie. And she never told anyone else. Ever. I never questioned it. I trust her.

Forgive me if this half is badly written; I'm a barrister (lawyer) not an author.

In the wake of all this, the whole story coming to light, I first met my wife, Charlie. My origin story continues it's strangeness. I decided that I needed to stop being so terrified of being stopped by cops. Soon after I started driving, I t-boned a cop. Oops. From there we went to dinner. Soon afterward I was married, or re-married depending on how you see it, to her. Here I'll tell you her backstory. She was a foster kid from day one, literally. She had a hard childhood, even for a foster kid. She got in trouble with the law as a child, a lot. She hates to admit it. But let me tell her story here in this book. She estimates that she spent nearly 3 1/2 years in minor prison, and I don't care, it's not detention, however some detention is prison, its prison. And that's not counting when she was 16. Tried as an adult for attempted murder; it was really self-defense. She was innocent. No one posts bail for a foster kid. She was 16, so Michael W. Sackett didn't even care, or maybe he was busy I never have been sure. Like him, not counting his pervious marriages that ended in death, I too was married to a cop. And like him, I have a very large family, many of which I initially defended. I also look after from time to time, or more like a social worker, except with competence, more such kids, just as he did. At 17 she was exonerated, though it was nothing short of a miracle. When she hit 18 she left everything. Like me she just walked into a brand new world. She simply checked into a homeless shelter; and went on to become a cop. Along the way her sibling came out of the woodwork. Other Charlie. Other Charlie started going by Charlie at 4, but it wasn't until 18 Other Charlie could change it. Other Charlie nowadays has re changed it and goes by another name, but I'm still calling Other Charlie "Charlie." Well, actually I always refer to Other Charlie as Other Charlie, even when Charlie's out of the room, because Charlie was Charlie Charlie first. Other Charlie is 4 years older than Charlie, or to hairsplit, 3 years 364 days. Charlie was born, unless records are wrong, which they probably are, on New Year's Eve, Other Charlie was born on New Year's Day. Charlie and Other Charlie, I would think to be Identical twins otherwise. My wife has no go-t or buzz cut, but, as much as she loathes it to be mentioned, a lot of freckles on her face, and two scars, one on her right cheek going horizontal, and one on the left forehead going vertical. Other Charlie has no

(insert mule picture here)
Houston

freckles, ever so slightly paler skin, and no scars I've ever seen. You know how I said Uncle Pierre was Uncle Pierre. Well, Other Charlie is Other Charlie even more so. I regard Other Charlie as my best friend, but I'm also good friends with Other Charlie's husband Bruce. How those two got together I'll never know, not because of what you already know, everything in this book being so high profile, not because of what makes those two so laughable. But because they were prefect opposites in terms of personality. It's like the stereotypical married couple; only perfect reverse. Bruce used to go by Carlos (different Carlos) but his 7 siblings, all sisters, did a dare when he was 4, or perhaps five, no one can remember, and from then it was force of habit. Except for the abundantly obvious Charlie and her sibling are quite similar. And no; I'm not making fun of anyone; this is really true, you get used to it. In case you're wondering where Charlie's family was her growing up. She has no family, as I always tell her, her biological parents, who to this day we've never met, and probably never will, are just that. Just biological parents, not real parents. No one raised her. She once had a real big brother when she was 7, who led her to Christ. She's been looking for him ever sense. As for how Other Charlie came up. Other Charlie looked for, and sued for, record. Charlie was all Other Charlie could ever find. They did a DNA test, it later turned out that they were really half siblings, but that makes no real difference, sharing a common mother. I'm sure they both look like their biological mother. Other Charlie was also a foster kid, but it wasn't as horrific in that case, nor did Other Charlie run into as much trouble with the law. After I married her Charlie became the real mother of my half siblings. Thought they never referred to her as such.

Fast forward again. 5 more years have passed. Me and Charlie were by then married. About to adopt. My half-brother was 13, Mersedes was 12. My half-brother saw someone being burgled. And to answer the question you're about to ask; I never really think of Charlie as a cop, I just think of her as Charlie. Technically they were searching a locker; but without a warrant it's really just burglary. He was sent to an alternative school. I told them that I was withholding him from school until he was pardoned and cleared. He was going to be sent to jail for not coming to school. That's the ultimate cheap shot. You can't go after (course in this case; they really could) someone; so you just go after their kid. I started to give in, but alternative school is really just jail. I told him he'd never have to go back there. He went to jail. I still to this day lie awake; wondering why I didn't just send him far off; where they couldn't get to him. My half-brother had juvenile diabetes. He needed to have the medication with him at all times. He died in jail. Captain W.X.Y.Z. Olaf went after the jail; as he perpetually does. But he was a friend, so he was afraid of the appearance of corruption; so he didn't go after the prosecution. In fact he, to avoid the appearance of corruption, did so little any less would have been nearly undeniable corruption, and even then it was just supervisees on the front lines of it all. I still remember when the cop came to my door. If Charlie hadn't been there I probably would have beat him up, assuming of course I would have been able. In moments like that It's hard to not kill the messenger; when their just another agent of the same machine. Fortunately it was an honest cop so I wasn't arrested. Jail for him was a fate worse than death, albeit not by much; I've seen a lot of children and teenage children in jail; I don't know that I've ever seen anyone take it so hard. He tried to put on a brave face, he seriously did. Yet, I can confirm the camps that my sister raided, well just one, were even worse. I can't even imagine what my sibling went through; and I'm just glad those PTSDing memories have been blotted out by the pearly gates. I am so proud of my late sister.

It has been said that negative karma is, well, I don't like to talk that way. I also don't believe in karma. But that is so often the truth. I was in such a state of shock because of a case that I had. My half-brother knew how important the case is that I was working; and we both figured I shouldn't lose that case in order to take the time to get him out of jail. Like Michael W. Sackett, I knew I and I alone could win some cases. This is one such case. I'll spare you all details of said case; as is so often the case; that I was having to seek professional help. I eventually, and being me, could, get a delay. And like Michael W. Sackett, all legal work I didn't choose to do, but did for money just went to pay for my costs in doing cases that could bankrupt a rich man to win. It's my purpose in life, and nowadays there are getting to be others like me. It was the same case. I've been told of how I wondered the complex.

Transcript of Juvenile Court Proceedings:

Bailiff: "All rise for the Honorable Judge -"

Justice - enters.

You're probably wondering what cut that short. Or what that even was in the first place. Well I have sense learned that in any academy of court reporting, they never teach how do document it if a class A felony occurs during the proceedings of court. That Judge put my brother in jail. Not my half-brother; by jailed brother. His chair had had the padding removed; in its place was a bombesque device that shot shrapnel straight up. Much like some form of whoopee cushion of death; by all rights it was a whoopee cushion of death. It being a bomb became a federal matter. I handled it much the same as I handled the death of the judge I blamed for the death of Uncle Pierre. I lawyered up, however in this case I was my own lawyer, but otherwise helped as I could. Being innocent they had nothing on me, so they had to release me. Later that evening I heard that the prosecutor had been beheaded, he was found almost instantly. And while Houston Police didn't release any details. I could tell that it had to have happened while I was in the interview. I knew they'd think I wasn't working alone, but couldn't bust that kind of alibi. Someone was looking out for me; I just worried who it was. Then I realized 2 things. First Charlie had been suspended pending investigation into all that happened. Charlie wasn't a stranger to investigation and suspension. First thing she did was arrest her partner. Her next and, at this time, current partner had the same name as me. Her last suspension had been when she arrested her superior officer during initial, start of shift, orders. And the time before that she lightly tapped a juvenile prosecutor and a fellow officer on their heads (no bruising at all!) with her service piece, regarding an alleged scandal involving "good cop bad cop" She was in the right. That's how it went from day one till she finally

(insert mule picture here)
Houston

made internal affairs, where she belonged. And her next suspension would be testifying for me in favor of a girl with HLHS (similar to my sister and Lili's heart condition) who wore a Taser proof vest. But I ramble.

But what I then realized that was more important was that Mersedes was missing. I feared the worst. I didn't know what to do. I called 911. The police imeadatly assumed that she was behind it. I still strongly remember to this day that an amber alert was never issued. And in case you haven't figured it out yet: Mersedes is my little sister/ half-sister/ half-brother's half-sister/ relative person's name. I had to switch mental gears fast, to defense attorney. They also thought me to be in on it. And through it all I still didn't know what really had happened; literally anything could have happened to her.

While there I ran into Carlos. And here I think I must tell his backstory. Carlos came from a very large family, 7th of 11. Around the time Uncle Pierre was indibted they moved into the apartment underneath us, where Shenequa's mother had lived, and Uncle Pierre as well. He only met Uncle Pierre a couple of times. Being in such a big family, he often could fade into the faces, or as his siblings tried to do often, sneak off completely. Eventually if he was with us in our apartment, and hadn't been given dispermission, it was ok; they eventually gave up on him letting them know. Those kids just ran wild. But Carlos was really a part of our family. Mersedes and her brother were like twins. And Carlos was the 3rd twin in many ways. As opposed to the 3rd wheel. He was to us as Justine was to the Frankenstein Family, except he was in no way a servant. While I was there I ran into Carlos.

Here's what happened:

"Carlos!" I said, "I guess they brought you in as well!"

"Oh! Yea, hey - I'm just a little distracted," he said.

"I take it you got the news Car," I said, the misunderstanding beginning.

"Yea, horrifying," he said.

"Little surprised you were brought in. Suppose it's smart," I said.

"Oh, no, I was dragged in for a different reason," he said.

"What?" I said.

"Well, I may or may not have been caught taking a leak in a drinking fountain," he said.

"Doh!! Carlos! That's Gross!" I said, "I'd have arrested you!"

"Oh come on! I was discrete, and I made sure the drain could handle it. And there was no bathroom in sig-" he said.

(insert mule picture here)
Houston

"Oh! That's just gross! But all things being equal it's a pleasant distraction-" I said.

"In the Old Country-" he said.

"And that's why I don't eat things made there," I said.

"What a double whammy," he said.

"You're telling me Car!" I said, "And reminiscent of Uncle Pierre."

"In so many ways," said Carlos, "Just, call me a sissy, but it's just so much grief."

"What do you mean?" I said, scared he knew something I didn't.

He looked at me like I had, and in hindsight, I probably had, and said, "He died."

"I assume you mean my brother," I said, and I am so glad that I could tell by the pronoun that he was only referring to what I already knew.

"Who else?" he said.

"Wait?" What was the double whammy, then?" I said.

He shook his head and said "My brother."

"Oh, I'm so sorry, what happened?" I said.

"He wanted out, my parents wouldn't let go. He wouldn't get back in the car. Dragged-" he said.

"I'm so sorry," I said, "If you need a guardian-"

He shook his head, said, "Don't sweat. No justice. WAIT! What did you mean about 'double whammy?!'"

Then I told him the whole story. He said he's stand by her.

After that, to change it to a brighter subject I said, "I've always noticed that thing on your upper arm, and while I normally avoid tattoos I must admit that that's a cool one. But I've never been able to tell exactly what it is?" I said, and it really was all I said," It'd think a cloud of lightning; but even that's not quite right."

"Actually, it's just the coolest electrical burn scar ever, happened when I was so young I can't remember anything about what happened when I got it. And I've really grown into it. It really had begun to attract the-" said Carlos.

Then an officer let us know that the prosecutor's head had been found on a spike, outside, at 1PP.

(insert mule picture here)
Houston

Sometimes I would have an innocent client. And often, though sometimes I would have to then defend them, I would pull a Perry Mason. As such I had long sense obtained a PI's license. As such they couldn't boot me off of the case. Bruce was listening to police scanners, and Other Charlie was taking the other shift. Mersedes' aunts, and cousins were out looking like any other lost child. I was worried that she was guilty, so I did a stake out. Apparently the police also got the idea to stake out Uncle Pierre's PAAAsacutor. That was quite interesting; but after a very, shall I say, interesting, talk, I got to talk to him.

There's what happened:

"I'm surprised you didn't bring your pet police captain-" he said.

"Well, a police officer drove through a bus stop while dead, after being poisoned in an internal cover-up, so he's a little tied up," I said.

"Yes, I hear it was a cover-up of a Juvenile Hall that was a house of unspeakable horrors," he said.

I quickly learned that it wasn't where Mersedes' brother had been. Meanwhile back at the ranch.

"You know, He'd be 17, if it weren't for you," I said.

"If you can't do the time, don't do the crime, and I bet his suicide was your-" he said.

"I should bash your skull in," I said.

"What? And finish the job that your little sister didn't-" he said.

"You think she killed-" I said.

"I don't think, I know," he said.

"Then, why didn't you call the police?" I said, truly baffled.

"Why do you think I'm in a wheelchair?" he said.

"Make sense!" I said.

"It all happened soon after whatshisname-" he said.

"Pierre!" I said.

"Whatever," he said, "I just found her in my house, with some big, weird, gun-"

"A flare gun?" I said.

"I suppose, probably," he said, "She was babbling on about murder and manslaughter-"

(insert mule picture here)
Houston

"A 7 year old understood manslaughter?" I said.

"A, no, she really didn't, b lawyer father, c as I was saying. She was babbling on about murder and manslaughter. Saying that I committed a murder, something about a life for a life, it, and it's been 5 years. I reminded her I was just doing my job-" he said.

"Didn't have to do so hard, could have kept it in child court, and could have shown mercy-" I said.

"How did you quote her word for word?!?!" he said, memory must have come back.

"I think you have the chicken and the egg wrong," I said, "Then what?"

"I told her that the judge did have a choice in everything he did. She demanded to know where judge - lived, and a hairpin. I later found that she smashed one of my windows. And after I even took her-" he said.

"So let me get this straight, you set someone up to be murdered by a child, admittedly someone who deserved it, just to save your own a-" I said.

"She stabbed me in the back! I'm still in a wheelchair-" he said.

"You call this cruelty; I call this mercy," I said.

"WHAT! You think I belong in a Wheelchair!! I was just protecting mys-" he said.

"She was 7, and no, you don't belong in a wheelchair; you belong in a refrigerated drawer," I said.

"Making a terroristic threat is a-" he said.

"Telling someone that you want to kill them is not a 'terrorist threat'" I said leaving.

Official victim statement from - as documented by the Houston Police Department. Sgt. - Pct. -

"So, Mr. - can you describe to us what happened tonight on the night of -" Sgt.

"I heard a weird sound at the front door, like someone was using a key to open it. But there's no way she had a key." he said.

"Then what happened?" Sgt.

"I saw it was a child, trying to get in," he said.

"Then what?" I said.

"I, at first didn't know what to make of it, I have seen a lot of bad children and teens-" he said.

"How so?" Sgt.

"I work in Juvenile court, I'm a judge," he said.

"Oh, please, go on," Sgt.

"She babbled something about what I did to her brother," he said.

"How so? Was it at all true?" Sgt.

"No," he said.

"Is it possible that she had the wrong person?" Sgt.

"No, you see her brother was skipping school, I just did what the law said," he said.

"Oh, what then happened?" Sgt.

"I told her all that. She wanted me to 'defend myself' but she was judge, jury, prosecutor, and executor," he said.

"She tried to kill you!" Sgt.

"No, no, she simply put a rag over my face, with some sort of sweet smell to it. Must have been chloroform," he said.

"That's the last thing you remember?" he said.

"Yea, next thing I knew, I was in the back of an ambulance.

*Attacker appears to have called the ambulance.

*Paramedics found victim with left hand cut off, tourniquet applied.

*Suspect appears to not have switched from original plan

*suspect is a juvenile, female, ages 12-13...

Official victim statement from - as documented by the Houston Police Department. Det. - Pct. -

(insert mule picture here)
Houston

"So, Mr. - can you tell us what exactly happened earlier this evening?" Det.

"I was pulling in my driveway, and I saw a little girl trying to pick the lock to my front door," he said.

"Then what?" Det.

"I called 911, but she tazered me. That's when it all gets, crazy," he said.

"That when it Gets crazy?" Det.

"Yea, we got to talking, or more arguing. Claiming I kidnapped and abused her brother," he said.

"You think she had the wrong person?" Det.

"No, And! And before you start think I'm well. It's a, or was a case I worked. It was a truancy case," he said.

"I don't follow?" Det.

"Revenge, And I'm not sure I do easier, err either. Said that she was going to cut off my foot. Later claimed she was 'reducing my sentence' and now I have no right thumb...

You know what case that judge and prosecutor worked. My wife had to help make sense of that on the police scanner. I later got ahold of those victim statements for this book. And if you've been worrying, like I was / would. Carlos was, being 12, soon released. Everyone else was out looking for my sister; I went home because I knew that someone needed to stay behind to hold down the fort, so to speak. Boy was I right. 5 minutes in I heard a knock. It was Mersedes.

"Mersedes!?!?" I said.

"Hey bro, I can't stay long," she said.

"Wha?!-" I said.

"Call the police, just do it," she said.

"Police, they-" I said.

"That way they won't suspect you," she said as she called them.

"For what?" I said.

"Hiding me," she said.

I couldn't even get a word out.

"I'm sure you're wondering where I've been," she said.

"Yea, what's going on. This is going to be one of my most difficu-" I said.

She just shook her head.

"Wha-" I said.

"You know how these sort of things end up," she said.

"What sort of things, what's happening?!" I said, by now I was sufficiently freaked out.

"I'm not getting out of this one alive; and I know it," she said.

"You're too young-" I said.

"This is beyond the law," she said.

"The law is trying-" I said.

"I know I'm about to die, the law is just watching it all happen," she said.

"Mersedes, what's going on?" I said.

"You remember when Uncle Pierre passed?" she said.

"Not exactly when it happened, but at the same time, all too much," I said.

"You were just glad he was free, though still grieved-" she said.

"I told you?" I said, "I don't remember anything from time point zero."

"Yea, you missed him. You breathed a sigh of relief. But when it happened. I just felt something inside of me just break," she said.

"What are you saying-" I said.

"Please, don't even bother organizing a defense," she said.

"Because, you going to, die?" I said.

"I don't know when or how, and no, I'm not going to kill myself. But I'm sure I'm going to get killed in this ordeal," she said.

(insert mule picture here)
Houston

"You might end up in jail," I said.

"Possible, and that small possibility scares me. Everything about this scares me, though I know I will soon be better off than ever," she said.

"I-I" I said.

"As you always said 'to answer the question you're thinking' Yes, I did kill that judge. With all that grief and guilt, you never realized anything," she said.

"And the PAAAsacutor?" I said.

"Yea, I did that, and everything else they think I did. I'll have to go soon, but just had to say goodbye," she said.

"You, you were 7, that must have hurt!" I said.

She did that mostly one shoulder shrug, implying some confusion, and said, "From an extremely young age. I knew that I was capable of things most people could never do."

"What? What did that feel like?" I said.

"Like opening a pickle jar," she said.

"Guess this technically makes you a serial killer-" I said.

"Well, we prefer the title 'Unlicensed executioner'" she said.

I responded about as you'd expect and she re-responded "Just kidding, but yea, I'm a serial killer, I suppose."

"You know the media has already given you a serial killer name. Lucafess," I said.

"Well, I guess the Prosecutor's head on a spike does encourage that," she said.

"Pretty bad hu?" I said.

"I don't know. I hope what I'm doing isn't too wrong. As that Justin Biber song goes, 'Only God can Judge me.' Whole song represents that whole situation."

"What happened?" I said.

"Well, when I heard about my brother. I had been able to put whatever that was, in most people it's some form of internal holdback, not quite a conscious, but close. Mine was always weak. But when you told me, I, right then, fell it break; I just felt it fall apart. I knew it had never been whole, especially ever sense. But now

(insert mule picture here)

Houston

I knew I'd never be able to put it back together again. I'm just trying to keep it at a minimum, and only those that dearly deserve it," she said, "And about the name, I've renamed myself, so. I'm sorry for what I've done to ya-"

I just let my mouth run, and I'm sure that this was something that the cops really wanted to nail me for, 911 overhearing this whole conversation, I said, "I'm just trying to not be proud of you. I wish I could give you at least a sandwich; but I'm sure you wouldn't take it. What's the name?"

"Copslayer," she said.

"Say hi to your brother and Uncle Pierre for me, and that I love them; and miss them." I said as she left, "Oh! And my siblings too!"

"I will, said Copslayer, "And for the record, you'll probably bemoan my short life. But other than Mom and Uncle Pierre's deaths. I've had a better life than I could have asked for. Only regret is that I couldn't marry my fiancé."

"Carlos?!" I said.

"You knew!" said Copslayer.

"Do I look like an idiot! I knew you were a couple; I just didn't know you were engaged. It was bound to happen, you 3 always being so close, and your brother being your brother, and him and Carlos being both boys and not Uncle Pierre; and it was just plain obvious!"

"Then how come you never said anything?!" said Copslayer.

"Because I could've been wrong," I said.

"Bye bro, thanks for everything," said Copslayer.

"Wait, one last thing," I said.

"Yea bro?" said Copslayer.

"I heard from your aunts that when your mother first laid eyes on you. She knew you'd be a great person, someone who was loving, and not afraid to stand up. Or a serial killer. She misspoke. She said "Or"; she meant to say "And.""

"Thanks," said Copslayer.

"No, thank you," I said. I didn't think I would ever see her again; I was half right.

(insert mule picture here)
Houston

The police arrived almost as soon as she was just out of reach. They really wanted something against me. But they all knew how good an attorney I am. I won't

repeat back that interesting argument. Everything in it was obvious that it would be in there; and there was nothing worth repeating. You already basically know the content. And they had known for some time they had known about the flare gun; stole it from an aunt. Took months for it to be realized that it was missing. Also it's worth noting that I think, had they been the same age at the same time Captain W.X.Y.Z. Olaf's sister and my sister would have probably been great friends. Except that my sister wanted to be a classic noir detective; rather than a ninja.

For reasons I don't need to go into I knew she also met Car that evening. In the morning I got word that he had died. The Medical Examiner concluded that he was running with scissors and fell. I never believed it. I, being so glad I didn't really know anything, always told the police everything. I suspected his parents, and the police. But I was never certain against either. And I certainly had no proof. Worse ways to go I suppose. Just ask justice - - district court; New Orleans Louisiana.

Admission of guilt, signed by Copslayer - A.K.A. - Lucafess - A.K.A. - Mersedes -   Found at crime scene by NOPD. (New Orleans Police Department)

To Police or Whomever it may concern;

Greetings. I'm sure you are aghast at a gruesome crime scene. For the sake of the family I would only confess. Instead in the interest of truth and history I will tell you the whole story; so that the whole story will at least be known. Albeit unbelieved. First of all I am sure that this is not legally binding. Legal Smegal. It all began when I was 7 years old. A judge in my hometown of Houston Texas killed a relative that was for all intensive proposes my brother. I killed him. Fast forward current times. My brother brother was sent to jail for reasons all too trivial. He needed his insulin right with him at all times. When he died I killed the judge that tried to PAAA (Prosecute As An Adult) my, for all intensive purposes, father's big sister's brother (No, I'm not crazy or lying, or making it up). Neither of those people I ever knew. He, (my for all intensive purposes father) committed no crime, legally, ethically, or morally. While I knew he'd have an alibi; I killed the prosecutor. Making me a serial killer. Then I made two vengeful attacks. Though I'm sure, being as the alleged victim survived to tell about it, you already know all about it. I didn't go after the jailors that killed my brother, or to be very technical, father's big sister's brother. In both cases the actual real police went after them; so I didn't. As for my for to be very technical, father's big sister's PAAAsacutors. She won. I only left a little, I was here. Almost no permanate scaring. I plan to let a more detailed account of my alleged crimes

(insert mule picture here)
Houston

come to light soon. As for this crime you are responding to. And I have held off on confessing till the end so that you'd read the whole thing. I picked the lock to get in, tazered him. He was an evil Juvenile Court judge. Records prove he ALWAYS convicted and ALWAYS gave the maximum sentence, look it up, it's true! I was going to break all his fingers and toes, in two places each. Then rotate the breaks. Then take a sledge hammer to his rib cage. Then everywhere, except most of the skill and all of the spine, except tailbone, bone comes up close to the surface. I'd fire a nail gun into the bone. Many times. Finally I'd drain all of the synovial fluid from his back. And I'd leave him where he'd have water as to not die of dehydration; instead he'd die a slower death from starvation. We got to talking. He knew it was all over. But he did get me to reduce his sentence. Yes, I killed him, and yes, I didn't make a peaceful death. But it wasn't as bad a way to go as possible. I threw a rope end out the window. Then climbed out on the ledge, and threaded it in the next window. In side I then took the rope in and out and tied the ends around the wall. I used a good knot and pulled it tight. Then I put an s hook in the celling. I made sure to hit a stud, and use a good s hook. I then handcuffed Judge - and cuffed his ankles together. I took the end of the rope and tied it to the chain holding his ankles together. Then I put the rope through the S hook. As I'm sure you know; he didn't even touch the floor.

Keep Calm and Kill Cops,

(signature)

Copslayer

It was a few days later that that happened. After she did that she called me from a pay phone on the edge of the Big Easy. The police were stalking us. Nothing anyone could do about it. Here's a transcript of that call.

"- Residence," Resident (r)

"Bro?" Lucafess (L)

"Mersedes?!?! Err, Copslayer! I-I thought I'd never see you ever again!" r

"You probably won't," L

(insert mule picture here)
Houston

"Oh, man, I can just picture your face in my head, and I've never before seen someone in as much pain," r

"Yea," L

"And never as mad- no. There was one time," r

"Really whe-" L

"When Captain W.X.Y.Z. Olaf found that judge briber. His eyes and nose bled. He was covered in blood. Couldn't let himself near that man. Later learned that what happened did permanate damage to his heart; much like a heart attack. And to-" r

"Answer the question you're thinking," L

"Yea, he didn't have a heart attack," r

"I can't talk long," L

"I understand," r

"How's things?" L

"No arrests. Won't be. Charlie'll be back at work soon," r

"All that remains, its gone. I can only use intelligence to keep myself from being a huge danger to the public," L

"I take it you got the news," r

"I did," L

"He didn't suffer," r

"Who killed Carlos?" L

"I don't know. It was-" r

"Ruled an accident," L

"How you?" r

"Ready to join him," L

"What happened? I mean in the meantime," r

(insert mule picture here)
Houston

"Found one, an admission of guilt will surface. But I will take the time to tell you that it was much like the first time, only slower," L

"First time?" r

"Yea, PAAAsacutor / judge - You remember?" L

"Yea, more than I'd like to. I never had any idea that the two cases were even connecte-" r

"I picked the lock into the loft," L

"How'd you get away? Or get to the prosecutor's-?" r

"He shouted what I was doing there. I pulled the flare gun. I didn't know if I could... we briefly argued," L

"How so?" I said.

"I told him what he had done, and asked how he could. He said he had done nothing wrong, and turned to call for the cops. I pulled the flare gun. He told me I'd go to jail. I told him 'How will that make you any less dead?' He put up his hands to shield himself and pathetically said 'Come on! I've given lots of victim's justice. I-I've been in-involved with lots of different charitable efforts. Any judge would-' I said 'Fine, give me back Uncle Pierre's live. With full exoneration, and healed of the memories of what had happened. And we'll call it even.' It wasn't a fair argument. That I do regret; He then 'WAIT!! Wait! wait, How could I?! That's not even possible!-' I coldly replied 'not my problem' paused for a moment, and pulled the trigger. Then calmly left the loft, and then main hallway, by that point it was filling with flare smoke," L

"Ouch,' r

"I still miss Uncle Pierre,' L

"So do I," r

"I even miss the parts of him that drove me nuts!" L

"I miss the boys he was constantly bringing home," r

"I miss the smelly exercise junk he'd leave laying around" L

"I could leave my dirty laundry laying all over everywhere (chuckle)," r

"Gota go, love you," L

"You to," r

"I-I have to go," L

"God bless you," r

(disconnection)

While that was the last I heard from Copslayer; it wasn't the last the world heard from her. She made a stop in Port Arthur; if you aren't familiar with the motive, once again that is a little backstory.

As you may know, when a cop stops you; you're supposed to just blindly do whatever they say. Well, we all know the old adage "absolute power corrupts absolute." And if they do something they shouldn't have; you just blindly go along; and supposedly get justice after the fact. Well, let's get real; a lot of bad things that could happen wouldn't even break with procedure. And if something that did break procedure did happen; then they'd probably never even believe you. And even if they did; what would they do? A suspension? Please. Only if it was something so over the top as to border on absurdity would you have any shot at any real justice. Even in civil court, you'd be doing fantastic to drain your own financial resources (assuming you to have the monetary and timely abilities) and merely cost the cops money; but never actually see any of it yourself. And suppose hypothetically that you could actually get justice; the damage has already been done; what good, beyond seeing them obtain their comeuppance, does that really do you? But, like I think I said. I have recently begun rambling and babbling.

Anyway, basically when you're stopped by a cop. You're enclosed in a Nano-dictatorship. At least to some undeniable degree. And even if you see it as a benevolent dictatorship; still a dictatorship none-the-less.

Meanwhile back at the ranch, Copslayer found a micro-ring reminisant of the superscandal; at least to some degree. But they were mostly Ranke file; but they understood what I have just articulated above. When they pulled people over, they abused that power in every way that they could think of. Oh how I wish there was a practical way to enumerate all the ways that they abused their power. First draft of this portion I tried to just list all the biggies, but I either found it radically wanting. Or I could make it more exhaustive. But it would just be so long! It would be much like that "Piece of Reference that's actually a good read" as I mentioned in Slay. Only as literature, it would begin terrifying, no matter what I did. And quickly devolve into extrodinarally, distressing. As such I have elected to withdraw any such list. Also it would just be so extrodinarally long! Bit I will leave you with this one little tidbit to give you an idea just what was going on. I have though on all the ways they took advantage of their power since the day, well. Unlike Lemony Snicket; I won't plot spoil my own ending. Up until as I type out these very syllables. And I am yet to think of a way; barring only the most preposterous, and not even all thereof, that they didn't in some way abuse their power! It's undeniable that they did likewise and then lived it for the exact same reason a typical serial murderer kills.

Pardon the language; I just finished reading Varney, the Vampyre by James Malcolm Rymer.

Well, Copslayer; the how is yet to be determined; became aware of this situation. Within a span of 34-38 hours she killed 5 PAPD officers. In the course of the investigation it was found that all four officers within the scandal were killed. At the last crime scene she left a note. It said "For ever the police have make plee bargins with criminals; now they're making plee bargins with me," These so called crimes being what she is most remembered for I won't go into any more detail; that and I've gotten so rambuly enough as it is. But for those of you in the past or who just crawled out of a rock, well. If you've just crawled out from under a rock, might I recommend a bath? But that's another matter. As for the 5th officer. He, among other duties, was supposed to go after corruption in his own department; internal affairs in an area that was too small for traditional internal affairs persay. But instead, all the years that scandal had been going on. He had instead been taking bribes to cover it all up. It only surfaced in the course of the homicide investigations.

In the interest of full, and might I add, forgotten, disclosure. It is conceivable that they really just told a few cheap lies; took advantage of a convenient situation, and merely pinned it on Copslayer. However I don't think that happened. And to answer the question you're thinking; no, there's no way the superscandal could have had a hand in that investigation

The amount of time from when I last laid eyes on Copslayer, and the last call is about equal to the amount of time from the call enumerated above to when I head the Copslayer was found dead. Allegly she was sitting on a bench in Hermann Park, and shot herself in the side of the head. But I'd never seen that gun in my life! I knew she was really murdered. In a big outdoor space, like a park. I imagine I'd be easy to fire a second bullet up in the air to put gunpowder residue on someone's hand. In fact I had a lab test just to be sure. It was fired twice. But I knew the police would do nothing. But I did tell them anyway, in the interest of full disclosure, you know, avoid the appearance of evil. But I never hired a private investigator. Michael W. Sackett's acquitted serial killer son was murdered; but because of what he had done, not what he was, he got off. However in the interest of full disclosure; I'm a strong believer in mitigating circumstances. Copslayer didn't deserve to die. Whenever anything big happened in my life; it's been a door I walked through. Good or bad. Always at least to an ever so slight degree. But at least this time I had people to stand by me. Charlie, Other Charlie, Bruce, Shenequa's sisters and nieces... When it came time to ID the body; because of how things change right when someone dies, I couldn't say for sure that it was her that they had found in the park. So they tried DNA. That complicated things, because they found that my brother and her shared a common mother, but not a common father. So she had no biological relation to me. Hence little sister/ half sister/ half brother's half sister/ relative person. But, as I always say "biological smioligical." Weeks later I realized that Copslayer's, and for that matter her brother's, birthday had also been her death day. And I, albeit sillily and superstitiously wonder if Carlos was also 13, I haven't dug up those records, to see if a mistake was possible.

When Uncle Pierre died; I felt a weight lifted; he was free; at least for a time. When my brother died; that hurt. When Carlos died; it was a painful insult to injury. But Copslayer; It's weird. I don't believe in ghosts.

(insert mule picture here)
Houston

And I don't think she is. But I do feel that she is watching this city; the City of Houston, much like a guardian angel. A bit like how she did at the end of her life.

Introduction by editor

First Houston Police Department, Internal Affairs division, Captain W.X.Y.Z. Olaf wrote "*Internal Affairs*." Then - wrote a nonfictional spinoff "*External affairs*," Telling two long continuous stories. But it has come to the attention of this publishing house that this is truly a trilogy. We have collected up a collection of stories about the famed Houston Police Department, Internal Affairs division, Captain W.X.Y.Z. Olaf. Each chapter is told from a different perspective. Do not be confused. 1. This is not a biography of Houston Police Department, Internal Affairs division, Captain W.X.Y.Z. Olaf. 2. Each and every one of these stories have been told by a different person, or persons. And while each of these has probably been heard somewhere else before; and may overlap with stories told in Internal Affairs or External Affairs. But they are not the same stories; guaranteed or your money back.

Also fair warning. We have, at least attempted, to break with previous customs of this work and instead follow the common style of all entertainment of our time. That is; keeping things as short as possible; even in this very introduction. Unfortunately a problem arose. Thoreau cried "Simplify Simplify." In your time people cry things such as "If you can't do the time; don't do the crime." In ours it is cried "Do Not Get Me Caught In The Weeds!" Though often worded instead with language we have opted to remove. In all such synareos it forgotten or ignored what may be lost in simplification; that is / A.K.A. oversimplification. As a result many of our chapters we have had to allow to be longer, and in one case, far longer than would normally be acceptable. Pleas pardon this inconvenience.

Also: names, places, and dates may be omitted to protect the innocent; or innocent enough.

Chapter A Good Cop Bad Cop

We've all read Captain W.X.Y.Z. Olaf's series "Internal Affairs." Then my husband wrote a nonfictional spinoff "External affairs." I was really surprised when the publishing house called me up. They were putting this book together. I will follow my better half's style and tell the back story; while assuming you to have read Internal and External Affairs.

You remember that alleged pistol whip that got me suspended. Let me start from the beginning. I hate to talk about this; but I will. As you know I was a foster kid; and had a very hard childhood. You try that and not get in trouble with the law! Once I deliberately went to jail one foster home was so bad. I got in trouble with the law a lot; and also did some things I'm not too proud of. A few I deeply regret. The last time I went to jail I was 15. It was a long time, and after that I was accused as an adult of attempted murder. It really was self-defense. But let me go back to one of the most haunting things that ever happened.

(insert mule picture here)
Houston

I was found in possession of something I shouldn't have been; you try living in that world! And not having escape! It was classic Good Cop Bad Cop. One of a few things that I still haven't been able to forgive. First the first cop scared me so bad; not something easy to do. Then I thought the second cop was really going to help me; I thought, and a few other times I had thought this before; I thought I had found a real home. I then confessed and even gave up my dealer and then boyfriend. I had had a lot of boyfriends. He duped me, perfectly; it was a perfect delusion.

Olaf was a funny person. While people do remember that he was a body builder; they don't remember just how tall he was. And his family was interracially adopted to the point of rediculas. He also believed that to conquer a fear you should become the thing you most fear. I did Olaf's "become the thing you most fear," and became a cop when I aged out of foster care. Like him, I was arresting cops before I was in IA. I would go on to become his successor after he died. And he was the only one that ever sided with me when I was in trouble, like below; well, also most of his IA officers. But enough backstory.

I was getting ready for vacation, seeing I was on suspension anyway for the shooting death of a juvenile court judge, in his own courtroom; he was going to call for S.W.A.T.-Bailiffs that were like police-solders who carry out the raids that get innocent people killed; see Epi. 6.

(I was cleared). The homicide detectives came to my door and arrested me. That, and the time I was tazered, really brought back some really bad memories. Fortunately my better half is a very good lawyer. Within 24 hours I was out on bail. First time I'd ever had bail posted. At the time of this, the dust was still seteling from Copslayer's death. To make matters worse I couldn't account for my whereabouts at the time of the homicide (coincidence).

My better half thought it might have been Mersedes. That made the cops wonder if he lied and she was really alive. As he put it "Do you really think being dead could stop someone like her?" For all intensive purposes; she and her brother were my kids; and Carlos was officially an unofficial 3rd member. Unofficially; he was an official member.

What had happened was that "Good Cop," who I had allegedly pistol whipped, was found dead at his home. No real evidence left; or for that matter no witnesses. Also my better half had allegedly threatened him. He had been shot with my spare service weapon. It was a home burglary; so good that we never even knew anything was missing; till we went looking. The police nearly destroyed that safe-sized crime scene. But my better half knew good defense crime scientists. They were able to get evidence; and found one set of prints that didn't match anyone that should've been there. He didn't want that death to be avenged; but to clear my name. He did. To be honest I felt the same way.

Turned out Bad Cop took the threats seriously; thought it'd be a "kill two birds." It was; for me.

Houston

Chapter B Elope

Hello. My name is unimportant. I will start off by letting you know that I'm not in this story, I'll explain later. This is one of the least known Captain W.X.Y.Z.O.ean stories. As such you've probably never heard it before; so you may not even want to bother trying to remember which one it is.

Let me begin from the beginning:

An older couple was driving to an important meeting; I have never been able to determine what. Actually in a real rush But they saw a homeless person sleeping. But it was a prime begging area and time. They were worried and stopped. They were cautious, but when he wouldn't respond they called 911. When the paramedics arrived they found 2 things. It was 1. a teen; and b, or 2. that is, 2. dead. The then officer, WXYZ Olaf, was the responding cop. He then ended up investigating the death surrounding the boy's death. My facts regarding the investigation are fuzzy. But I confirm a few things. It was a long slow process. He had been homeless. He didn't have the police backing him. Which was probably for the best. In time he found the boy's wife. But first when he notified next of kin.

I don't have a transcript of what happened. None exists. But I can tell you that she asked if it was her fault. He said "Of course it is" He had too much ethics to arrest her for assaulting an officer.

By now I'm sure you are getting baffled. Let me start from the beginning.

He had a sister that was a drug addict. She had it bad. Her / his / their mother asked one too many shaming questions. Absolutely forced her to answer. "Socratic method" Pushed her over the edge. The next morning across town there was a raid at a crack house. She was found dead. Overdose. His mother was trying to determine how he was reacting. He asked her "Why couldn't you have just shot her?" A physical fight ensued, he grabbed a glass art / decoration, and more in anger than anything else, clobbered her good. When she came around he had grabbed the girl her he loved, and ran off with her. Hence the title of this. His dad, who had been searching, but not ever finding me, I'll explain later. He wouldn't take her as family. If only they had. Couldn't afford military school, so they planted something on him. Thought they could get him sentenced. He ran off. He took ill; and died of some form of strep throat; couldn't get health care without going home. In time his wife was told, and soon had a miscarriage. She is now my sister. After his sister died, her mother fast became an addict; which is why it's good he came at the time of day that he did; otherwise she wouldn't have even been able to talk to him. The mother wasn't indicted by the grand jury. The hospital and workers were. The legislators that crafted the law that kept him (a minor) from getting health care without a guardian also were never charged. In time harmony was restored; and they all lived happily ever after.

As for me, where was I? That's an equally long back story. I'll save you the canned rom com to say that I ran off with a girl that both our families wanted to keep apart. That's where I was throughout this whole story. My father was trying (with absolutely no luck might I add) to chase / find us. Eventually I came back.

Tru dat

Chapter C Sweat

Official Court Reporter's Record. Harris County Criminal Court No. -

- Court reporter

- Judge

- Prosecutor

- Assist. Prosecutor

- Defense attorney

- Assist defense attorney

- Defendant No. 1

Count 1: Kidnapping of a minor child

Count 2: Abuse of power and authority

Count 3: Psychological abuse of a minor child

Count 4: official oppression

Count 5: wrongful detainment

- Defendant No. 2

Count 1: Kidnapping of a minor child

Count 2: Abuse of power and authority

Count 3: Psychological abuse of a minor child

Count 4: official oppression Count

Count 5: wrongful detainment

- Defendant No. 3

Count 1: Kidnapping of a minor child

Count 2: Abuse of power and authority

Count 3: Psychological abuse of a minor child

Count 4: official oppression

Count 5: wrongful detainment

- Defendant No. 4

Count 1: Kidnapping of a minor child

Count 2: Abuse of power and authority

Count 3: Psychological abuse of a minor child

Count 4: official oppression

Count 5: wrongful detainment

- Defendant No. 5

Count 1: Kidnapping of a minor child

Count 2: Abuse of power and authority

Count 3: Psychological abuse of a minor child

Count 4: official oppression

Count 5: wrongful detainment

Prosecutor's opening statement:

    Jurors, you have been told of your duties and abilities as jurors of this case. The defense will claim that they were simply doing their jobs as police officers. They will claim that a brovdignagian Internal Affairs division is simply trying to put them in jail for something was at worst a procedural fowl up. I will be honest. This is a very difficult and unusual case. But the facts are these. At approx. 8:40 Am Central Standard time - was found by his teacher to be in possession of a contraband substance. At 9:50 Central Standard time he arrived at the - Pct. His parents' attorney worked out a deal, by which he would receive full immunity; of which he personally never agreed to anything. But one stipulation of the deal was that he had to give over the name of the person that sold him the substance. He refused. The police decided to hold him until he gave over the name of the dealer. - was 11. After 4 1/2 hours he gave over the name; and was released. He was in tears, and guilt ridden. He gave then his brother's name. He is now experiencing extreme guilt. He is a 5th grade student-

    Defense attorney's objection:

    This is grandstanding.

    Sustained. Continue

Continuation of Prosecutor's opening statement:

    Social services has conformed plenty of examples in which the victims of child abuse have been less emotional. And these are not alleged; because the abusers were found guilty. We will be providing an expert witness. In fact everything we will be presenting will be undeniable–

Defense attorney's objection:

    Nothing is undeniable in court

    Denied. Continue

    There is no further statement to be made, your honor.

    Very well them, Defense. You may begin

Defense opening statement:

    Thank you your honor. It is very interesting what the prosecution has said. Because it is records that will exonerate my clients–

    Prosecuting attorney's objection:

    Both of those statements would be alleged.

    Sustained. Continue

    They were doing their jobs, when Internal Affairs decided that what they were doing wasn't good; and made the choice to trump up absurd criminal charges–

    Prosecuting attorney's objection:

    That would be alleged.

    Sustained. Continue

    In fact no police procedure was broken in the course of the case in question. As such is it illogical to believe that they broke the law–

    Prosecuting attorney's objection:

    Actually police officers that wrote the police procedures were later charged and convicted for having written procedures that led to wrongful tazing deaths

    Defense attorney's objection:

    I only asked rhetorically 'is it logical?'

    Sustained, denied, continue

Yes, your honor. And as this case goes on, you will see how the leading investigating officer, Captain William Olaf, is nothing more than a cop hater with a badge-

Prosecuting attorney's objection:

That would be alleged.

sustained. Continue

Yes, your honor. However I intend to prove that he is every bit as insane as I intend to portray him. And I also intend will prove that the alleged victim's age is irrelevant-

Prosecuting attorney's objection:

That would be alleged.

sustained. Continue

I have finished my opening statement, your honor

Prosecution, you may begin your response

Thank you your honor, you the jury will see, as the defense has admitted, that Captain W.X.Y.Z. will be portrayed as a brovdignagian cop hater; to paraphrase that is. But, he isn't-

Defense attorney's objection:

That would be alleged.

Denied. Continue

Thank you your honor. In each case you will see that, while occasionally arresting the book; rather than by the book. Captain Olaf has broken no law-

Defense attorney's objection:

That would be alleged.

sustained. Continue

Thank you your honor. He simply does what needs to be done. He has done nothing wrong-

Defense attorney's objection:

That would be alleged.

sustained. Continue

And he will be able to show, despite whatever story the defense attempts to tell, he has done nothing wrong. No doubt the defense will also try to convince you that this is another such story. But you're smart

Defense attorney's objection:

That would be alleged; and this is sickafantcy

sustained. Continue

(Pause)

No further response, your honor.

Prosecution - err defense, you may begin your response

Yes, your honor. Just as the prosecution has said that what we said was interesting. What they have said is interesting in the same way. But what is really interesting is allegedly interesting Captain Olaf is guilty of arson-

Prosecuting attorney's objection:

That would be alleged.

He said alleged.

No no your honor, it being interesting is technically alleged.

sustained. Continue

Yes your honor, he is guilty of murder-

Prosecuting attorney's objection:

That would be alleged.

sustained. Continue

And he is an accomplice after-the-fact to numerous crimes-

Prosecuting attorney's objection:

That would be alleged.

sustained. And if you do not stop; I will hold you in contempt Mr. - Continue

Yes, your honor. And we intend to prove these very things. Captain Olaf himself being the main witness to this. The defense will make no further statement at this time, your honor.

To be clear, all of your clients are evoking their 5th amendment right to not testify. Is that correct consoler?

Yes your honor

Prosecution, you may present your first witness

Your honor, the people present Houston Police Department, Internal Affairs division, Captain W.X.Y.Z. Olaf.

The Witness walks to the stand.

The witness has agreed not to take an oath of testimony on religious grounds; but agrees to be truthful.

You may be seated

Captain W.X.Y.Z. Olaf, tell us when you first became informed of what was happening.

My people were looking through different police records for signs of police mis-conduct or blue crimes. Something we do a lot of. Lot of hay to sort through to find the needle

Who exactly stumbled over this case?

My assistant

But you took the lead?

That is correct

Why was that?

Because, this, I could tell from the start, would be a specialty case.

Please, explain

Well, just as you said 'This is a very difficult and unusual case.' But I would also add, unorthodox.

Ok, what happened then?

we looked closer into records. When finished, we probably already had proof. But we weren't finished

Your honor, the people present the following police and legal documents and records, as well as these video recordings

Evidence is approved, shown to jury

After you collected this evidence, when then happened?

I sent my assistant, the only other officer on the case-

Why was only 2 officers on a 'very difficult and unusual case.'?

All that was needed, it's all in interpretation, you can't deny what happened

Defense attorney's objection:

That would be alleged.

sustained. Continue

Yes your honor, what did your assistant do?

She cut a deal with the victim's brother, who was by then in jail for-

What kind of deal?

She got the DA to offer him immunity

Did she have to?

No, But! but but! she might as well have. Following the proceeding events, the case was cooked and served with lemon butter, anyway.

Defense attorney's objection:

That would be alleged.

sustained. Continue

What were you doing at this time?

I was taking the victim statement from the victim, when I'm working a case I normally do that

Your honor, the people present the following police and legal documents and records, as well as these video recordings

Evidence is approved, shown to jury

After these statements were taken. What did you do?

I made the usual arrangements to arrest the suspects

Have you recently worked a similar case to this?

Unfortunately, yes

Please, explain

It keeps me up. It's the only time I ever lied in a professional capacity- well. I simply allowed an officer to lie.

Please, explain

No one would do anything, well, Gergor Mendal would. But he'd dead. And so's his crew. It was a scared straight program. We told the warden his son had brought a gun to school. If he signed an admission of guilt to the accusation his son would get off and we could perform an entrapment. If it hadn't been absolutely essential to stop that, monster, that ani-

Defense attorney's objection:

This is grandstanding.

sustained. Continue

We succeeded in stopping the program. However I need not tell anyone in law enforcement that justice doesn't actually undo anything. I suspended myself and involved officers for 12 weeks. If it hadn't been absolutely essential, I would have had to indibt us.

I rest my case your honor, permission to recall this witness

Permission granted, defense you may begin questioning the witness

Thank you your honor, Mr. Olaf-

Please, call me Captain Olaf

Captain, Olaf, are you sure the case against the brother was 'cooked'

I suppose not against a reasonable doubt

But you flushed it-

No, your clients flushed it-

Defense attorney's objection:

That would be alleged.

sustained. Continue

Captain Olaf, tell us the story of officers Dury and Lenin

They tried to take evidence, using the old cop trick of 'offer them a drink.' Officer Churchill realized what was happening, and it

ended badly, he tried to stop them; and was shot dead. Officer
Thatshare then returned fire, but was unable to save her partner.

What happened then?

She was sentenced to life, but a few years later after I arrested
1/3 of HPD at once. Jurisdiction became so squishy, that I was able
to go back and clear her and him of any wrongdoing.

Where is she now?

She's a Deputy Captain in my IA

So, to be clear, you took a cop killer from jail, to Internal
Affairs

Technically

Prosecuting attorney's objection:

There's video that clears them of any wrongdoing

Sustained. Continue

Are you guilty of arson?

I would say no, but you would object and say that that is alleged

Explain,

Well, for starters, it's true.

Defense attorney's objection:

That would be alleged.

sustained. Continue

I rest my case

That's what I say, this is a hostile witness. Is it not true
that you once burned down a courthouse?

Technically,

What technically?

I was rescuing 3 children

no further questions

Your honor, the people present Houston Police Department,
Internal Affairs division, assistant Captain Macy Dillard.

Assistant Captain Macy Dillard, do you solemnly swear to tell the truth, the whole truth, and nothing but the truth?

I do

You may be seated

Miss Dillard

Like, just call me Ms.

Ms. Dillard, can you tell the jury about your involvement in this case?

Shah

Will you?

Like, you asked Can? Not Will?

Ms. Dillard, if you don't answer the questions, I will hold you in contempt

Sure

Ms. Dillard, kindly tell the jury your involvement

Like, I found fishy meanness, and the boss said 'Weave onea those cases' and I like, helped him bring justice

Juror number 11 stop laughing or I will hold you in contempt

How so?

Where r we?

Mamm—

Like, Chillax, no dusty manners needed—

O-k, can you - no - will you tell the court what has happened? Details please

Totally, He was like, caught. But the cops were so totally super mean. So much so that we're like trying to right that wrong. You, like, saw that videos? right?

Totally, so? What made the DA do what he did?

He was totally scared of being charged as an accomplice, perpetually. #Asperususal

I rest my case

Defense, you may begin questioning the witness,

What can you tell us about the death of Officer Churchill?

Nothin' like, totally fore my time. Didn't do that case.

Did your boss kill his brother?

Like, doubt it. But like he said he'd let the killer go if the killer was a child at the time. So like probably not totally best relationship

No, no, I mean his twin brother

Like, he was murdered by a sniper

No further questions, on the grounds that I can't take any more of this

I ·an offended!

Please step down Ms. Dillard

The defense calls Bailiff Marcus Anthony as our only witness

Marcus Anthony, do you solemnly swear to tell the truth, the whole truth, and nothing but the truth?

I do

You may be seated

Mr. Anthony, how did you get so burned?

The fire started by Captain Olaf

Prosecuting attorney's objection:

Objection to relevance

Denied, continue

Didn't that fire, and the so-called escape cause the case to have to be thrown out of court?

That it did

Prosecuting attorney's objection:

Objection, it was arrests made in that mission that caused it the case to be thrown out of court

No further questions, your honor

Prosecution, you may begin

Thank you, your honor. If they raided the courthouse like under normal circumstances, about how many people could have been killed?

Approx. 20, give or take

How many people were killed

I nearly was

But how many were?

Zero-

I rest my case

You may step down

But-

That's the courtroom way of saying, Get Out of the Box; you of all people should know that!

Your Honor, The people call - as our victim witness

- do you solemnly swear to tell the truth, the whole truth, and nothing but the truth?

I do

You may be seated

- Your family has evoked their 5th amendment right to not testify? Is that not correct?

Yea,

Why?

Too scared

But you decided to testify?

Without me, case is dead.

And you're here for justice

I'm here to keep other cops from, doing that again

And as for what happened you've made a victim statement? Correct?

You know that!

Your honor, the people present the following police brutality victim statement,

Evidence is approved, shown to jury

Was that statement accurate?

Of course it was,

So they tried to 'sweat' the answer out of you

That's what I said

No further questions

Defense, you may begin questioning the witness

Little boy, is it not true and your brother were guilty of-

If I'm old enough to go to jail, I'm too old to be called 'little boy'

Very well then, but, you and him were guilty

Please answer the question

WHY COULDN'T YOU HAVE JUST KILLED ME!!!!! WHY'D YOU HAVE TO MAKE ME JUDAS!!!!!!

Order!! Order in the court!

No further questions,

Your honor, the people call - as an expert witness in Child Abuse

- do you solemnly swear to tell the truth, the whole truth, and nothing but the truth?

I do

Please tell us, how does this compare to More normal cases of child abuse?

Actually, this is not that unusual-

I rest my case

Defense, you may begin.

He was uninjured, and no law was really broken-

Prosecuting attorney's objection:

That would be alleged.

You cannot object! She's your witness. Continue

Actually, Child Abuse comes in many forms, and what happened speaks for itself

Are you su-

Yes I am-

No further questions, your honor

Prosecution closing statement:

Everything speaks for itself; all evidence provided supports what we have been claiming all along. And review the witnesses Captain William X.Y.Z. Olaf says he carefully collected the evidence, and the alleged victim was totally shaken up. Assistant Captain Macy Dillard, ok that one didn't say much. The defense's own witness regarding the courthouse being burned down himself admitted that about 20 people would have been killed had it been conducted like a normal raid. And its undeniable there wasn't time to try to just wait them out and wait for them to come out; by then they would have been convicted. The alleged victim wished he had simply been murdered. Murder, an offence punishable by death. And the expert witness, she said this is not even that unusual a case of child abuse.

End of closing statement

Defense closing statement:

The Prosecution had tried to go over everything, and show you how it proves my clients guilty. I will do likewise, and instead it will prove IA to be the brovdignagian thing I have been portraying it to be.

Prosecuting attorney's objection:

It allegedly will prove that.

sustained. Continue

The Captain has been shown to be an accomplice after the fact to unspeakable crimes; just because the alleged perpetrators have been young.

Prosecuting attorney's objection:

That would be alleged.

sustained. Continue

And had taken convicted cop killer, from jail to his own division

Prosecuting attorney's objection:

She was cleared of all wrongdoing; and he, being dead, wasn't convicted; and was also later cleared of all wrongdoing.

Defense attorney's objection:

They were cleared of any and all wrongdoing by Mr. Olaf

sustained. sustained. Continue

His dingy assistant-

Prosecuting attorney's objection:

She is allegedly dingy.

Denied. Continue

She has been a fine representative of the brovdignagian thing that IA truly has become.-

Prosecuting attorney's objection:

That would be alleged.

sustained. Continue

In fact those he 'busted' in the 'superbust' were right in their intent to try to do away with Internal Affairs altogether. As they said 'Everybody in the police department is a cop, no real point, except for stuff like this'

Prosecuting attorney's objection:

That would be alleged.

sustained. Continue

And going back to the fire itself, they fire department was kept from doing their job properly, just so they could get in-

Prosecuting attorney's objection:

If that was true, you would have supplied someone to support that.

sustained. Continue

The alleged victim is just a little boy having a fit because he didn't get his own way-

Prosecuting attorney's objection:

That would be alleged.

sustained. Continue

Prosecution response to defense closing statement

The following statement form the defense was just further proof of how weak their case is-

Prosecuting attorney's objection:

That would be alleged.

sustained. Continue

At no point in this case have they attempted to take on the issue of their own guilt, or lack thereof. Head-on. Instead, they have simply tried to place the officers and their division into a poor light. But if you remember one thing from this statement, make it the ages of the boys rescued in that courthouse fire 12, 13, and 14.

Defense attorney's objection:

This is grand standing

Denied

Defense response to prosecution response to defense closing statement

This whole case is built on emotions, a crying 11 year old. Monsters-

Prosecuting attorney's objection:

That would be alleged.

sustained. Continue

Those Charged with otherwise severe offences, but supposedly should get off, because they're not old enough to drive. That's it.

Prosecuting attorney's objection:

That would be alleged; and there was a child abuse expert witness

sustained. Continue

End of trial

Question asked by jury to prosecution, via the bailiff

What are the details of the 'burning courthouse case?'

Response to question asked by jury to prosecution, via the bailiff

They were 3 brothers charged as adults for gang rape and murder.
But there was no proof that their parents didn't just try to cover up
their crimes, or they just walked in and misunderstood, and were
covering up. But a. acquittal was unlikely and b. if convicted they
probably would never be set free, ever. What you thought about what
would have happened had they raided the courthouse was correct. They
called in Captain W.X.Y.Z. Olaf's Special opps identical twin brother
to carefully set the courthouse on fire. Such that there'd be a lot
of fire fighters. They themselves, but not the captain. Too tall to
fit in. Disguised themselves as fire fighters, they rescued those
boys, and all those that had done them bad were arrested. But in the
interest of full disclosure, the grand jury said 'no' to any charges
against those arrested in the courthouse raid. Also the bailiff was
wrong, but was the only person with real injuries. All damage
couldn't be avoided, but they did good considering it was a fire that
could, and did, burn the courthouse to the ground in the course of it.
But as we said 'the bailiff was wrong' the twin brother was mistaken
for Captain W.X.Y.Z. Olaf; but the Captain was more muscular and an
inch taller.

2 hours later:

Has the jury reached a verdict?

We have your honor

Foreman hands verdict to bailiff Bailiff hands verdict to judge

–

We the jury, find the defendants, on all counts, guilty.

Chapter D Personal Life

Signed and notarized affidavit from -

- Attorney

- Notary Public

- 2nt Notary Public

Most of the chapters of this book will be about Captain W.X.Y.Z. Olaf; this one, and this one only, is About Mr. W.X.Y.Z. Olaf. In other words, it will show that he lived his personal life just the same as he lived in his professional life.

It all began when I was a teenager, my mom was gone in Afghanistan, and my sister had been rejected. There was nothing I could do; she was lost to foster care. You see, I had a dad that was one of those parents that you could never live up to. My sister he disowned, and I couldn't help her; but my youngest brother decided that he had failed her. I gave up on appeasing dad a long time ago, did a lot of dumb things, and while I won't go into detail, I also won't make excuses. I was sent to military school, my brother, other brother, between me and our youngest brother; he had been one that tried to live up. He finally saw all that was happening; ran away. Said he wouldn't come home till I was brought home. Dad was so mad, but he brought me home. I should have provoked him till he snapped, and simply called the police. I'll always have the guilt over that. My brother then came home. It was a set up. We were then sent to a boot camp, even worse. We would have run away from home; but we only had 10 minutes' notice. It was simply impossible; instead something happened that no one could have predicted. Something the youngest brother did. He grabbed a knife and killed him in his sleep. He was eight years old.

That's when W.X.Y.Z. Olaf pops up in this story. I and my other brother left that horrible place. But we ended up in foster care. Nobody would have anything to do with my brother; and his brothers and sister could do nothing for him; nor could have W.X.Y.Z. Olaf have stopped him from going to jail. But W.X.Y.Z. Olaf visited him in jail, at least twice a week. Everything from this point on was told to me by W.X.Y.Z. Olaf, so it was probably more; he was humble and modest. Not one to brag. Right before he was going to get out, he was poisoned to cover up unspeakable crimes being done to the inmates where he was, in exchange for money. Not the only person killed in that great scandal. I know one victim got out, recitivised, and then to avoid going back killed a cop. Later the scandal was held responsible for that death; I believe more cops may have been killed. That was the big case W.X.Y.Z. Olaf was working during the Lucafess catastrophe; the same mega scandal briefly mentioned in the second half of "External Affairs". My brother was having it done to him more than anyone else. And it couldn't have helped that my brother was having it done to him half by creepazoids, and half by people obsessed with power. The guilt I fell over what happened to my brother, words cannot describe.

(End of affidavit)

But beyond tying up a loose end from *External Affairs* there is another lesson to be learned in all this. I learned it myself some time back. It's an established fact that of all the numerous horrors of world history; the greatest ultimately and / or in some way boil / boiled down to some form of abuse of power. However, perhaps the cruelest of all horrors are those that have no interest in causing or bringing about death. The genocide's victims' suffering ends at the grave. The murder victim, assuming it to not be a cruel manner, merely succumbs to an inevitable fate early. Meanwhile on the other end of the spectrum; just because you died of natural causes, doesn't mean you didn't suffer. Possibly even more so if not suffered immensely. There's a reason many people want to die a quick death. But the horror that has no interest in death is so cruel; because it lasts so long. If you remember the prison camps of Vietnam; they were denied even the ability to take their own lives. Tis better to be overwhelmed by serial killers. Because at least Jack the Ripper eventually took up an interest in something else. The vampire's thirst for blood could possibly be satisfied, Varney the Vampyre would sometimes have a pang of conscience. But the contrary either will most likely have an unquenchable thirst for power, as some of my brother's "clients" had. And / or they torment, attitude adjust, and / or reeducate with the approval of conscience, and possibly also with a strong-armed chairman's strong-arm on their cast. Those at the

(insert mule picture here)

Houston

sanitarium and military school were tormented without end; meanwhile the
triangle factory workers plummeted away from the flames.

Chapter E Oops

(Partially translated from heavy acient for ease of mainstream understanding)

It began a normal slow-to-boring day. It stayed as such till I was chillin' with my bros-stinky timing.

It seemed initially like another minor drug raid that went sad. An officer was non-life-threateningly shot; under normal circumstances, virtually no investigation needed; but Captain W.X.Y.Z. Olaf, that wasn't his style. Why we were there was a suspect was life-threateningly shot, being rushed to Ben Taub; excellent, albeit charity, trauma hospital. In the Texas Medical Center, probably the best in the world; I once needed it. I was a teen, don't ask.

That was cut short by another officer involved shooting. Well, technically that was what we had to call it. A body had been washed up from Galveston bay. Been dead for days, so everything had been washed clean. Also dental records had to be used to identify him. It gets more complicated. In all such cases, the autopsy would be done by the chief medical examiner in Harris County; only wrench was that that was also Captain W.X.Y.Z. Olaf's wife. Coincidence, but always complicated things, because whenever the boss would be working a fatal case, she'd have to do the autopsy. What brought us in, or even HPD, was that it was a ballistic match for an HPD officer's service weapon. Rats! Thought I'd never b able 2 clock out!

And we weren't able to finish that up because the first case, the suspect had died. And while the boss always kept a few IA officers on duty at all times, whatsoever; but that's the difference between a beat cop working the graveyard shift. And a homicide detective. Rough translation, no real investigation had been done yet. But the investigation had done us. There had been a teenage boy, 13, tazered 4 blocks from the raid.

But Olaf, being a non-fatal tazing, sent others to that one. He went to inform the family. When something like this happened he always made sure to do it himself. Said something like "Least he could do" After that it was morning; and we needed sleep.

When we got back to work next day the day crew had already begun initial investigation into all 3 cases above. That's where things veer off into crazy town.

The first case the cops had the wrong address, and some indiscrepincies in paperwork regarding pre-raid procedures. All too boring to relate. It gets worse. The boss made it standard prodigal to double and triple check all warrants and court orders. For once it paid off. There was no record of them going for the warrant. So the judge had been brought in. He signed some legal something or another, basically it said he never signed the warrant. We've seen forged warrants, mostly by fake cops we mistook for real ones. But that was called "The work of an evil genius" Now I was exaggerating; but that's the only time I've ever seen a real judge's signature forged.

The second case, there had been a crime stoppers tip around the time, like hours after the victim vanished, saying they saw a fake cop throwing a dead body off The Cosway, a bridge to Galveston Island. Also the cop, who's service weapon matched, GPS put that squad car on that bridge after the vic. vanished. Not even in city limits; no reason at all to be there. When we arrived CSU was already sweeping the squad car. As for later that evening; the officer was in the hospital. Soon after those events he got in an accident caused by shock. The cause of shock he had no idea.

But the third case was Crazytownest. The tazing officer was the same girl that wrote Chapter A of this very book. As such, being a personal connection the boss had to step back from the case; but at the same time he couldn't. To explain what happened. I will have start at the beginning. You have probably heard the saying, quote, whateveritis, "The enemy of my enemy is my friend." The boss is a strong believer in that, whatever it is. As such many of us in IA are still gang members, and the boss is, mostly just officially, a member of about every gang in town. As such he could tell something was extra fishy when some extra senseless gang crimes came up. A normal cop would've not smelled anything amiss. He was able to, finally, get outside tests done from different crimes. It proved that the perpetrators had been on drugs at the time, no surprise right? WRONG! These were, and don't expect me to say what exactly what they were, I don't remember exactly what. But these were drugs that could, and apparently were used to make people do things they wouldn't have done. Loss of free will drugs. Crazytown indeed. And every defense attorney's dream; and prosecutors worst nightmare. Regular detectives launched, not led, but, assisted by Captain W.X.Y.Z. Olaf, a super investigation. And with witness statements figured out who it was. It was a gang hating old lady. But, being every defense attorney's dream; and prosecutors' worst nightmare. They had do proof, no probable cause. A smart cop would have simply watched her like a hawk; but they decided she was too great a threat. They took a lead from some show called Castle, and put that 13 year old boy up to attack her; obviously behind the boss' back. But the for mentioned officer, - was too ethical, she wouldn't have anything to do with that. It was all made to look like a homicide; and she would have shot him. But it was a teenage child. She showed him mercy and tazered him, while apologizing!

Only one profitable thing happened during the day, we realized that the accusations against the old lady gang hater, were illogical. About everyone could fall victim to one of those crimes. There were irrelevant victims, and those that were members of the same gang; and had no internal disputes. Which was mostly thanks to the boss. So much so he had in the past arranged even peace treaties; something otherwise unheard of in Gang wars. Just something more on the side, or at least off the books. He said we (the police) our only concern was public safety; justice that was the (and the only) concern of the prosecutors. And it all gets crazier still. It made sense her framing them to get rid of them. But that much collateral damage? Things stopped adding up.

The next day the first thing that happened was we got a witness to the killer cop case. He had simply assumed, and he demanded immunity for, D.W.I. that what he saw boiled down to something that boils out. But news stories conformed otherwise. He said the officer had been attacked by a drunk, and when he couldn't beat up the cop, he pulled a gun. If this doesn't make sense know this. Later that evening someone called the police having found a gun in that parking lot; ballistics found it to have a scratched out serial number. Different records showed that a bullet had been found logged in a bumper, and it had been parked there that night. But almost nothing was done; and it even took 2 days for it to be noticed. We sent a better view into that parking lot, found a logged. But security was closed circuit; and no witnesses saw the shooting; and the officer still said "Can't remember a thing from that evening."

Also that day we offered immunity to the real dealer, in exchange for knowing what happened at that raid. Turns out; it was extremely violent. The officers were later charged. Never thought I'd see cops saying that an officer involved shooting was started in self-defense; but the cops were not the ones acting in self-defense.

But the 3rd case, remained Crazytownest. We were able to search the old woman's apartment. She had such drugs hidden away. But it still smelled a little wrong. A warrant was obtained, and we took samples of her hair, what there was left of it. Turns out she had been on such drugs. So, to clarify, an old woman was drugged and hypnotized into drugging and hypnotizing known gang members to go out and commit horrific and senseless crimes. SuperCSU came in and found a hair belonging to someone who had no way to justify his being there. It was a lead gang task force officer. The boss had made them be a lot less brutal and corrupt; and would stir up public sympathy for gang members whenever he was made Time magazine man of the year. Everyone was exonerated; except for 2 boys. That sad tale is better told by one of them's sister; in the next chapter. And I know that this seems crazy and just a big lie; but I never was a great writer, most of the people in this book never had those skills. And as for content. You must first remember this whole thing; you must remember from when this story is told. Second when the super scandal broke; it was found that this was one of a few cases that was individually broken before we knew what was going on

Chapter F Oops 2 The Chandler of San Louis Ray

WARNING!!:WHILE THIS IS A SECULAR BOOK IN A SECULAR TRILOGY; THIS ONE CHAPTER ALONE IS NOT! IT MAY OFFEND YOU!!!

(insert mule picture here)
Houston

Pardon that preface, you can think the National Department of Hate Speech prevention. Course not too far back this could get you arrested. And, what was it they kept saying in book 2 "To answer the question you're thinking" no this, like everything else in this trilogy, takes place approximately when it is being published, not when it is written.

This is the story of what, among other things, happened to my brother. One of Captain W.X.Y.Z. Olaf's few failures. He put the police commission in jail regarding established procedures that later resulted in tazings. He "rounded up" all school district workers for stealing A.K.A. confiscation. He took over a federal checkpoint in Kingwood. But he just couldn't save my brother, or his friend. I will explain but I will start at where it all began; furthermore you should know that, like book 2, the spinoff, this is an extremely unpleasant story; you've been forewarned.

It all began when I was younger than when our sad tale takes place. The book 2 superscandal, I heard the stories of some of the victims. One really stuck out in my mind. Wasn't a little kid; was a little older, but not that much; guess it gave it a touch of realness. Or perhaps being older I simply knew no one would really care—would really see her as a child-crime-victim. Full disclosure: she probably was guilty. She ended up having to cut a deal, waving all right to any appeal. As she said "Don't like seeing perfectly good keys get thrown away." In time, too much I might add, she was released. And many people questioned if the superscandal ever really happened. As such when she was finally released, she died. Shot down on the steps of the courthouse. Same courthouse where Olaf was, thank the King of the Universe, unsuccessfully, PAAAed, my brother died, and eventually had to be burned down.

After that I started reading news. And thinking, too much. Psyawhacamacallits, or shrinks as I call them. Where was I, oh yes. I started roominating, the technical term, about it. The thought of children in adult court, locked up for life, and later at times it was extended to Juvenile Halls, military schools, even just being very grounded. It wasn't like I lost my faith, but I was just bothered that God had allowed it. You'd think of the atrocities and injustices throughout world history and modern day; but in a weird sort of way, they almost helped. Guess no matter what you do disconnect form those sorts of things, at least on some level; and / or I merely assumed I could except better here in America.

By the time I was 12, I had still been able to put on a brave face for longer than I'd liked to have to. Being the only daughter, and soon the only child, I had screechy, microaggressing, and otherwise unpleasant parents that sure didn't help. I-I can tell you one thing; something I doubt you'll ever hear anywhere else on this cruddy rock. "All it takes for evil to prevail is for good men to do nothing." But, at some point you absolutely have to say "Not my problem." Not being able to do so, and when I did I felt some guilt like I was ignoring. Nearly caused my death. Also I took some probably illegal vices; anything to not think about it. Well, even now I'd rather not admit what they were, even now, it in a book. But that became an addiction. And at the worst possible time, the worst possible thing happened. The only person I was really close to was my new brother and longtime classmate. He was about a year and a half older than me. Allegedly he and some other gang members had, and did, commit some murders. But while waiting for them to arrive to carry it out he allegedly killed 5 people in about as cruel and heinous a manner as he could, just to kill time while he waited for someone to show up. In fact news crews said it was reminiscent of the T.C. Jester Park murders of decades ago. But one of the victims was a fellow gang member and a would-have-been accomplice, that he was good with, with which was going to commit the other premeditated murders; one more was just a witness. The other 3 were just convent bystanders. When his friend showed up, together they finished up. There was a ton of forensic evidence; no attempt to cover things up. First hole. He was him, not Prince Vlad the Impalor. Second hole. He may have been on drugs, making him essentially a service robot. But the captain couldn't get proof of such drugs, and in a case this emotional, the burden of proof is basically on you (albeit unofficially). Furthermore, exoneration would be the only possible way to liberate my brother, or his friend. It bothered me a bit that that happened. And a bit more that that happened at the hands of someone that age. It also bothered me a bit bigger bit that he did that. I didn't know any of the victims. And merely knew of the friend. At first I could just pretend, like I sometimes would, that it just wasn't happening. But in time, Before he was convicted I was able to have a good talk to my brother.

You'd think I'd have gotten mad at God. Jane Doe's twin brother said to God he'd "defect." And was briefly involved with devil worship, though he came back before she died. Not so with me. It was more like me and my Heavenly Father weren't on speaking terms, more like. Though at times I found myself having to force myself not to be mad at God. I began to see the world as a car driven by God, on cruise control, and with no one sitting in the driver's seat.

Those drugs were my brother's main defense. But he couldn't prove it. The prosecutor later bragged that it was the most open and shut case ever. There was no prayer for an insanity plea, saying someone else didn't do it was so impossible, and self-defense; impossible! The defense went over as well with the jury as you'd think. To paraphrase James Malcolm Rymer It was such an open and shut case; the defense was just a formality. Though unlike when Varney the Vampyre was on trial, or after the Great Experiment went sideways in The Jewel of Seven Stars I was not spared the pain of hoping.

Up until then I had been good, I was able to keep it bottled up. Almost never did anyone see any hint of all that what happening. Till the day we all knew the guilty verdict would be pronounced. My parents were so off, my dad wore slippers to the courthouse. I think I got up early and walked. Maybe I took the bus. I only think I got there my own way because of a stop I made. I thought I had time. I probably would have; but for how long I took.

(insert mule picture here)
Houston

I stopped at the St. Something Something Cathedral of Something Something (who cares what it was really called). I was just going to pray for my brother and light a candle for him and his friend, each. I broke. I doubt a word I said the whole time could be understood. Eventually the priest came out and tried to comfort me. I saw what I was. A pathetic sinner, asking a prayer for a lost cause that probably didn't even deserve it, though if my case was wrong and my brother did deserve it, ultimately that would have been worse. It seemed like forever that I was there and at the same time mere seconds.

As long as I shall live, I shall never know how I got to that courthouse. When I got there I must have been crying; because my closes were wet, but I didn't smell. Or, at least not much. I was really late, by time I got there they had already had been found guilty. But I knew something weird was up. Had no clue what, though I hoped, what for, I don't remember. But at the same time understanding the pain of hope. Eventually I got someone to tell me. A Chandler had fallen in the courtroom. My brother was killed. As long as I live, I will remember standing over the fallen chandler, seeing the puddles of blood. But I know that my mind must've been messed with. I could never have seen what I remember for 2 reasons. I know that the bailiffs weren't letting ANYONE in the courtroom after that happened. I believe even the judge, thought I can't be sure. Second, the friend made it to the hospital. But soon afterward died.

And I know many people will look at the crimes themselves. Think maybe my brother should have been convicted as an adult. But what they don't take into account, and no, I wouldn't say this to a relative of a victim, was that here in America, we don't execute in a cruel way, we try to make it painless. But, serial killers, like Jeffery Dommer that have killed 100+, you could justify it. That does not mean you should. Second. He's DEAD; didn't get away with it.

Afterward, Captain Olaf took me out for Fro-Yo to take my mind off what happened. We went to some place in a bookstore in some mall out somewhere.

(insert mule picture here)
Houston

For reasons I can't remember Captain Olaf's geisha aunt had to drive us. Car problems of some kind, I think. Honestly everything about that day is either a blur, or burned in my memory; so who knows. Like an Asperger reading something bogus in that couldn't possibly be more obvious. But the one thing that I am relatively certain about may give you a chuckle. I remembered Olaf as a "The Beast." A nice beast, but a beast. And I can now for once and for all confirm that he could and did out-eat Garfield (Cat, not president. Don't know how much the president ate). Being a bodybuilder like that it should be no surprise; but he wasn't one to brag, guess that's why it never came up in his novel. He was absolutely huge with blond hair down to his shoulders; frankly he could've been something out of one of my vices; but that's enough of that.

As I began looking into the details, it was ruled an accident caused by sloppy maintenance. Though an involuntary manslaughter case couldn't be built. 2 others were also killed, my brother died instantly. A bailiff bled out before they could get there. And the public defender only made it till the paramedics arrived. The bailiff had just been diagnosed with alztimers; a disease he greatly feared. And the public defender probably was the worst in town. A better case might have been able to be built by his clients, by themselves.

I heard about the camp mentioned in "External Affairs." It was great at "Breaking rebellious spirits: totally and completely" among other unspeakable acts. Some were sentenced there; other were sent like military school. Many inspected, no one understood what was happening, and no one wanted to do anything. It took some siblings, and their boyfriends and Girlfriend, plus a family friend, and a brother of a girlfriend to come in shooting, hot AK47's a blazing. That's what it took to expose and stop it. It was a battle. I believed my brother would end up in a similar place, or not much better. I still do. Though I was able to have a good talk with my brother; he actually had to ask me to stop coming to see him. Reason was was that my visits were like taking oxygen when climbing up Everest (his words not mine). This is a

(insert mule picture here)
Houston

happy ending. I wasn't out of the woods. But I instantly was "mending fences" with the almighty. This proved once and for all "My ways are higher than your ways. My thoughts are higher than your thoughts." And to respond to what I'm sure you're thinking "Why couldn't they just exonerate them" Even when it hit the fan, this one case, they could never prove that they were on those drugs. And they'd have to prove it to win an appeal. A actually thanked God.

Chapter G Vehicular Manslaughter of a Sort

Signed and notarized affidavit from -
- Attorney
- Notary Public
- 2nt Notary Public

It all began on such a normal day. Most juries would have exonerated him. There were partial prints at the scene of the robbery. Otherwise no other evidence against him. I convicted him. He was just some kid.

My prosecutors said "Jail is hell." They were right. Nevertheless I would spend the rest of my life in solitary confinement if it could bring that boy back.

I'm a middle aged old man that's about to make parole; he was, he was, he was just a child!

I gave him what I thought to have been a lighter sentence considering his age, and the value of the stolen property.

About 8 months later I read in the news that the police had tried to talk him off of a ledge. When he saw the trampoline being set out; he decided "Now or never." And fell to his death.

The next day I was working a similar case; Bailiffs decided to not let the place be raided. Grand jury inquiries take time; Captain W.X.Y.Z. Olaf needed to catch me in the act. His IA officers weren't enough, and the juvenile courthouse of ill repute was made so as to prevent the fireman trick he used, and ended up burning down the courthouse and getting his twin brother killed. Where was I? Never mind; and no. This isn't sickafancy in the hope of parole. It isn't needed.

(insert mule picture here)
Houston

```
     The Captain; he couldn't get cops to help him.  But he said "the
buck stops here"; and "We don't leave a man behind."  He assembled
nearly 300 gang members, police brutality victims, general thugs, and
etc... And gave them all a weapon.  It was later shown half of them
didn't even have ammo.

     Thank God, we all knew it was over.  Everybody just ran. Myself
included.  I was acquitted of other charges, but was convicted of
voluntary manslaughter.  In time I came to see the error of my ways;
the guilt is worse than jail.

     At least that was the end of anyone being tried without a jury;
against their will.
```
(E n d   o f   a f f i d a v i t)

Chapter H An Internal Affair

The sequence of events that led to the deaths of seven police officers started farther before this story begins. But I will begin with my sister's death.

I was there when she died. My little sis, when she died; her and my little, her big, brother. I now realize it should have been me. They were all I really had. Well, that and terrorizing fear. I still struggle to forget what happened; but I will tell you that we 3 had run away from our parents. I would have rather not spent the rest of my life in jail; but I would rather have spent the rest of my life in jail than go back home. You can probably guess why.

We were on the street; which was not a great place. But far preferable to home. We took our little baby sister with us when we ran away from home. Couldn't let her meet the fate we knew she would. Soon afterward she died in a railroad accident; stay off the trains.

I'll tell you how my sister died. We were stopped by a cop. My brother was tazed, we were running. What else could we do? My sister tried to stop her. Fortunately her partner wasn't there. The officer pulled a gun; my sister tried to take it away. Was just trying to keep us safe. She was shot, but was able to wrestle it away. She had to shoot the officer in the head to save her own life; and her older brothers. Oh God! What I'd give to go back! To help her! I had to carry my brother off. It wasn't easy. We got away and my brother recovered. But my sister died a slow painful death from a liver wound. There was nothing we could do to save her. Soon afterward we were caught.

We were immediately separated, they pulled the usual intimidation. They made me think my brother rolled over. But when they tried to figure out who we were, the thought of going home broke me. I confessed just so that me and my brother wouldn't have to see our parents.

(insert mule picture here)
Houston

A kind officer, who proved to be a new rookie, tried to arrest a detective for disorderly conduct, forcing us to talk. He wasn't to cooperative, and even tried to arrest her. When he pulled his stun gun, she shot it. His partner shot her, dead instantly. A different officer then shot the partner. When the first officer tried to return fire, he was shot. He alone survived, well him and the surviving good cop. The good cop had to shoot the 3 other detectives working this case in order to save his own life. And another officer that just misunderstood what was happening. I will always remember him radioing "Officer in need of assistance. Seven suspects shot. Please be informed, suspects are police officers, I repeat suspects are police officers."

Captain Olaf offered me immunity. The cameras didn't see what happened. I did. Not only was the good cop quickly cleared of any wrongdoing, though he had to serve a long suspension. Just standard protocol for when an officer has to kill someone; so that they can get their bearings. Wasn't even a punishment. It was extended because of how many. Not only all that, but when the surviving officer; all they had him on was a disorderly conduct charge, and possibly resisting arrest. He went back through his carrier. He was able to prove 1527 different cases of disorderly conduct and in in the process countless appeals were dredged up. Not really enough; but better.

Chapter I Another Internal Affair

Exherts from Houston Police Department Internal Investigation Report

Chief investigator: Captain W.X.Y.Z. Olaf

Nature of investigation: Officer involved shooting

Please note; the best representative portions have been taken for this chapter. We opted to not include the entire Internal Investigation Report; seeing as it was very long.

Witness statement from uninvolved officer -

He told us that a fellow officer had been murdered in the heart of known gang territory. He had me pass out a list of known gang members. Then, as usual, he asked if we had any questions. She asked "Should we drag in every gang member just because they're a gang member? Despite no proof of anything?" He just started to go on about what an evil thing it was, hammer of justice. She stood up, and interrupted him to arrest him for wrongful arrest. He got super mad, and ordered her to sit down.

(insert mule picture here)
Houston

Said he was going to get a detective on the case, she reached for her stun gun. What happened next is such a blur, he reached for his weapon, I think, I think as just a threat, I think. Next thing I knew he was on the ground. Bleeding but not breathing, and she were pointing her service weapon at the spot of air that had just been where he was standing. Then we all gasped, and I realized I was standing, and everyone else was.

Witness statement from uninvolved officer -

We were started off hearing about the murder of officer - We were ordered to be on high look out for all the known gang members we were told of. Should we be able to find one, we were to arrest then, immediately. As information was being distributed; one new recruit; you know who; stood up, asked a question hinting that she was about to cry "misconduct" to Internal Affairs. He was furious, and probably pushed her too far. She stood up, ignoring his orders. And proceeded to attempt to take him into custody. When he didn't cooperate, she went with the procedure to stun him. That is I guess she was attempting to be procedural; but what followed could possibly be the least procedural thing ever. But he reached for his gun. I don't know if he shot; but she acted automatically. He was killed instantly; even though we tried to save him. It went straight through his badge and heart. I meanwhile tried to comfort her. She was hysterical with guilt, and fear of going to jail.

Conclusion: No wrongdoing found

Chapter J Twofer

It began when I was much younger than I deserved to be. Bear with me; this is a long and complicated story.

It all began, oh, I already said that. I had fallen victim to cyber bullying; so bad I faked a suicide attempt just so I'd be in a padded room (they still have those!) instead of that horrible place called school. And my uncle being the police commissioner I was able to get things investigated.

Being after the superscandal, See External Affairs, There were a durth of police officers. Leaving police working all kinds of odd jobs. Detectives on beat. Beat investigating murders. And Captain W.X.Y.Z. Olaf investigating my case. Actually wasn't the first time he'd help me. My sister got it even worse. He couldn't control my sister, so he planted on her. Framed her for dealing drugs. And when the judge wouldn't let the secret tape recording I'd taken of my dad forcing someone to steal those drugs; and they got killed in the process I might add. Then he

(insert mule picture here)
Houston

simply bought them himself, very expensive. As I was saying: when the judge wouldn't let the secret tape recording I'd taken of my dad forcing someone to steal those drugs, The Captain stood up and arrested the judge in the middle of court (no; the judge hadn't taken a bribe). Charged him as an accomplice, somehow my parents got off. I've heard of those that couldn't afford military school, so they got planted on. But that, well, there is no mitigating factor for any of this.

Meanwhile back at the ranch, just a Captain (W.X.Y.Z.) was beginning his investigation. He was arrested for locking the police commissioner into a bomb to force him to force the district attorney to drop charges. They even produced recordings of him saying planning it and saying things like- "You're right; we can't sacrifice 10 lives to save 1. But we can sacrifice 1." and "We Can't Leave A Man Behind." And "God won't compromise his principles; maybe that's why he hasn't already won his war with Satan." That last line was almost proof that it was a hoax. That and the new police commissioner was locked into a bomb vest and forced to force the new DA to drop the same charges.

I was surprised to learn it was found to be a hoax. Just to frame him; even Olaf admitted that he would have done it (though he had a different plan. Revenge for the superscandal bust. Nevertheless. the charges couldn't be undropped.

As they said in book 2 "to answer the question you're thinking" the charges actually went back to the superscandal. A girl was going to be sent to military school. No prior warning. Just "This Conversation is Over. My Decision is Final" type ****. She reached for a knife, had to I believe. Ended up dead, and dumped. Just another "Can't solve, so let's frame. But who was on trial was her sister who knew something to be up. Couldn't trust the cops. Charged for not talking. After all this happened, she later got a civilian award for NOT talking to the cops.

Meanwhile back at my ranch. What happened was I went behind my parents backs to do social networking. And I got hacked. They hacked me. They were finally convicted. I meanwhile got a new school; and unofficial witness protection.

Chapter K Micah; Boy of the Streets

"*It all began months ago. Micah was a normal kid. But, well when people talk about underprivileged kids, they normally don't literally refer to privileges. But in this case I do. His parents, but especially his mother. They were determined to raise a proper southern gentleman. Thankfully, he wasn't shipped of somewhere. But unthankfully his own life turned basically into that. Acceptance was*

(insert mule picture here)
Houston

simply out of the question, and he just couldn't come to live with tyranny. His brother and sister, to closely paraphrase Thoreau, tried to clog with their own weight. But they just couldn't wear the machine smooth. Soon he ran away. He was desperate, so desperate. I-I wish I could describe his extreme desperation. He eventually committed some armed robberies. And was soon arrested. But now an actual investigation has taken place; led by yours truly. As such he has now received full immunity; and he and his siblings will soon be moved. Not by a CPS psytoinvestigation. Rather by the fact that the dictators of Micah's household will now be charged with his armed robberies. And seeing as they are adults; they will be charged as adults. "

--- Houston Police Department / Internal Affairs Captain W.X.Y.Z. Olaf speaking at a press conference

Chapter L The Rebellion Or Screwtape's Squad Car

For all too long our schools; the students had been deliberately getting in to as much trouble as possible. It had been such a nightmare; and they were trying to wear us smooth too! Then I finally remember hearing that Cap. Olaf had been arrested; I thought finally! Thank God! After all his encouragement of this, was about time; would've been sooner, but everyone was too scared of him.

Then I heard the news. There was a violent rebellion in Wisconson. Turned out two 12 year old girls were being tried as adults for attempted premeditated murder. They were ripped out of the hands of law enforcement. And by ripped I mean that they came up to the police central station and when the cops stood their ground. Over 100 officers were massacred, but fortunately in was the Alamo in terms of the winner's losses. They fully took command of that station and did so running in screaming non-sense like "The Buck Stops here" "We Don't Leave a Man Behind" and "Principles before Principals" It was the Cuban Missile crisis afterword and we lost. I was happy to hear that one of the two died in it all. Unfortunately the governor pardoned the other, and anyone that had participated in the rebellion. Oddly enough the cops and other law enforcement were also pardoned.

We ended up letting Olaf out; and he went up there in the wake of all that. But I must give Credit where credit is due. Here (and a couple other places) we nearly had another rebellion; which would have spiraled into a true civil war which he may very well have been enough to prevent. Unfortunately after a literal surrender treaty went through Olaf locally headed up the enforcement thereof; which oddly enough more affected schools. But it stood to reason seeing as it was all junk he had been pushing for.

Chapter L How Could They Have Known

I apologize for how short this story is. I can't bear to give the details that haunt me so. But I will try to tell this story. We've all heard it. But it needs to be in this book.

We were taking our kid to the doctor. One of those specialists at the hospital, in another building. Something stupid happened in a gift shop. Our son was nearly tazed to death. I think it was over a petty theft. My wife tried to make a citizen's arrest of the other officer. But it backfired because, being old, she couldn't get down on her knees; she was also shot, didn't pull through. I was handcuffed; and they ignored that I had severe slipping rib syndrome. Cartilage was torn. We got cleared, course we aren't cops. Him, not so much. Olaf.

Chapter N Coulda done better

Fair warning: This chapter is depressing, distressing, and may even be called sick. But I assure you that it all really happened.

It began farther back, but to me, it all began the day I was nearly shot. And I got a bullet in my blender. I will call him Bernard, though that's wasn't even close to his real name. His sister had just been fatally shot, and the bullet went through the wall. She had just been so tired of her dad running her life. Bernard got her a gun to keep her out of military school, or worse. If such a thing even exists. I never knew if she shot herself or her dad shot her in some sort of sick twisted self-defense. He would only ever say "I don't want to talk about it." I wouldn't press it. Also he was charged in relation to her death. He was a tween. Once again I never knew exactly what law he was charged with breaking. After he got out he was seeming super jumpy and bothered. But we became friends. And I would take him out for fro-yo. And I happened to see something he didn't mean for me to see. I discovered that he was cutting himself. After that terrible discovery I saw to it that he got some help. Soon afterward he and his dad had had the fight to end all fights. I called 911 fearing someone was going to get murdered. After that I took him in. He confessed that the only reason he hadn't killed himself was so that he could be there to keep his little sister from meeting the same fate. But I didn't have him put in a mental hospital because I thought being locked up in any form in his state would be cruel. He seemed to be getting better. He broke. He, for reasons all too trivial, was sent to "alternative school." See jail school. I had to see to it that he pulled out of the public school system all together. And he lost was vestiges of friends he had. In all that he got desperate, needed a break. Wasn't a good or right thing. But he fell into a police drug trap. He was quickly bailed out.

(insert mule picture here)
Houston

But he would be convicted; and he would get far worse. Putting him. after all he went through. back there! He broke. Committed suicide by cop. Never even got to be a teenager for a day. I will never forget getting the last message he'd ever send. I won't include it, but I will tell you a few things it included. Something like that, impossible to not memorize. I wanted to be there for my sister...I broke...Can't go back...Forgive me...You did all you could for me. But there's no point in trying now... and so on. Where THE IA Captain comes in is he not only got the officers that hurt him charged. He was always trying to help kids like Bernard. But sometimes it never would even make it to his desk. But Bernard's death. He not only got those officers that shot him charged with murder. He got a conviction. I was the one that made the victim's family statement. I felt a lot of guilt myself; while fearing some form of charges. And even to this day, at different random times of the day. I just stop, usually for only 2-3 seconds; and wonder. If he was still alive. What would he be doing right now?

Chapter O Finale

Well, the publisher let me know that this is probably going to be the last chapter in the last book in this genre starting book. But they told me maybe not. Who knows? Maybe there'll be a 17th author; or maybe can make this a quartet. So in conclusion, no pressure here. I've also been told that this book will probably make sure it stays a trilogy; and not a qua-whatever. And while I'm rambling I should let you know that while the first story in Internal Affairs was written in your future; our present day. So is this one. Here goes.

My dad got stopped; and the cop told him to take a snort of an illegal substance. There is no point in saying its name; seeing as it hasn't been invented yet in your time. I've heard of cops planting things. We even have trunk cams standard on all vehicles for that very concern. But this?! Dad shoved him in front of an oncoming vehicle. Where does Olaf Come in? Why even tell this story? Well. This was the very last case he ever worked. Actually he wasn't even able to finish it. But @ least he lived a long, good, accomplishing life.

Chapter P Chron

Preamble

This is a compilation of relevant news stories and articles made by and compiled by the Houston Chronicle. In the on-going spirit of keeping this a brief and non-redundant book we have not included much; including some of the most memorable stories. If you wish to read something a bit more exhaustive, you may read SUPERSCANDAL, The Firsthand reports. In that book you will find every news article we have ever published regarding the superscandal, up until its own

(insert mule picture here)
Houston

publishing of course. If you are simply interested in the work of Captain W.X.Y.Z. Olaf, then we have also published, The Unabridged Olaf, covering deep and in depth all his work throughout is historic carrier. Through the eyes of our newspaper. Also it is worth noting that while our publishing and newspaper do not do redactions; the publisher of this Novelette has required it.

We will begin this chapter with two brief news articles from the superscandal. They are listed as were published.

Death in the Family

By Amy N. X.

Here at the Houston Chronicle two nights ago we have suffered a great loss. We have lost the industry acclaimed - at the age of 39...His last work involved police misconduct and violence. While not much is known at this time; what little he had determined has been turned over to law enforcement to aid in their investigation.

Separate Suspects

By Zelda Z.

In all this talk of omnigate and those being framed and gross acts of paraunspeakable violence; let us discuss just one specific case with no particular great horrors about it. Take the framing case of longtime friends - and -. One night - mother was murdered. The killer left no evidence; and this being towards the start of the scandal; the police did do some degree of investigation.

- & - had spent that evening playing video games in - apartment. They were called in for questioning. They were kept separate, thereby unable to keep their story straight. Instead of getting justice; they got a confession. After being the two were turned against each other - turned on his friend. Ratted him out for sneaking out and requesting that leave of absence to be

(insert mule picture here)
Houston

kept quiet. Both men were sent to prison. A source tells the Chronicle that he had been convinced that his friend had already ratted on him; however we cannot tell whether or not this is true, seeing as this is not a very trusted source.

While away in prison - is said to have experienced psychological trauma. - on the other hand is said to have changed. He is said to have been made into a criminal, and his sentence went merely from accomplice to life after he bragged about his other crimes to a jailhouse snitch. There is no evidence to support these accusations made either by the jailhouse snitch; or the accused.

There are undisputed facts in this case however. 1 - daughter fell into great emotional distress as a direct result of this court case. She had been doing quite well in school; but soon started flunking. She also entered therapy. 2 - mother was receiving elder care in a facility. Following her son's arrest and incarceration she went as long as 13 ½ months without a single visit. Also she herself was very nearly put onto the street or arrested after her court appointed elder guardian failed to pay some of her care related costs. There is also statements and minor evidence in favor or elder abuse, or at least neglect; however at of currently this remains undetermined. 3 two statements have now emerged that were not presented nor investigated in when they came out during the course of the trial. The statements were support both men to have been completely innocent. 4 there never was any solid proof or strong evidence beyond the obtained confessions.

We will now begin miscellaneous stories regarding the IA Captain Olaf.

Justice Not Served

By M. B. Johnson

There has been a reopening of the investigation into the death of -; who you will probably not remember. - was stopped by a police officer 3 ½ years ago come Monday after next. In which he was ordered to uncross his arms. After a brief and miserably failed attempt at a lawsuit; he committed suicide by jumping of a parking garage in TMC.

(insert mule picture here)
Houston

When it initially went down, he put out a listing for an attorney. "Normally an attorney would not take such a hopeless case without cash up front." said – attorney. - Put out a listing on Craigslist for an attorney. "admittedly it's a difficult case, as such upon success all judgments against plaintiff will serve in whole as payment (100%)" the listing read in part. One barrister responded in part; and was hired immediately. "I had never even seen a case with such high" said the victim's attorney. The victim told friends and co-workers he simply wanted justice; to prevent it from happening to someone else. He also said that he really didn't have to win; if he cost the cops lots of money, they he won. The case was thrown out of court immediately.

While this may seem a bit far-fetched, the victim had oppositional defiant syndrome; which our resident expert on such matters says could have made the experience of having to take military style orders to the letter and blindly with nor regress quote "cruel."

There was, as a result of the lawsuit an internal investigation. The investigation was small and brief. The officer received a one day suspension; he received a second day's suspension following the suicide. But now Internal Affairs has reopened the case. Led by the head of IA, Cap. W.X.Y.Z.C. there have already been charges regarding official oppression and abuse of power. A grand jury inquiry had been called to determine if the officer, his superiors, or the department itself may be held criminally liable for - death. The family says that if only it had been sooner; then maybe their loved one might still be alive.

Interrogation

By Timothy Montgomery H.

Olaf had done it again. Officer - has been charged with making a terroristic threat. It all began with an interrogation. The suspect requested an attorney, but was told that if they would have to wait in "zoo holding." Many more extreme cases, discussing what they would find, or even what would happen to them. But this is different. Usually a case as small as this will not stick; but this officer has in the past been accused. The last time - had allegedly demanded a suspect hand over their shoe; - then banged it onto his chest, then said "You kicked me." The suspect was a minor.

Afterword

"*History is not made by those that followed the flawed paradime of their day, but by those who did not.*" – S. Days, author

"*In a mad world, only the mad are sane*" - Asylum, By Madeleine Roux

"*All change is not growth, as all movement is not forward*" - Ellen Glascow

"*Don't find fault, find a remedy*" - Henry Ford

"*In matters of principle, stand like a rock*" - Thomas Jefferson

"*Only two things are infinite-the universe and human stupidity, and I'm not so sure about the universe*" - Albert Einstein

"*Of all tyrannies, a tyranny sincerely exercised for the good of its victims may be the most oppressive. It would be better to live under robber barons than under omnipotent moral busybodies. The robber baron's cruelty may sometimes sleep, his cupidity may at some point be satiated, but those who torment us for our own good will torment us without end for they do so with the approval of their own conscience.*" - Clive Staples Lewis

"*Here at the Central Intelligence Agency we like terrorism. We encourage it. That's not to say that we actually go out and make attacks. Oh no, no that's conspiracy theory. No we simply look the other way. Belittle a threat. Deliberately do a B grade job. That way we can get the funding and mechanisms, such as date mining, that we really need to protect the people.*" - common concern regarding American intelligence.

"*MIND YOUR BUSINESS*" - Fugio cent

(insert mule picture here)
Houston

"*To Serve and Protect*" - universal police motto

"*Petty Thieves get hung; great thieves go free*" - Russian Proverb*

"*The Truth shall set you free, but first it will make you miserable*" - adage

"*Dictators to and fro upon tigers, which they dare not dismount. And the tigers are getting hungry*". - Winston Churchill

"*The Road to Hell is paved with good intentions*" - adage

"*Good must destroy evil or cease being good*" - paraphrase

"*We hold these Truths to be self-evident, that all men are created equal, that they are endowed by their creator with certain unalienable rights, that among these are Life, Liberty, and the pursuit of Happiness. That to secure these Rights, Governments are instituted among Men, deriving their just powers from the consent of the governed, that whenever any Form of Government becomes destructive of these ends, it is the Right of the People to alter or to abolish it, and to institute new Government, laying its foundations on such principles and organizing its powers in such form, as to shall seem most likely to affect their Safety and Happiness. Prudence, indeed, will dictate that, Governments long established should not be changed for light and transient causes; and accordingly all experience hath shown, that mankind are more disposed to suffer, while evils are sufferable, than to right themselves by abolishing the forms to which they are accustomed. But when a long train of abuses and usurpations, pursing invariably the same Object, evidences a design to reduce them under absolute despotism, it is their right, it is their duty, to throw off such Government and to provide new Guards for their future security*" - United States of America, Declaration of Independence

"*Those who stand for nothing will fall for everything*" - spiritual adage*

"*The right of the people to be secure in their persons, houses, papers, and effects, against unreasonable searches and seizures, shall not be violated, and no warrants shall issue but upon probable cause, supported by oath or affirmation, and particularly describing the place to be searched, and the persons or things to be seized. No persons shall be held to answer for a capital or other infamous crime unless on a presentment or indictment of a Grand Jury...nor shall any person be subject for the same offence to be twice put in jeopardy of life or limb; nor shall be compelled in any criminal case to be a witness against himself, nor he be deprived of life, liberty, or property, without due process of law...In all criminal prosecutions, the accused shall enjoy the right to a speedy and public trial, by an impartial jury of the state and district wherein the crime shall have been committed, which districts shall have been previously ascertained by law, and to be informed of the nature and cause of the accusation; to be confronted with witnesses against him; to have compulsory process for obtaining witnesses in his favor, and to have the assistance of counsel for his defense...Excessive bail shall not be required, nor excessive fines imposed, nor cruel and unusual punishments inflicted.*" - Constitution of the United States of America

"*Just as evil never walks in and announces itself as evil; rather portraying itself as something positive; so Tyranny also portrays itself as Liberty; liberty from crime, liberty from "The Man", liberty from offence, Etc...*" - Speaker Unknown

"*Don't Tell Me What To Do!*" - Neoadage

"*Innocent until proven guilty*" - universal motto of criminal justice

"*The difference between stubbornness and determination is whether or not the person speaking thinks it to be a good thing in that context.*" - me

"*Do not accept a bribe, for a bribe blinds those who see and twists the words of the righteous*" - The Torah (may be poorly translated)

"*The Search for truth is never ending.*"

"There are more things...In heaven, and on earth, than are dreamed in our philosophy" - Varney, the Vampyre, by James Malcolm Rymer

"Compliance kills" - instant adage

"*Why do Teenagers put up with Curfews and screen time limits? Why do workers go to work every day? Why do New Yorkers put up with Stop and Frisk? Because, as long as you take their Data, you take their Paycheck, you take their protection, you may as well be their slave; because you are.*" - expansion and Paraphrase of common adage.

"*The ONLY duty of the police officer is to protect. The ONLY duty of the prosecutor is to provide justice. Keep that straight; and nothing will ever go wrong. Confuse that even a little; and it's the two halves of an atomic bomb.*" - future adage.

"*Judge not, lest ye, too, should be judged*" - Christian Scripture (translations vary; derived from Varney, the Vampyre, by James Malcolm Rymer)

"Sometimes a cigar is just a cigar" - Sigmund Freud

"*I think that we should be men first, and subjects afterward...Unjust laws exist; shall we be content to obey them, or shall we endeavor to amend them, and obey them until we have succeeded, or shall we transgress them at once? Men generally, under such a government as this, think that they ought to wait until they have persuaded the majority to alter them. They think that, if they should resist, the remedy would be worse than the evil. But it is the fault of the government itself that the remedy is worse than the evil. It makes it worse. Why is it not more apt to anticipate and provide for reform? Why does it not cherish its wise minority? Why does it cry and resist before it is hurt? Why does it not encourage its citizens to be on the alert to point out its faults, and do better than it would have them? Why does it always crucify Christ, and excommunicate Copernicus, and Luther, and pronounce Washington and Franklin rebels?*"

"*One would think, that a deliberate and practical denial of its authority was the only offence never contemplated by government; else, why has it not assigned it definite, its suitable and proportionate, penalty? If a man who has no property refuses but once to earn nine shillings for the State [to pay his poll tax], he is put in prison for a period unlimited by any law that I know, and determined only by the discretion of those who placed him there; but if he should steal ninety times nine shillings from the State, he is soon permitted to go at large again.*"

"*If the injustice is part of the necessary friction of the machine of government, let it go, let it go: perchance it will wear out smooth-certainly the machine will wear out. If the injustice has a spring, or a pulley, or a rope, or a crank, exclusively for itself, then perhaps you may consider whether the remedy will not be worse than the evil; but if it is of such a nature that it requires you to be the agent of injustice to another, then, I say, break the law. Let your life be a counter-friction to stop the machine. What I have to do is to see, at any rate, that I do not lend myself to the wrong which I condemn...the only house in a slave state in which a free man cay abide with honor [is the big house]. If any think that their influence would be lost there, and that their voices no longer afflict the ear of the state, that they would not be as an enemy within its walls, they do not know by how much truth is stronger than error, nor how more eloquently and effectively he can combat injustice who has experienced a little in his own person. Cast your whole vote, not a strip of paper merely, but your whole influence. A minority is powerless while it conforms to the majority; it is not even a minority then; but is irresistible when it clogs by its whole weight. If the alternative is to keep all just men in prison, or give up war and slavery, the State will not hesitate which to choose. If a thousand men were not to pay their tax-bills this year, that would not be a violent and bloody measure. As it would be to pay them, and enable the State to commit violence and shed innocent blood. This is, in fact, the definition of a peaceable revolution, if any such thing is possible. If the tax-gatherer, or any other public officer, asks me, as one has done, "But what shall I do?" my answer is, "If you really wish to do anything, resign your office." when the subject has refused allegiance, and the officer has resigned his office, then the revolution is accomplished. But even suppose blood should flow. Is there not a sort of blood shed when the conscience is wounded? Though this wound a man's real manhood and immortality flow out, and he bleeds to an everlasting death. I see this blood flowing now* " - On the Duty of Civil Disobedience A.K.A. Resistance to Civil Government A.K.A. The Relation of the individual to the state A.K.A. Civil Disobedience, by Henry David Thoreau   This is one quote I must discuss. In that I mean that I mean that many of these quotes require some thought; food for thought if you will. But this one I will, take the time to point out that this affect we have seen put in practice BY ACCIDENT! By that I mean that we no longer lock people up for marijuana possession; prison overcrowding leads to early release, and on it goes. And they weren't even clogging with their entire weight!

"*Those who don't know history are doomed to repeat it*" - adage

"*Some mysteries are best left unsolved*" - saying

"*Industries and defense teams are all bad because one has industry secrets, and the other doesn't want the prosecution to have a heads up. Thus since both have secrets, both must be up to something, thus both must be bad*" - food for thought

"*With great power; comes great responsibility*" - neoadage

"*I think that we should be men first, and subjects afterward*" - Civil Disobedience, by Henry David Thoreau (also known by other titles; the book, not the author. See above)

"*You don't know what you've got till it's gone*" - Eddie Money

"*Some people leave their party for their principles, more people leave their principles for their party*" - Winston Churchill*

"*I am perfectly in favor of getting that which is dangerous out of the hands of those whom are deranged; let's start with power*" - paraphrase of Frank Lloyd Wright (meaning changed)

(insert mule picture here)
Houston

"*Few things are harder to put up with than a good example*" - Mark Twain

"*The difference between fiction and reality? Fiction has to make sense*" - Tom Clancy

"*Efforts and courage are not enough without purpose and direction*" - President Kennedy

"*Be sure to put your feet in the right place, then stand firm*" - President Lincoln

"*In the middle of difficulty lies opportunity*" - Albert Einstein

"*Common sense is the knack of seeing things as they are, and doing things as they ought to be done*" - Harriet Beecher Stowe

"*If you can dream it, you can do it*" - Walt Disney

"*Our lives begin to end the day we become silent about things that matter*" - Dr. Martin Luther King Jr.

"*Great works are formed nor by strength, but by perseverance*"

"*In business you don't get what you deserve, you get what you negotiate*" - Chester L. Karrass

"*You will never do anything in the world without courage It is the greatest quality of mind next to honor*" - James Allen

"*It is a fact that those who are not up to anything, have nothing to hide. Everything should be out in the open. Therefore the government must be up to lots of bad stuff because it has classified intelligence*" - food for thought

"*Loose lips sink ships*" - military proverb

"*You only need the light when it's burnin' low; only miss the sun when it starts to snow...only know you've been high when you're felling low; only hate the road when you're missin' home*" - Passenger

"*The fault is not in our stars; but in ourselves*" - Julius Caesar, By William Shakespeare

"*Some legends are told, some turn to dust or to gold*" - Centuries, By Fall Out Boys

"*Fear is the foundation of most governments; but it is so sordid and brutal a passion, and renders men in whose breasts in predominates so stupid and miserable, that Americans will not be likely to approve of any political institution on which is founded on it*" - Thoughts on Government, By John Adams

"*Do ⊡ 2 other as u would have them do 2 you*" - do I really have to say?

"*Anything that causes displeasure, injury, pain or suffering; misfortune; calamity; mischief; injury; the negation or contrary of good*" - from the definition of evil, from, Websters New Twentieth Century Dictionary of the English Language Unabridged (Standard Reference Works Publishing Company. .c 1957)

"*In a time of universal deceit, to tell the truth is a revolutionary act*" - 1984, By George Orwell*

"*Journalism is simply putting out there what someone else doesn't want to be known; the rest is just public relations*" - George Orwell*

"*The law is wrong*" - saying

"*When the rights of one man are impeded; than the rights of all are endangered*" - Dr. Martin Luther King Jr.*

"*And so he bragged that he had killed one man for hitting him; and a boy just for striking him!*" - The Torah (attribution imdefinite; reworded)

"*All that Hitler did in Germany; was legal*" - Dr. Martin Luther King Jr. (Somewhat paraphrased)

"*The most dangerous weapon in the world is power.*"

"*The bigger they are; the harder they fall*" - neosaying

(insert mule picture here)
Houston

"*A half-truth is a whole lie*" - a fortune cookie*

"*Unto every rule there is an exception*" - hairsplitters universal slogan / motto

"*The only easy day is yesterday*" - written on a wall in an undisclosed furniture store

"*Of all human nessaties...perhaps the greatest is to be free*" - the narrator of the new Outer Limits*

"*Just because someone says __; does not necessarily mean that it is true*" - abundantly obvious

"*Better the devil you do know; than the devil you don't know*" – neoparable

There was once a woman who, growing up, her family gave refuge to Jews in the Holocaust. Many years later when she was asked what does it take to do that, she simply said (in so many words) "*When the world goes off the cliff insane; you simply don't follow*"

"*You can't believe everything you hear*" – wise saying

"*They were monsters with human faces, in crisp uniforms, marching in lockstep, so banal you don't recognize them for what they are until it's too late*" – Miss Peregrine's Home for Peculiar Children, by Ransom Riggs

"*It always amazes me when I listen to politicians say, 'we are going to win the war on drugs by building prisons, appointing more judges, and putting more police on beat'...Having spent seven months in prison, there wasn't one night that I did not smell marijuana burning. If you can get marijuana in prison, with watchtowers, inspections, and prison guards, you can get it into a country. You can send the U.S. Marines to Columbia to burn all the fields, seal all the borders, and build all the prisons you want, because you won't stop drug use in this country*" – from a speech made by Charles Colson

"*Just because someone means well, does not necessarily mean that they do well. In fact that could be even worse. With someone is doing evil for evil's sake; there is always at least some possibility of a pang of guilt, or their thirst of blood to be saturated, or for them to come to another interest, or, or, or. But if they believe that they are doing good, then they do so with the approval of their conscience. In fact the very mechanism [that is the conscience] that should be holding them back is in fact egging them on! While people may end up merely looking to how they are well meaning, they really shouldn't; seeing as*

(insert mule picture here)
Houston

they can make a real hell of earth; worse than if they merely intended harm " – strong paraphrase of earlier quote

"*But though men, when they enter into society, give up the equality, liberty, and executive power they had in the state of nature, into the hands of the society, to be so far disposed of by the legislature, as the good of the society shall require; yet it being only with an intention in everyone the better to preserve himself, his liberty and property; (for no rational creature can be supposed to change his condition with an intention for the worse) the power of the society, or legislature constituted by them, can never be supposed to extend farther, than the common good; but is obliged to secure every one's property, by providing against those three defects above mentioned[2], that made the state of nature so unsafe and uneasy. And so whoever has the legislative or supreme power of any commonwealth, is bound to govern by established standing laws, promulgated and known to the people, and not by the extemporary decrees; by indifferent and upright judges, who are to decide controversies by those laws; and to employ the force of the community at home, only in the execution of such laws, or abroad to prevent or redress foreign injuries, and secure the community from inroads and invasion. And all this to be directed to no other end, but the peace, safety, and public good of the people.* " – Section 131, Chapter 9, Book 2, Two Treatises of Government, by John Locke

"*If the world's only gonna see a fox as shifty and untrustworthy, there's no point trying to be anything else* " – Zootopia the Junior Novelization, adapted by Suzanne Francis

"*In loco parentis means 'acting in the role of parent'… It is a legal term and it applies to Count Olaf. Now that you are in his care, the Count may raise you using any methods he sees fit…Count Olaf is acting in loco parentis. Understand?"*

"But he struck my brother!…Whatever Count Olaf has done…he has acted in loco parentis, and there's nothing I can do about it. Your money will be well protected by myself and by the bank, but Count Olaf's parenting techniques are his own business. Now, I hate to usher you out posthaste, but I have very much work to do" – Chapter five, The Bad Beginning, A Series of Unfortunate Events by Lemony Snicket

"*No Buts!*" – every dictator ever

"*Sheriffs, those unfeeling blood-suckers have, under the watchful eye of the legislature, committed the most horrid and barbarous ravages on our people. It has required the most constant vigilance of the legislature to keep them from totally ruining the people; a repeated succession of laws has been made to*

---

[2] Essentially; 1. Being able to do whatever he pleases. 2. The right of vigilante justice. 3. Must assist in government in some way / to some degree

suppress their iniquitous speculations and cruel extortions; and as often has their nefarious ingenuity devised methods of evading the force of those laws: in the struggle they have generally triumphed over the legislature" – Comments at the Virginia Ratifying Convention, by Patrick Henry

"The devil in disguise is redundant" – truth

"A decent and manly examination of the acts of Government should be not only tolerated, but encouraged" – William Henry Harrison

"Nothing to see here" – This is a statement that has been said many, many, *many* times; as of the time of my typing this, it is yet to be said truthfully.

"Pay no attention to the man behind the curtain" – The Wizard of Oz

"What I want to know," said the young mule, who had been quiet for a long time, "What I want to know is, why we have to fight at all."

"Because we're told to," said the troop-horse, with a snort of contempt.

"Orders," said Billy the mule, and his teeth snapped.

"Hukm Hai! [It is an order]," said the camel with a gurgle, and the Two Tails and the Bullocks repeated "Hukm hai!"

"Yes, but who gives the orders?" said the recruit mule.

"The man who walks at you head–or sits on your back–or holds the nose rope–or twists your tail," said Billy and the troop-horse and the camel and the bullocks one after another.

"But who gives them their orders?"

"Now you want to know too much, young 'un," said Billy "And that is one way of getting kicked. All you have to do is to obey the man at your head and ask no questions" – The Jungle Book, by Rudyard Kipling

"But if they all only ever spoke when spoke to, how would any speech begin?" – Alice Through the looking-glass; and What She Found There (attribution imdefinite; reworded)

"Sometimes you have to stop listening to what people say and start listening to what they do" – The Search for Wandla [trilogy] by Tony Diterlizzi*

(insert mule picture here)
Houston

"*There's nothing worse than being locked up. It just kills your soul*" – This statement was made by a character named Pip in the book trilogy, the apothecary series (Maile Meloy). He came from a very large and very poor family; as such he ended up turning to being a pick-pocket. Nevertheless the police had regaurdlessly locked him up countless times *by fourteen*. (I know for a fact that the psychological element is real.)

"*Justice is blind*" – legal adage

"*We must not permit our respect for the dead or our sympathy for the living to lead us into an act of injustice to the balance of the living*" – Davy Crockett

"*Crisis is the rallying cry of the tyrant*" – Madison

"*The privilege of the Writ of Habeas Corpus shall not be suspended*" – Constitution of the United States

"*The important point is not to dare to do, but to dare to do right*" – Party Terrorism, from Harpers Weekly (May 30, 1868)

"*[The sentence is] capital punishment on a judge or arbiter legally appointed who had been found guilty of receiving a bribe for giving a decision*" – Twelve Tables of Roman Law

"*Too often we excuse those who are willing to build their own lives on the shattered dreams of others...Some who accuse others of inciting riots have by their own conduct invited them. Some look for scapegoats, others look for conspiracies, but this much is clear; violence breeds violence, repression brings retaliation*" – Robert Kennedy

"*We are a nation of laws, but, what if, the laws, themselves, also, became dictators?*" – Food for thought

"*For there is another kind of violence, slower but just as deadly, destructive as the shot or the bomb in the night. This is the violence of institutions; indifference and inaction and slow decay...But we can perhaps remember–even if for only a time–that those who live with us are our brothers, that they share with us the same short movement of life, that they seek–as we do–nothing but the chance to live out their purpose and happiness, winning what satisfaction and fulfillment they can.*" – Robert Kennedy

(insert mule picture here)
Houston

"*Left in the care of a heartless puritanical woman and her weak husband, a retired seaman, Kipling spent five long years, bullied, tortured, and unloved his eyesight deteriorating and his spirit close to being broken. Only after a visitor noticed the boy's pitiful plight were his parents summoned back from India; when is mother arrived and entered the room, the child's first gesture was to raise an arm to ward off the expected blow*" – Introduction [to The Jungle Book and The Second Jungle Book A.K.A. The Jungle Books] by Alberto Manguel

"*Who knows who is good or bad; only with the passing of generations will you be able to tell who is and is not richous*" – paraphrase of a quote (original quote not enumerated here)

"*In this state of things, if any evil happened to Mrs Zant, silence on Mr Rayburn's part might be indirectly to blame for a serious misfortunes*" –The Gost's Touch by William Wilkie Collins

"*'He declares that he will not lose sight of me until his mind is at ease. It is useless to attempt to alter his opinion. He says my nerves are shattered - and who that sees me can doubt it? He tells me that my only chance of getting better is to try change of air and perfect repose – how can I contradict him? He reminds me that I have no relation but himself, and no house open to me but his own - and God knows he is right!' She said those last words in accents of melancholy resignation, which grieved the good man whose one merciful purpose was to serve and console her*" – Mrs Zant and the Ghost by William Wilkie Collins

"*{[don't let your life end before doing] / [your life has no meaning / value / purpose until you do]} something for your fellow man*" –This quote I believed came from the only continental army chaplin (and was the only thing he was remembered for saying) Later knowledge contradicted it. All I know is I heard (and poorly remembered) this from a funeral. It clearly has not been well preserved into this here

"*Uncle Pio never exactly beat her, but he resorted to a sarcasm that had terrors of its own*" – The Bridge of San Luis Rey, by Thornton Wilder

"*I took them out to dinner one evening and asked them why they had acted so badly in class. They said my class was boring and that I had nothing to teach them…I asked if anything I taught in class interested them. One fellow responded that I had caught his attention when I had discussed my import-export business. He rattled off various figures I had mentioned in class, calculated my profit margin, and concluded that my business was doing well.*" – Steve Mariotti (from what was originally a speech)

(insert mule picture here)
Houston

"*The average human being has a strong tendency toward concern about what he sees before him, and toward lack of concern about what the does not see*" – Fire, by George R. Stewart

"*Today my grandmother hit me again. She bashed me like a hundred times with a wooden spoon, and then with a tennis racquet. I have cuts and bruises all over. It takes all I have not to just haul off and knock her one, but I know they throw me in jail if I do. The last time I stood up to her she called the police, and when they came she acted like a sweet old lady who got stuck with a low-life juvie. Of course the police took her side. Once you have a record, cops just bother to think. Every time I tried to say something they just told me to shut up. One of them threatened to tase me. Sometimes I fell like this crummy world is just completely stacked against me and I want to give up*"

"*Then I think about my best friend Jack…If it wasn't for him I probally would have just ended it a long time ago. I know Jack will never read this, but if he did, I'd say "I love you man."*" – exherts from a journal entry in chapter 47, Battle of the Ampere, Michael Vey, by Richard Paul Evans. (This quotation otherwise unrelated to earlier reference to this work.)

"*Did You See That?! He was Gunu hit me back!!*" – David Miscavage*

"*I say you're not injured. And if you say {otherwise / that you are injured} then you're defying me!*" – Anotomas*

"*'Well, looking back all these years later, I really would have liked to have married her; but maybe it's for the best that they kept us apart and we weren't able to marry. I mean, she was rich and I'm not, we're from different backgrounds, and, and,' he said; clearly still somewhat hurt*" – Varney the Vampire, by James Malcolm Rymer (Adapted)

"*It is generally true that an individual is responsible for everything that happens to him*" – Scientology: the fundamentals of thought, by L. Ron Hubbard

"*You may say 'I know what you're going through' but you shouldn't. No matter what how close your experience is; you don't know what they're going through*" – Rabbi Harold Kushner*

"*It's one thing to tell a story to tell a story, for me. It's another thing to actually do something that's actually going to help people. What can we do? What can you do? What can you do? What can our lawyers do here? I don't know what those things are but I have to find a way to to bring justice to some of these people who have been victimized; and to prevent anything in the future form happening. This*

(insert mule picture here)
Houston

cult or another cult I don't want people to feel powerless because something seems more powerful than you. Do something. You can do something" – Leah Remini in Leah Remini Scientology and the Aftermath

"Each time a man stands up for an ideal, or acts to improve the lot of others, or strikes out against injustice, he sends forth a tiny ripple of hope" – Robert F. Kennedy

"Trumpets didn't sound. Bluebirds didn't sing. Angels didn't call my name. Nothing changed at all...But I felt good inside. Like I had done something right" – The Case of the Missing Snowman (a Jigsaw Jones Mystery) by James Preller

"The truth is that all men having power ought to be mistrusted" – James Madison.

"This is the way the world ends; not with a bang, but with a whimper" – T.S. Elliot

"When one is abused, we are all abused" – JFK

"Injustice anywhere is a threat to justice everywhere" – from a Human Rights Day Rally in Calcutta India (2015)

"We know the rules; we just hate the way that ya told em" – a rap song

"The only thing necessary for the triumph of evil is for good men to do nothing" – Edmund Burke

Author's Note on the Text

As you may have noticed; this work is written in many different fonts; assuming of course that is has not been republished according to some other manner. The different fonts are intended to highlight the different (ostensible) authors. There is one exception and one sorta exception made deliberately. The exception being External Affairs and chapter A having been written in the same font. And the sorta exception being Chapter K was merely a modified version of the font used in Internal Affairs. Both such cases were done to highlight a connection.

Also full disclosure; this work likely will not be published in the exact same font as it was originally created in; not that no doubt is the intellectual property of a major and nameless computer / software company. As such it may have lost some degree of the original feel. Furthermore in later publications (Penguin Classics, Bantam Classics, Signet Classics, Barnes & Noble Classics, Publishing House X That Does Not Exist in the Point In Time I'm Writing This Classics, Dalmatian Press Classics, Etc…) it will

(insert mule picture here)
Houston

likely be republished in just one, one size fits all, font. If so, then all feel derived from the font will be lost; and / or all bets will be off. Furthermore likely this entire note will be edited out; if so what I am typing here is moot.

About the author

I am someone that was born; and I will eventually die. I started on this work on either 11-16-2015 10-24-15 depending on what you consider the beginning; initially this was going to be something wholly and almost completely unrecognizably different. (Insert when work finally completely ceased.) This is the first thing I've ever written with any real thought toward publication; and even then not initially. All of the stories in this work, except the last chapter of the last book was first written in notepad; stories that simply had to be written, don't wait for an easy means of creation. I will and shall forever be completely and totally anonymous. Though it will seem that there are 22 total different authors, assuming *External Affairs* to have just one author, and not counting the afterword at all. But in fact it was just me; and I did almost exclusively by myself. With virtually no assistance from anyone else. What I did get help for is very small and / or slight things.

Also if you're reading this in some boring obnoxious lit. class years down the line; I'd like to apologize.

Bonus Sneak preview into this author's next work *BOOK OF TEXTS*. Soon to be banned from a public school near you.

Read and see the most seditious novelette you may ever read. Arriving soon.

BOOK OF TEXTS

By Anonymous

(insert mule picture here)
Houston

In coming

Out going

(Due to the fact that Book of Texts is (as of my typing this) a work of progress I have opted to not actually place the text here. Also I will want it to appear on the page as it would on a smartphone; so I can't do that here. Best I can do is organize the text (no pun intended) Just use your own judgment on how much to put in here, I was thinking the first like 7 pages, just until you arrive at Tuesday.)

Other Titles Coming Soon From This Author

Book of Texts

Your school is guaranteed to ban *Book of Texts*. If you liked *Last Grafts* you will also enjoy this one; another thought provoking and ground-breaking piece of ideological horror; told in a method unlike almost anything else. Many times throughout history people have turned to civil disobedience; but what about if it

(insert mule picture here)
Houston

escalates to a true and full peaceful civil war? An
unorthodox epistletory Novelette. Also with a bonus
sneak preview of Thou Shalt Not Judge, Nureal
Steinbeck's Hiding Place and Victoria Strongneck's
Home for Juvenile Delinquents, and Fire

Thou Shalt Not Judge

Muck like how brother Juniper investigated the
ultimate cause of the bridge collapse, so a landlord and a
paramedic go out investigating a septuple (seven) suicide.
Read and see the strong-arm and parental overreach that
strangled them to death; literally. A dangerous and
thought provoking piece of ideological horror.

Nureal Steinbeck's Hiding Place and Victoria Strongneck's Home for Juvenile Delinquents

First, a rabbi, in training, in 1950, pulled of the train by
Rolph Wallenberg, has decided to try and "Pay it
forward"; But After one volunteer session he finds a new
secret calling, sheltering would be mental patents.

Then, 50 years later, a protectee of Nureal's decides to
herself carry on the tradition. This time however, instead

of a mere handful, she has far more protectees and even her own witness protection program. Read and see as tough love and juvenile justice are turned into a horror story.

The Most Frightening Book Ever Written

Many people and groups have been persecuted over millennia. But this one is different. See what happens when a religion is declared a dangerous communicable mental illness. A stellar blend of horror and ideological horror.

Fire

Fire has always had its place in the horror genera. But never has it been its own sub-genera of horror; till now. A bone chilling book of terror like nothing else.

Made in the USA
San Bernardino, CA
14 July 2019